Allegiance to Liberty

Allegiance to Liberty

The Changing Face of Patriots, Militias, and Political Violence in America

Barry J. Balleck

 PRAEGER

AN IMPRINT OF ABC-CLIO, LLC
Santa Barbara, California • Denver, Colorado • Oxford, England

Library of Congress Cataloging-in-Publication Data

Balleck, Barry.
   Allegiance to liberty : the changing face of patriots, militias, and political violence in America / Barry Balleck.
      pages cm
   Includes bibliographical references.
   ISBN 978-1-4408-3095-2 (hardback)—ISBN 978-1-4408-3096-9 (ebook)
1. United States—Politics and government—1945-1989.   2. United States—Politics and government—1989-   3. Patriotism—United States.
4. Militia movements—United States.   5. Dissenters—United States.
6. Political violence—United States.   7. Government, Resistance to—United States.   8. Political culture—United States.   I. Title.
   E743.B325 2014
   322.4'20973—dc23   2014026381

ISBN: 978–1–4408–3095–2
EISBN: 978–1–4408–3096–9

19 18 17 16 15   1 2 3 4 5

This book is also available on the World Wide Web as an eBook.
Visit www.abc-clio.com for details.

Praeger
An Imprint of ABC-CLIO, LLC

ABC-CLIO, LLC
130 Cremona Drive, P.O. Box 1911
Santa Barbara, California 93116-1911

This book is printed on acid-free paper ∞

Manufactured in the United States of America

To my wife and best friend, Deana, and our children
—Jeremy, Brittany, Joshua, and Alexis
—who have always supported me through the years.

Contents

Introduction

"I believe in the United States of America as a government of the people, by the people, for the people; whose just powers are derived from the consent of the governed; a democracy in a republic; a sovereign nations of many sovereign states; a perfect union, one and- inseparable; established upon those principles of freedom, equality, justice, and humanity for which American patriots sacrificed their lives and fortunes. I therefore believe it is my duty to my country to love it, to support the Constitution, to obey its laws, to respect the flag, and to defend it against all enemies."
                        —William Tyler Page, The American's Creed, 1918[1]

The United States of America was founded upon principles that were only historical abstractions in the 18th century. Yet the fundamental ideal behind the American experiment—that the natural rights of man inherently endowed human begins with the right to govern themselves—was a radical ideal of its time. Pure democracy—based upon the ancient Greek principle of one man, one vote—was not the answer. As noted by Elbridge Gerry, there were evils that flowed from an "excess of democracy."[2] Democracy was not a trusted form of government, as the vast bulk of the people possessed neither the intellect, skill, nor inclination to directly involve themselves in the processes of governance. To a propertied class of individuals who would become known as the "Founders" or "Framers," democracy was "experimental, scary and based on the belief—not inherently appealing to an elite group— that men of less property, less learning, less breeding should be allowed to govern themselves."[3]

Yet the United States in 1787 was the hallmark of democracy as compared to the rest of the world, where "hereditary monarchies prevailed."[4] As noted by author Eric Black,

The American experiment in government by the consent of the governed was a turning point in world history. The American and French revolutions of the 1770s and 1780s started a democratic trend that has never stopped. Before those revolutions, the divine right of kings was the basis of governmental power. Two centuries later, even the most despotic rulers feel obliged to make some pretense of possession a popular mandate.[5]

The Founders firmly believed that a democratic majority could exercise as much despotic power as any monarch.[6] Drawing upon the inferences they drew from ancient texts and more contemporary theories, the Founders proposed ideas that consisted of limited government, checks and balances, freedom, liberty, and notions of civic virtue. Though these ideas had been written about for centuries, they had never yet been put into practice anywhere in the world. What was unique about the American experience was the notion that these ideas could actually be written into existence and that citizens could be governed by ideas that had hitherto been only abstractions. In the American case, these ideas flowered into a government unlike any other in the world up to that time. In the 18th century, the world was dominated by only a few recognized "states." Most of these were monarchies that had dynastic characteristics that had remained unchanged for hundreds and in some cases thousands of years. These governments were of the few and not the many. They did not take account, nor were they likely to, of the average citizen found in the state. The government serviced the needs of the monarchy, the extended royal family, and the aristocracy. The desires of the people often went unmet.

Yet with the creation of the American system of government, expectations were quickly raised to a point they had never been before. The Founding period of the mid- to late 18th century brought about the creation of a new lexicon of American politics that included ideas of "freedom," "liberty," "limited government," "checks and balances," and the like. Expectations of government, which had to this point been minimal, were now raised. Citizens began to see the value of government, and they began to desire to defend government against tyrannical forces. It was well known to most astute political observers of the 18th century that governments inevitably decay and that average people suffer as a result. Yet the American system was meant to mute the forces that negatively impact government and that would eventually bring about its demise. As this promise played itself out over the years, the American citizen became a jealous advocate of the ideals of government and the manner in which it had been instituted. At the same time, the Founding documents of this period became tantamount to scripture as an American citizenry recognized the uniqueness of its government and its differences from all other governments then in existence. The people and not the actual stakeholders of government became the most vocal supporters and proponents of government. Yet when government fell short of expectations or the people supposed that government was not fulfilling the purposes for which it had been designed, the people would undertake actions to remind the government who it served.

This "reminder" often came in the form of political violence. Such violence has occurred between opposing groups since the beginning of time. In the field of political science, researchers have long sought answers to the causes of interstate and intrastate wars (e.g., Ted Gurr's work, *Why Men Rebel*).[7] Yet with revolutions of all kinds happening in recent years—eVelvet, Orange, and the like—and the recent Arab Spring that occurred in the Middle East, it seems necessary to ask the question why people rebel against their own governments. In the case of dictatorships, authoritarian rule, or monarchies that have lost their appeal, the answer seems quite clear. Yet in the case of democracies—where people have the right, indeed the obligation, to participate in their government—why does violence occur?

Thomas Jefferson once quipped that "The tree of liberty must be refreshed from time to time with the blood of patriots & tyrants" (to William Stephens Smith, Paris, November 15, 1787).[8] This basic idea has given voice to much of the political dissent and violence the United States has experienced over its nearly 240 years of existence. The country itself was birthed through violent revolution, and those who fomented such revolution were hailed as heroes. Indeed, from that day to this, they are often referred to as "patriots." In the beginning, political violence was never intended to overthrow the government of the United States. Rather, it was meant to hold government to the ideals that had been articulated in the Founding documents. American citizens, unlike their fellow citizens of the world, could, during the years following the Founding, demand accountability of their government, for it was a government "of the people, by the people, and for the people." Never before in history had such words been so forcefully put forth as the outline of an entirely new relationship between those who were to govern and those who were to be governed. Within the Founding itself was an expectation of governmental accountability and governmental limitations. That is, citizens demanded of their government that it fulfill its promises, but there was also the expectation that government would not do that which other governments prior to it had done—that is, trample upon the rights and liberties of its citizens. In such cases, again as articulated in the Founding documents, it was the right of the people to "alter or abolish" government.

Of course, those who demanded accountability from government did not ordinarily act with malice or with the thought of overthrowing government. Such individuals fought to preserve and protect the government. In the American lexicon today, these individuals are commonly viewed as "patriots." Indeed, the term "patriot" holds a special place in the hearts of Americans. Elementary school children learn that it was patriots who jumped aboard English ships and dumped tea overboard into Boston Harbor in 1773. The men who risked their "lives, fortunes, and sacred honor" to forge the Declaration of Independence are considered patriots. George Washington, who selflessly put aside a life of leisurely retirement to serve his country as the first president of the United States, was a patriot. Patriots were once thought of as those who supported and sustained their government despite its shortcomings. Even the Framers of the U.S. Constitution knew that the government that they were constructing was not perfect.[9] Yet they supposed that citizens, through civic virtue, would rally to the new government and support it. After all, the alternative was the uncertainty and chaos that were evident throughout much of the world in the late 18th century. To support the fledgling government in the face of uncertainty was, in and of itself, the act of a patriot and a patriotic undertaking that would be passed down from generation to generation.

Throughout its history, however, there have been Americans who felt it their duty *not* to unquestioningly support their government but to ensure that government did not become that which the "original" patriots feared—expansive government that grows unchecked and continually tramples on the rights and liberties of its citizenry. Thus, throughout American history, there has been another strain of patriotism that has walked side by side with the more traditional notion accepted by most Americans. This is the patriot who does not accept the broad interpretations of government that have come to characterize U.S. politics today. Whereas most Americans will accept the notion that the Founders could not possibly have envisioned the complexity of life in the 21st century and the manner in which government must be mobilized to meet such challenges, there is another segment that believes that any change to the original structure of the government does damage to the intent of those who so carefully crafted it. These individuals point to the innate fear and distrust the Founders had of large government and the abuses that accompany it. The justification for the break from Great Britain was put forth in the Declaration of Independence. In it, learned men elucidated the pitfalls that come from a large and unresponsive government. Their goal was to throw off such government and construct a new government that would "provide new Guards for their future security…" (Declaration of Independence). Many self-proclaimed "patriots" of today embrace this notion. Moreover, because such individuals believe that it is their right to "alter or abolish" government, as their patriot forefathers outlined, they arm themselves and form themselves into self-styled militias to prepare for the eventuality of a government that will no longer be able to tolerate their obfuscations.

Patriots of the ilk outlined here come in many forms and follow many persuasions. Yet there seem to be at least two consistent threads that run through the narrative of the 21st-century patriot. The first is an affinity for the thinking and writing of Thomas Jefferson, third president of the United States. Jefferson, author of the Declaration of Independence, stands for many as the paragon of the patriot cause. After all, it was Jefferson who, in putting pen to paper, articulated the notion that government is first and foremost a creation of the people and should be responsive to them. If it becomes destructive to its ends, it is the right of the people to alter or abolish said government. For many patriot and militia groups of today, this sentiment resonates in that they believe that the current incarnation of the U.S. government has become unresponsive and unchecked by any of the conventional mechanisms designed to keep the government from usurping power from the people. Jefferson is also a hero to these groups because of his unflagging support of the right of all Americans to keep and bear arms. Jefferson once remarked that "For a people who are free, and who mean to remain so, a well-organized and armed militia is their best security."[10] Another quote often attributed to Jefferson—"The beauty of the Second Amendment is that it will not be needed until they try to take it"—cannot be found in any of Jefferson's personal papers or writings.[11] Nevertheless, Jefferson was a strong advocate of small and limited government, believing that the best chance for the United States to preserve its bucolic character was to be found in an agrarian and pastoral setting. His sentiments leaned toward frequent elections, a small central government, and the rights of the people to be represented by that government closest in proximity to them—state and local government. Though he had some qualms about it, Jefferson was largely an admirer of the Constitution. He remarked to Amos Marsh in 1801:

I join cordially in admiring and revering the Constitution of the United States, the result of the collected wisdom of our country. That wisdom has committed to us the important task of providing by example that a government, if organized in all its parts on the Representative principle unadulterated by the infusion of spurious elements, if founded, not in the fears & follies of man, but on his reason, on his sense of right, on the predominance of the social over his dissocial passions, may be so free as to restrain him in no moral right, and so firm as to protect him from every moral wrong.[12]

Together with their admiration for Thomas Jefferson, the patriots of today look to the literal text of the U.S. Constitution as their guide and inspiration. From its inception, the Constitution has inspired devotion because of its simplicity and originality in constructing a government for such a far-flung geographical area as is the United States. That the text has remained largely intact with very few alterations is testament to some of its "divine" nature and the belief that it was a document inspired by deity.[13] Even the Founding Fathers marveled at what they had done:

The virtue, moderation, and patriotism which marked the steps of the American people in framing, adopting, and thus far carrying into effect our present system of government has excited the admiration of nations. (George Washington, 1789)[14]

The example of changing a constitution, by assembling the wise men of the state, instead of assembling armies, will be worth as much to the world as the former examples we had given them. The Constitution, too, which was the result of our deliberations, is unquestionably the wisest ever presented to men. (Thomas Jefferson, date unknown)[15]

The individual known as the "Father of the Constitution," James Madison, warned against violating the text and spirit of the Constitution:

In bestowing eulogies due to the particular and internal checks of power, it ought not the less to be remembered that they are neither the sole nor the chief palladium of constitutional liberty. The people who are authors of this blessing must also be its guardians. Their eyes must be ever ready to mark, their voice to pronounce, and their arms to repel or repair, aggressions on the authority of their constitutions. (James Madison, 1792)[16]

It is remarkable that since its articulation in 1787, the U.S. Constitution has only been amended 27 times. Ten of these amendments, of course, occurred within the first two years of the Constitution's existence, the subsequent 17 being added to the text over the last 223 years. This feat is remarkable when one considers that over this same period of time, only one of the original 13 states, Massachusetts, has not completely rewritten its constitution. All of the other original 13 states have rewritten their constitutions at least once, and most have done so multiple times. The following illustrates the number of times each of the original 13 states has completely rewritten its constitution since 1787:

Connecticut—2

Delaware—4

Georgia—9

Maryland—4

Massachusetts—0

New Hampshire—3

New Jersey—3

New York—4

North Carolina—4

Pennsylvania—4

Rhode Island—2

South Carolina—6

Virginia—7[17]

Several commentators have remarked about the place of the Constitution in the collective historical narrative of the American people:

There's a strong strand of divine-guidance thinking about American exceptionalism. People have certainly seen the texts of the Constitution and the Declaration of Independence as the equivalent of a secular religion, with the idea then that you don't challenge these texts. (Mary Beth Norton, Cornell University, 2010)

In a country as fragmented as the United States is—we don't have a national religion, a really shared ethnicity—the kinds of emotions that would be directed at organic nationalism are displaced on the Constitution. (Sanford Levinson, University of Texas law professor, 2010)

The patriots of today long for the stability and the consistency of the past. They find it difficult living in the modern world and they take refuge in the familiar, the trusted, the consistent, the unchanging elements of society. Modernity, with all of its uncertainty, unfamiliarity, and revolutionary change, is upsetting and challenging to the paths and principles to which such groups cling. (There have been those who suggest that Muslim extremists hate the United States because it represents all of the negative aspects of modernity. See William Blum, *Why Terrorists Hate America*.[18]) What some might consider "counterpatriotism" or "antipatriotism" in today's context, then, is viewed as a solemn duty by those who embrace this philosophy. The result has been that throughout American history, there have been both strains of patriotism—that is, one that is unquestioningly supportive of government despite its misdeeds and missteps and one that is fiercely loyal to the original constructs of American government as they (patriots) interpret it. The latter view fosters bitter reaction to the policies and the programs that are meant to deal with the complexities of modern life, but that, for these patriots, are a bastardization of the purity that is epitomized by the founding documents of the American Republic. On several occasions throughout its history, the United States has found itself confronted by its own citizenry who wish to violently overthrow the government in its current incarnation and either (a) replace it with an altogether newly constructed government or (b) forcibly return it to the principles embodied in a strict interpretation of the Constitution without "elastic clauses," "judicial review," or "implied powers."

PLAN OF THE BOOK

This book shall explore the notion of the patriot in the American political lexicon and how the term, as understood by many today, is somewhat contrary to the normally accepted definitions of this term. From this alternate interpretation of what an American patriot truly is comes the justification for the formation of militia groups meant to check the power of an ever-growing expansive government that is deemed unresponsive to the true desires of the American people. The result has been that throughout American history, there has been political violence perpetrated in the name of a patriotic ideal that bases itself not on the protection of American government but on the desire to change and mold the government into some idealized version of what the government once was and can become again, if only through dedication and commitment to a cause. Too often, of course, such ideals have resulted in a conservative backlash to return to the values of the past. These values, it is believed, were pure in nature and maintained the natural order and balance of American society. Thus, in many patriot movements of today, there is a distrust and even intense hatred of all things seen as un-American. For instance, in the patriot world of political violence, the desire to return to a "pure" form of American government necessitates, indeed even demands, actions against those who do damage to such an ideal: immigrants, those of different religions (non-Christian), those who damage or destroy "traditional values," and the like.

This book shall be guided by the following outline. Chapter One will examine the idea of the patriot in the American mythos. This chapter shall more fully examine the notion of the patriot as both unquestioning lover of country and factious disturber of government. It will be demonstrated that these two notions of the patriot have gone hand in hand in American history. This chapter shall establish the idea that those who are "patriots" have either been "superpatriots" in Michael Parenti's sense (in that they follow government policy without question)[19] or they are patriots who agitate for change through violence or threatened violence. Even those who may fall into the former category may become violent (as in the case of individuals and groups who act violently toward those whom they believe are contravening government authority). The chapter will also lay the foundation for that which patriots "care" about: government. The construction of the U.S. Constitution will be examined, as will the violence that both precipitated and followed this seminal event in the hearts and minds of patriots. The "cult of the Constitution" will be established that provides a basis and justification for the acts of all patriots.

Chapter Two will examine the challenges that early American patriots faced as their government grew and evolved. This growth was problematic for some, as it meant a move away from cherished values of the Revolutionary period—small and limited government, states' rights, and the protection of valued cultural mores. The shift away from power being focused at the state level to power with a locus in the national seat of government would concern those who wished to remain loyal to the government as it *had* been constructed but who expressed serious concerns about *how* government was evolving. This tension between an idealized version of government and the reality of government would manifest itself first in tensions over slavery and then in a variety of reactions to the perceived "overreach" of governmental power. "States' rights" would become the rallying cry for patriots who wished to hold the constitutional government accountable to its original intent. And when it was perceived that government was overstepping its bounds, there were legislative means—for example, "nullification"—to rein in government, as well as violent reactions. These tensions would eventually culminate in the U.S. Civil War.

Given the historical context established in Chapters One and Two, Chapter Three will closely examine the factors that contributed to the making of the contemporary patriot movements. The rise of patriot groups will be examined in light of the end of the Cold War and the growing disenchantment with government and the frustration at the increasing involvement that government was believed to have had in both the public sphere and the personal lives of average Americans. Yet the movements that demanded something different from their government were not just found on the political right. That is, there was not just a longing for a return to the uncomplicated past where government was smaller and less intrusive. Indeed, during this time, there were violent political movements that expressed themselves on the left, which demanded wholesale change in their government because it had, in their minds, become "destructive to its ends." These groups, though they did not call themselves patriots, nevertheless had the same goal: to change government to one that was more reflective of the times and the aspirations of the people.

Chapter Four will examine various patriot and militia groups that formed in the aftermath of the Cold War and in reaction to the perceived changes in American values and the essence of American government. These groups were noticeably on the "right" of the political spectrum in that they shared a desire for smaller, less intrusive—and less obstructive—government. The violence in which these groups engaged differed from organized protests to militarized attempts to change the scope and nature of government. Despite the difference in their methods, however, they all seemed to be motivated by the overwhelming desire to return American government to the pristine past, where state and local governments passed laws that had direct effects on citizens' lives.

Chapter Five examines several patriot/militia groups that formed in the 1980s and the 1990s and the events that propelled their causes and led to the creation of new groups as the millennium approached. Two seminal events in the patriot/militia movement—Ruby Ridge and Waco—are examined and offered as the events that continue to inspire the patriot groups and the militia movements of the 21st century. The worst terrorist event perpetrated by an American—the bombing of the Alfred P. Murrah Federal Building in Oklahoma City—is also examined, as is the life of its perpetrator—Timothy McVeigh.

The Conclusion will discuss contemporary patriot/militia movements and what the presence of these groups means for today and the future. The notion that an "allegiance to liberty" has been the guiding force of patriot groups in both the past and the present will be a major concluding point.

NOTES

1. Page, William Tyler. 1917. "The American's Creed." April 3, 1918. http://www.ushistory.org/documents/creed.htm. (Accessed June 2, 2013).

2. Black, Eric. 1988. *Our Constitution: The Myth that Binds Us.* Westview Press, p. 47.

3. Ibid.

4. Ibid., p. 48.

5. Ibid.

6. Straub, Steve. 2012. "Alexander Hamilton, Real Liberty Is Neither Found in Despotism or the Extremes of Democracy, but in Moderate Governments." July 12. http://www.thefederalistpapers.org/founders/hamilton/alexander-hamilton-real-liberty-is-neither-found-in-despotism-or-the-extremes-of-democracy-but-in-moderate-governments. (Accessed May 21, 2014).

7. Gurr, Ted Robert. 2011. *Why Men Rebel.* Paradigm Publishers.

8. Kaminski, John P., ed. 2006. *The Quotable Jefferson.* Princeton University Press, p. 119.

9. "Benjamin Franklin to the Federal Convention." September 17, 1787. http://press-pubs.uchicago.edu/founders/documents/a7s3.html. (Accessed June 3, 2013).

10. "Thomas Jefferson on Politics and Government; Chapter 47: The Military and the Militia." http://famguardian.org/Subjects/Politics/thomasjefferson/jeff1480.htm. (Accessed May 25, 2014).

11. Http://www.monticello.org/site/jefferson/beauty-second-amendment-quotation. (Accessed July 10, 2013).

12. Kaminski, p. 51.

13. Benson, Ezra Taft. 1987. *Ensign.* (November). At https://www.lds.org/ensign/1987/11/our-divine-constitution. (Accessed September 1, 2013).

14. U.S. Senate. 80th Congress, 2nd Session. *United States Constitution, text, index, chronology, and leading quotations* (S.doc. 210). Washington, Government Printing Office, 1949. (Serial Set 11221).

15. Ibid.

16. Ibid.

17. "U.S. State Constitutions and Web Sites." http://www.constitution .org/cons/usstcons.htm. (Accessed May 20, 2014).

18. Blum, William. "Why Terrorists Hate America." http://www .thirdworldtraveler.com/Blum/WhyTerroristsHateAmer.html. (Accessed November 10, 2013).

19. Parenti, Michael. 2004. *Superpatriotism*. City Lights Publishers.

CHAPTER 1

What Is a Patriot?

SUPPORTER OR FACTIOUS DISTURBER?

In 2000, Mel Gibson starred in a movie titled *The Patriot*. Released only a few months before 9/11, Gibson's character of Benjamin Martin is portrayed as an individual who is tortured by his violent past in the service of the British crown and therefore hesitant to embrace the growing American colonial disaffection with Great Britain, Parliament, and King George III. In an early scene of the movie, a soldier/friend of Martin muses out loud about Martin's hesitancy to embrace the "cause" of revolution against the British Empire. His comment to Martin is, "I took you to be a patriot." Martin's reply is that he does believe in the cause of the American colonies but not to the extent of the lives that it will cost to take on the most powerful country in the world.

The list of characteristics that constitute a patriot probably seems straightforward to most Americans. Patriots are people who love their country and are willing to sacrifice themselves to a higher cause. That "cause" is whatever is in the best interests of the country and its people. In the case of *The Patriot*, Benjamin Martin fights as an American militiaman during the Revolutionary War. He fights unconventionally, often ambushing British soldiers from the confines of swamps, wheat fields, or densely covered forests. For the "cause" of independence, he sacrifices his home, two sons, and the easy life of a gentrified farmer he had enjoyed before the war. The love of country, however, spurs him to action. He is throughout the course of the movie, as many Americans would agree, a true "patriot," driven by an unswerving love of country.

Yet to the British who are his opponents, Benjamin Martin is not a patriot. Indeed, in his conduct of warfare against the British, Benjamin Martin does not abide by the "civilized" code of war. His targeting of officers, his unconventional tactics, and his unorthodox methods of attack earn him the scorn and the derision of his British counterparts. He could rightly be called a "guerilla" or perhaps even a "terrorist." How, then, is Benjamin Martin held up by one side as a patriot (hence the name of the movie) and by the other as a terrorist? The answer lies in the conflicted nature of what a patriot is and what he/she portends to represent.

The term "patriot" originates in ancient Greece. Its root is found in *patriotes* (fellow countrymen) and *patros* (father).[1] By the 17th century, a patriot was defined as a "loyal and disinterested supporter of one's country."[2] Though the "loyal" label here seems appropriate, the "disinterested" labels seems somewhat contradictory. By modern standards, patriots are not disinterested in the welfare of their country but are, at times, hypervigilant about their country's causes and survival. Yet in the early history of the American Republic, patriots were known more for their passive rather than active support of country. Bernard Bailyn (1965) points out that in the early history of the American experience, "formulas were suggested, tests outlined, by which *true patriots* [emphasis added] could be distinguished from conspiratorial dissenters."[3] Bailyn continues:

> Patriots never seek office; they have it thrust upon them. . . . They do not seek office because they do not need office; independent in wealth and opinion, they cannot be bought or meanly influenced. They are—palpably, transparently—lovers of virtue. . . . [t]he good magistrate "thinks it a great part of his duty, by precept and example, to educate the youth in a love of virtue and truth." The good magistrate seeks union and harmony in the public; *he is never found stirring dissension* [emphasis added].[4]

Bailyn notes that Benjamin Franklin, over the course of 14 elections for which he could have stood for political office, noted, "I never did, directly or indirectly, solicit any man's vote."[5]

Yet one who might rightly be called an antipatriot or "demagogue,"

> "fancies he is not made for the people but the people for him; that he does not govern for them but for himself; that the people live

only to increase his glory"—it is only the demagogue who stirs dis-sension. "He does not inquire what he may do for them but what he may draw from them; by this means he sets up an interest of profit, pleasure, or pomp in himself repugnant to the good of the public." He declares the active defense of justice to be "sedition and rebellion" and strives to "diminish that strength, virtue, power and courage which he knows to be bent against him." He is fearful of truth, and so "will always, by tricks, artifices, cavils, and all means possible endeavor to establish falsehood and dishonesty. . . [to] bring the people to such a pass that they may neither care nor dare to vindicate their rights."[6]

Thus, in the beginning of the American political consciousness, there is a clear meaning of the term "patriot" as one who quietly, behind the scenes, supports his country and does his best to promote public virtue and the general welfare of the people. By the mid-18th century, how-ever, there are at least two meanings for the term "patriot": "one whose ruling passion is the love of his country" and "a factious disturber of government."[7] In this context, a patriot may be one who is either (a) a passionate supporter of his country in its current iteration and one who is willing to defend the policies and programs of government despite vitriolic and constant criticism or (b) a detractor of current government policies and programs hearkening instead to some idealized version of past government that is deemed far superior to the current state of government.

In the American context today, both uses of the term "patriot" are common and deemed valid by the public. The first is applied to those who support the government regardless of their personal opinions or points of view. Military personnel, public servants (including local, state, and federal government officials), and average American citizens who support their government despite which political party is in power might rightly fall into the former category. On the other hand, members of the Tea Party, states' rights advocates, militia groups, and strict con-stitutional constructionists might also rightly be called patriots. These are individuals who wish to see a return to cherished political, social, and cultural values that have been subverted or replaced in the current version of American politics. Either of these "patriots" may use violence to promote their views and have done so on many occasions. Of particu-lar interest to this study is how such violence—most often political in nature—has been cloaked as "patriotic" and those who promote and justify such violence label themselves as "patriots."

It is the dual meaning of the term "patriot" and the accompanying political violence justified in the name of patriotism to which this study addresses itself. The former definition embodies the notion to which most Americans would associate the word "patriot." It is commonly believed that a patriot is one who loves their country and who would fight to defend its values, principles, and physical borders. This was the patriot of Mel Gibson's movie. The second definition of patriot, however, has always walked hand in hand with the first. A patriot may be one who is a "disturber" of government. A founding principle of the American Republic was limited government. There are individuals and groups both in the past and in the present who have deemed it their patriotic duty to hold the U.S. government to account and require it to fulfill the limited role upon which it was founded. Though they may be thought of as "disturbers," these individuals are, in their minds, protectors of the true values of the United States. Therefore, they are the true "patriots" because they do indeed love their country beyond what others do, particularly in the presence of an overbearing and interloping government.

The zealotry with which patriots act as disturbers of government sometimes manifests itself in violence across the decades. From Shays' Rebellion to the Whiskey Insurrection to the Bonus March to the rise of militia and patriot groups in the 1980s and 1990s, the common thread among these self-proclaimed patriots has been a distrust of government, its actions, and its inability to fulfill its obligations under an idealized version of the meaning of the American Republic. As noted by author Richard Abanes, the more committed individuals such as these display the following characteristics: "an obsessive suspicion of their government; a deep-seated hatred and fear of federal authorities; a belief in far-reaching conspiracy theories; and a feeling that for all intents and purposes Washington bureaucrats have discarded the U.S. Constitution."[8] Yet as sinister as these characteristics seem, for the patriot they embody the same ideal: an overwhelming love of government and a desire to return government to an idealized, pristine version of the past.

As a result of the reelection of President Barack Obama in November 2012, the political cause of the patriot was reinvigorated. In the aftermath of the election, political leaders in some 15 American states indicated the desire of their states to secede from the Union. During the off-cycle elections of 2013, one state—Colorado—saw 11 counties include "secession" from the state as an item on their ballots. According to the *Denver Post*, "Proponents say they have become alienated from the more urbanized Front Range and are unhappy with laws passed during this year's (2013) legislative session, including stricter gun laws and new renewable-energy standards."[9] As noted by the mayor of Fort Lupton, Colorado, the publicity of a secessionist vote would shed light on rural Colorado's grievances. "We not only want to be at the table," he said, "but we want a voice at the table as well."[10] The tension between rural and urban is repeated again and again by those who sometimes take a more aggressive route to expressing their patriotism. American history is replete with citizens expressing fear at an expansive and ever-growing government. Such attitudes are held by those that believe that they are living under the tyranny of government, which necessitates bold action. Moreover, the once forgotten notion of nullification—that is, the ability of states to disregard or "nullify" national laws when they conflict with state laws—has found new life in contemporary patriot movements.[11] In recent years, the idea that states can nullify actions of the federal government—encompassing issues such as gun control, health care, intrastate commerce, transportation security, and many others—have prompted state legislatures and governors to introduce legislation to overturn federal mandates that are seen as federal over-reach and not within the purview of the federal government's power as granted by the United States Constitution. Those who hold such views often couch their actions as "patriotic" and see themselves, legitimately, as "patriots."

These knee-jerk reactions may have many causes, but at the heart is the belief among many individuals and groups that the federal government has far exceeded its mandate as outlined by the Founding Fathers in the Constitution. The day after the November 2012 election, for instance, stocks in gun companies soared and people were buying guns and ammunition at record levels—stockpiling them for what they believe is the inevitable confrontation between the American government and the freedom-loving people of the United States. These actions were driven by the political rhetoric that swirled in the aftermath of the shootings of Representative Gabrielle Giffords in early 2012 and the shootings in a movie theater in Aurora, Colorado, in the summer of that year. The official rhetoric coming out of Washington intimated that stricter gun control laws were needed in the face of these tragedies. Such rhetoric, perceived as threats by a government intent on destroying fundamental freedoms, was pushed into hyperdrive after the shootings in Newtown, Connecticut, in December 2012.

Most, if not all, of the individuals reacting negatively to calls for more gun control laws would self-identify as patriots. They love their country. They idealize (and even worship) the Constitution of the United

States. They deem the 2nd Amendment to the Constitution inviolable and something with which the federal government has no authority to tamper. They also see an expansive and invasive federal government that has far exceeded the powers intended for it by the Founding Fathers. With recent events, there have been numerous threats of violence against the federal government if legislation is enacted.[12] Those expressing their anger and frustration view themselves as the true protectors and lovers of the American Republic, whereas government officials and the government itself no longer represent the interests of the people.

The question to be asked, then, is are such actions patriotic and do they represent the action of true patriots? Are patriots and patriotism the true love one expresses for their government and the willingness to stand by one's government, right or wrong? Author Michael J. Parenti (2004) has defined such patriotism as "superpatriotism." According to Parenti, "Superpatriots are those people who place national pride and American supremacy above every other public consideration, those who follow leaders uncritically, especially in their war policies abroad. Superpatriotism is the nationalistic hype propagated by officialdom, the media, and various flag-waving groups."[13] For Parenti, patriots who are "superpatriots" are dangerous, as they follow leaders and policies blindly, never questioning and never challenging the tenets and precepts of a government that may or may not be corrupt. "Superpatriots" are not patriots at all. In fact, they are dangerous pretenders of the democratic process, criticizing those who do not fall in line with government policy and disavowing the loyalty of anyone who has the temerity to question government policy.

On the other hand, a patriot who is a "factious disturber of government" may be the individual who means to hold their government to account. This may be the individual or the group that demands of their government fiscal responsibility and legislative and judicial minimalism on issues that are considered to be of a moral, social, or religious nature. These are the individuals who subscribe to the notion of limited government and the belief that government should be given no other powers than those that were acceded to the government in the Constitution.

Unfortunately, both notions of a patriot are often one and the same. That is, whether superpatriots or factious disturbers of government, such individuals have difficulty accepting the process of social and political change or the inevitable evolution of government systems. They become rigid literalists who believe that their interpretation of government is correct and that dissenting views are wrong or perhaps even treasonous. When they are unable to effect change in a timely manner, they resort to violence. This, in fact, is the *modus operandi* of the historical patriot movement and the political violence that has defined many patriot groups in the past and in the present.

REPUBLICANISM AND THE PATRIOT

The roots of the modern patriot can be found in the doctrine and philosophy of republicanism. As early as the Roman Republic, political theorists realized that geographically large political units were unwieldy and would need new forms of government rather than the traditional model—empires. Republics would have centralized government but would rely upon local governments to administer on behalf of the local populations. Thus, during the early Roman Republic era, there was the introduction of local provincial control where local governments would promulgate rules, laws, and regulations particular to each population but that would be consistent with the overall policies of the Roman Republic.[14]

This method of government was rediscovered during the Enlightenment and became the basis for what would later become the United States Constitution. Concentrated mostly in the ideas of John Locke, republicanism in the United States emphasized mixed government, federalism, separation of powers, and checks and balances.[15]

To the American mind, republicanism emphasized liberty, inalienable rights, a rejection of inherited power or aristocracies, the vilification of corruption, and the independence of each citizen who felt the natural need to perform civic duties as their patriotic duty.[16]

The American patriot of the Revolutionary period distrusted the large, aristocratic governments of the old world, particularly as manifested by the abuses of the British Crown. For these patriots, real government was small, responsive, and unobtrusive. These sentiments were evident at the Constitutional Convention of 1787 as delegates haggled over the notion of plans to (a) create a new government that would replace the Articles of Confederation or (b) revise the Articles of Confederation, which would maintain the balance between small local governments (i.e., states) and a national government. In the end, the delegates endorsed a plan that created a new national government that was far more expansive than the original intention. Within the new Constitution were ideas of expansiveness antithetical to the ideas of the patriot. For instance, when articulating the scope and power of the new legislative branch of government, Article I Section 8 introduced the concept of the "necessary and proper" clause.

Since dubbed the "elastic clause" because of the reality that has greatly expanded the powers of Congress, this idea has come to epitomize the overreach and expansive nature that have come to characterize modern American politics. Article VI of the Constitution is also problematic, as it states that "The Constitution. . . shall be the supreme Law of the Land. . . ." To individuals who had just fought a revolution against government power that never seemed to end, the idea that the new Constitution would trump the states and their elected legislatures sowed the seeds for future conflicts.

Some of the concerns of those who opposed the expansiveness of the new Constitution were assuaged by the passage of the Bill of Rights, or the first 10 amendments to the Constitution. Particularly, guarantees of the right to keep and bear arms (Amendment 2), civil liberty protections (Amendments 1, 4–6), assurances that nothing in the Constitution infringes upon the rights retained by the people (Amendment 9), and the notion that all rights not specifically granted to the new national government under the Constitution were reserved to the states—the reserve powers clause (Amendment 10)—mollified those who stood ready to oppose the expanded powers granted to the new government. With these assurances, opponents of the new Constitution could not then imagine circumstances under which the new government would trample the rights of the people. Nevertheless, over the decades, the rise of the power of the presidency and the role of the federal courts in strengthening national law over state law paved the way to patriotic sentiments that once again are ready to stand against intrusive and obstructive government.

CREATING THE PATRIOT MAGNUM OPUS–THE ROAD TO THE CONSTRUCTION OF THE U.S. CONSTITUTION

Patriots both supportive and critical of government view the U.S. Constitution as the foundation of the American system of government and the inspiration for their actions. The need for a new system of government was forged out of political violence. The Articles of Confederation, which had governed the states during the fight with Great Britain, had proven woefully inadequate when the country finally secured its independence. The Articles' failures led to perhaps the most quintessential event in convincing elite members of American society that drastic action was needed.

SHAYS' REBELLION

Post-Revolutionary conditions in western Massachusetts were dire for the average individual who had served the fledgling country in the American Revolutionary Army. Most of the rural inhabitants of western Massachusetts had little but their land to provide economic sustenance for themselves and their families. In the aftermath of the Revolution, Massachusetts's European trading partners had largely refused to extend credit to the state and demanded payment for their goods in hard currency. This demand led to a precarious debt situation in the state. Farmers, many of whom had found it necessary to place mortgages on their farms when they entered military service, now found themselves unable to extend their credit as merchants, themselves hit hard by the hard currency requirement, began demanding payment in hard currency. The result was a patriot farmer who now could not meet his debt and tax obligations, as lending institutions refused to extend further credit on overextended loans. As individuals began to lose their land and other possessions, a strong resentment arose against those who were in official employment of the government—tax collectors and the courts—where creditors obtained and enforced judgments against debtors and where tax collectors obtained judgments authorizing property seizures.[17]

Facing default, farmers became radicalized when they felt themselves and their livelihoods threatened by government policies. In 1782 and 1783, individuals who had fought for their country as "patriots" began to obstruct official government tax collections and property seizures. These activities came to a head in the late summer of 1786 when well-armed and organized forces began to prevent county courts from sitting as their sessions began. It was these courts that would hear the petitions from creditors to foreclose on farms whose mortgages were overdue or seize land if farmers were in serious default.

Daniel Shays, a veteran of the Revolutionary Army and by definition a patriot, was one of the organizers of what was increasingly being viewed by the Massachusetts state government as a rebellion. Participants armed themselves and began a march on the state capital in Boston to demand relief. The governor of the state, James Bowdoin, declared the protestors a "mob" and made preparations for military action.[18] Along the way, several skirmishes took place among the rebels and county militias that had been mustered to deal with individual acts of violence. The Supreme Judicial Court of Massachusetts indicted 11 leaders of the rebellion as "disorderly, riotous, and seditious persons."[19] Yet the acts of the dispossessed or soon-to-be-so farmers of western Massachusetts were not isolated incidents. Neighboring states also were facing their own violence as a result of the conditions present in the states as a result of the postwar depression (e.g., New York and Rhode Island). In short, the epicenter of the patriot movement to remove the British tyrannical rule from the colonies—Massachusetts and its close neighbors—now itself became the focal point of discontent. The state's determination to punish the ringleaders of the rebellion—as evidenced by judicial indictments and the continuation of the seizure of land and property—further radicalized the poor and dispossessed, who began to organize an overthrow of the state government. "The seeds of war are now sown," wrote one correspondent in Shrewsbury, and by mid-January, rebel leaders spoke of smashing the "tyrannical government of Massachusetts."[20]

So alarming was the rhetoric of the rebels that there was the belief expressed that Massachusetts was on the brink of civil war.[21] Samuel Adams, himself considered to be the penultimate patriot and agitator who almost single-handedly brought Massachusetts to the cause of liberty, claimed that treason was being sown among the "commoners." In response, Adams helped draw up the Riot Act, or an act that declared the unauthorized assemblage of individuals as riotous and prescribed punitive actions in the cases of those who refused to disperse. Moreover, Adams helped construct a resolution in the Massachusetts state legislature that would suspend *habeas corpus*, effectively allowing state authorities to keep people in jail without the promise of trial. There were additional provisions that suggest prohibiting speech critical of the government and offering pardons to protestors who were willing to take an oath of allegiance to the state.[22]

Inasmuch as the national government of the United States under the Articles of Confederation was unable to suppress the rebellion due to a lack of funds, Governor Bowdoin suggested the creation of a private militia funded by Boston's merchants. Some 125 Bostonian merchants donated nearly $10,000 to raise a militia of more than 3,000 men to confront the rebels.[23] As the rebellion moved from west to east, the privately funded state militia began to march west to confront the rebels. The first clash was at the national armory at Springfield. Though they had no permission from the national army to do so, the private state militia occupied the armory and took guns and munitions from it to fight the rebels. An attempted raid by the rebels in late January 1787 led to a skirmish that killed four rebels and wounded 20 more. A second attack by militia forces in early February 1787 scattered the rebel forces, though some elements continued to engage various militia units until the early summer in 1787.[24]

In the aftermath of the rebellion, several hundred participants were indicted on charges relating to the rebellion, but most were pardoned under a general amnesty granted by the state of Massachusetts. Such pardons were deemed judicious given the precarious nature of the state's finances and the possibility that protests could again erupt at any time. Eighteen of the individuals deemed to be ringleaders of the rebellion were convicted and sentenced to death, but most of these individuals either had their convictions overturned on appeal, were pardoned, or had their sentences commuted. Daniel Shays himself was pardoned in 1788,[25] but he was generally vilified by the Boston press, who painted him as an archetypal anarchist opposed to the government.[26]

Interestingly enough, only a decade before, Daniel Shays had been viewed as the quintessential patriot. He had risen to the rank of captain in the Massachusetts militia and had fought at Lexington, Bunker Hill, and Saratoga.[27] Having left his home and farm to fight in the service of his country, he left the military in 1780 after being wounded. Shays, who was vilified as the "archetypal anarchist" opposed to government, was never paid for his service to his country and died broken and penniless.[28]

Like those who would follow him in later years, Daniel Shays's armed opposition to the Massachusetts government was not intended to destroy but to hold government to account for the promises it had made to its citizens. Indeed, having served his country, Daniel Shays and others believed that there was a reciprocity due them for the patriotic duties they performed on behalf of the new government. Unfortunately, their belief that the Massachusetts government had become unreasonable and tyrannical in its treatment of former soldiers was met not with sympathy or promises of concession but with gunfire and threats of death. Such government overreach and perceived unresponsiveness would become the hallmarks of patriot movements from that time down through the course of American history. Indeed, the belief that patriots had fought for a government that would be minimally intrusive and represent the views of all people, including the "commoners," was the hope of every patriot. Many had their hopes dashed, however, with the creation of the new U.S. Constitution.

THE ANNAPOLIS CONVENTION

The political unrest punctuated by Shays' Rebellion was on the minds of delegates to the Annapolis Convention, which convened in September 1786. Attended by 12 delegates from only five states (i.e.,

New York, New Jersey, Pennsylvania, Delaware, and Virginia), the Annapolis Convention met to consider the deficiencies of the government of the United States as then constituted under the Articles of Confederation. The inability of the national government to confront the challenge posed by Shays' Rebellion illustrated to many of the business and merchant class the need for a stronger national government to ensure the monetary and fiscal survival of the new country. The convention proved to be a bully pulpit for Alexander Hamilton, who had long believed that the new government must shore up its financial situation if it were to survive as a national entity and not break into the constituent states.

The Annapolis Convention was timely in its call for stronger national government in light of the growing political unrest in many of the states and the small rebellions that had been taking place since the end of the Revolutionary War. It was the enormity of Shays' Rebellion, however, and the potential of an action such as this to spread that persuaded the delegates in Annapolis to call for a Constitutional Convention to be held in Philadelphia the following year to consider proposals to revise the Articles of Confederation. Such revisions would be necessary to quell the growing sentiment among the citizenry of government ineptitude and weakness.

But the final result of the Constitutional Convention would be a form of government many who longed for small and minimalist government would find disappointing in its final form.

THE CONSTITUTIONAL CONVENTION

No other single event or document inspires more passion among self-proclaimed patriots than the U.S. Constitution. For many, the Constitution is a document of perfect construction, birthed by individuals who were themselves the most avowed patriots of their time. Today, these individuals are called by many names: the Founding Fathers, the Framers (of the Constitution), or the Founders. But to today's modern patriots, they all embody one thing: the desire for a government "of the people, by the people, and for the people." Such a government was to be based on popular consent, not the capricious whims of a monarch. It was to be prescribed and limited and was to ensure the liberties and freedoms the country had fought and died for during the Revolution. The Founders knew and understood the foibles of men. They constructed a document that would ensure the financial solvency of the new union but would also give deference to the desires of the people. It would provide stability, harmonize the sectional interests of the country, and provide for popular representation. How this was to be accomplished was the subject of the Constitutional Convention that convened in Philadelphia, Pennsylvania, in May 1787.

Of the 55 individuals who initially attended the beginning of the Constitutional Convention, only 39 eventually signed the document that would be presented four months later. Some had drifted away over the long, hot Philadelphia summer, and some refused to sign when the final draft was submitted for approval. Though all of these individuals could be considered patriots given their devotion to the idea of a union of "united states," they had very different ideas about how to construct and maintain the government that would eventually be created.

The original intention of those attending the Annapolis Convention was to call upon the Congress, still operating under the auspices of the Articles of Confederation, to authorize a Constitutional Convention that was to revise the existing Articles. To many, the Articles of Confederation, though imperfect, were a legitimate representation of the will of the people. For instance, the Articles preserved the one facet of government that many patriots felt strongly about—that is, the role of the state governments in relation to the national government. The Articles of Confederation recognized the indisputable fact that state governments existed before any national government and that the loyalties of the people were first to their state and second to the nation. This single fact, the recognition of which was literally sidestepped when the Constitution was finally constructed, would plague intrastate relations up through and including the Civil War and would continue until the present day in one form or another.

But the document constructed in 1787 did not fully address the wide chasms that existed between the different states and the sectional differences that existed at the time among the various states. The New England and Middle Atlantic states had economies based on commerce and industry, and foreign trade was critical to the continued growth of these states. The southern states, on the other hand, were traditional, gentrified, and tied to the land in a manner different than their compatriots to the north. The southern economies were based on agriculture and slave labor. This cheap supply of labor allowed the South to maintain its position relative to the North, since the northern states needed the raw materials—which could be extracted cheaply—of the South to continually fuel the growth and expansion that was occurring in the North. Sectional differences reared themselves often during the

Constitutional Convention, and it became evident to many that the new government was being drafted to protect the commercial class and emerging interests of those tied to these interests.

Today, patriots view the U.S. Constitution as the magnum opus that defines the parameters of the patriot's view of the world.[29] Yet those who sat in the Constitutional Convention in Philadelphia during the summer of 1787 could rightly call themselves patriots as they envisioned a new form of government unlike any other in the world. Some supported a strong, centralized government, while others opted for the security of governance by the states.

At the outset of the Convention, a new plan was presented by the delegates from Virginia for a new national government of the United States. This plan, known as the Virginia—or large-states—plan, was put forth by the largest and most populous of the 13 states then in existence. Rather than amending or revising the Articles of Confederation as had been the original intent of the Convention, the Virginia plan proposed an entirely new government, one that would not recognize the then widely accepted idea of state supremacy over national government but one that would make the new national government coequal with state government and, in some cases, even make it superior to the states. Patriots on both sides had strong opinions about such a plan. Patriots who held up the sanctity of states' rights were fearful of the potential intrusions of national law into the realm of state law. Moreover, as many of the Founders themselves recognized, the history of national governments was inevitably expansionist, as such governments must expand or eventually wither away. Such expansion, however, comes at the expense of local government, as more and more power must be relinquished to the national government in order to perform the tasks of an ever-growing and ever-expanding government.

Patriots who favored small government put forth the New Jersey—or small-states—plan in order to counter the move toward more expansionist government. But the New Jersey plan did little but revise the Articles of Confederation at the edges (e.g., Congress was given the power to tax and spend and the addition of an "executive," though it was unclear what form this would take), making it less appealing to those who recognized that the fledgling country was in a precarious financial situation.

Those who favored a more robust national government became known as the "nationalists" and included many of the undisputed patriots of the Revolutionary era. George Washington, James Madison, Alexander Hamilton, and Benjamin Franklin had all played pivotal roles in the victory over Great Britain and had been instrumental in the life of the country as it had evolved after the war. No one at the time would have dared to call them unpatriotic, but many of their ideas certainly flew in the face of the smaller and less intrusive national government most people had envisioned with their victory over the British. After all, Great Britain had a centralized government that had trampled on the rights of the American colonists and been unable to make concessions to avoid war. Moreover, the presence of the king had exacerbated the ability of the Parliament to see beyond the needs of the state, thereby preventing the negotiations that were necessary to preserve the relationship between the colonists and the Crown.

Yet only four years removed from their victory, the nationalists were proposing a government that included a bicameral legislature (not unlike the British Parliament, which consisted of the House of Commons and the House of Lords) but that shared power between the two branches of government rather than making one more responsive to the people (as the House of Commons was in the British system). Small states, of course, bristled at the suggestion put forth in the Virginia Plan that both houses of Congress would be based on a system of proportional representation, thereby putting small states at a perpetual disadvantage. This was clearly at odds with the equality that small states enjoyed with large states under the system of the Articles of Confederation. The introduction of an executive smacked to some of the possibility that the executive would come to dominate the legislature, thereby doing damage to the idea of legislative supremacy. And finally, the provision put forth in the Virginia Plan of an independent national judiciary was seen as a direct threat to those who firmly believed that laws were best promulgated and subsequently adjudicated only at the state level.

Both the small-state advocates—those who mostly supported a revision of the Articles of Confederation because of the preservation of the status quo of equality that they enjoyed as a result of their provisions—and the large-state advocates—those who envisioned the need for a robust and vibrant national government to meet the growing demands of a country destined to play a role on the international stage—can rightly be called patriots. The former group advocated small government and government closer and more responsive to the people, while the latter group advocated large government that could protect the freedoms and liberties of the people not just in the current iteration of time but far into the future. Of course, there remain patriots of both these positions today. But those of the former persuasion—those who advocate smaller, less intrusive government—seem to have been more successful in coopting the moniker of "patriot" for their purposes, as shall subsequently be shown.

PORTENDING THE PATRIOT FUTURE: THE FEDERALIST–ANTIFEDERALIST DEBATE

Upon the construction of the Constitution, the debate over ratification took a turn between those who advocated larger government and those who feared the potential abuses that come from larger government. In a series of articles and essays written in support of the new Constitution, James Madison, Alexander Hamilton, and John Jay put forth their justifications for the new Constitution and urged the citizens of the various states to ratify the instrument as the last, best hope to secure the social and economic well-being of the new country. Using the pseudonym "Publius," the authors of the Federalist Papers attempted to persuade their fellow citizens that the new Constitution was an instrument for the good and benefit of all. Indeed, the pseudonym indicated that Madison, Hamilton, and Jay—all wealthy and influential—were, in fact, speaking for and on behalf of the common man—the public.

In contrast and by way of response, antifederalists published a series of tracts pointing out the deficiencies of the new Constitution, chief among them a perceived lack of protection and explicit statements regarding the protection of individual rights. Antifederalists held that the lack of an explicit statement of rights in the Constitution would inevitably lead to the abuse of such rights by an expansive government. Such abuses, invariably the consequence of a tyrannical and abusive government, would necessitate bold action. The authors of the antifederalist papers (historically assumed to be George Clinton, Robert Yates, and Samuel Bryan, among others) argued against large government and the provisions that aimed themselves at the protection of business and commerce.[30] The pen names used by the individuals—"Cato," "Brutus," and "Centinel"—are all suggestive of individuals who opposed the bastardization of traditional values and the taking of power not freely given. For instance, Cato the Elder was a Roman statesman who opposed what he viewed as the "degenerate" nature of Greek influences on the austerity and purity of Rome, while Brutus was the assassin of the ultimate tyrant—Julius Caesar.[31] Both federalists and antifederalists assumed for themselves the role of patriot in the protection of the interests of the country, but both came to it from very different positions.

In Federalist No. 1, Alexander Hamilton laid out six themes that the Federalist Papers would exposit in favor of the new Constitution: first, the utility of the Union to the political prosperity of the American citizen; second, the insufficiency of the Articles of Confederation in preserving the Union that had been so hard won through the struggles and trials of the Revolution; third, the necessity of an energetic government to meet the needs of the people; fourth, the conformity of the new constitution to the principles of republicanism; fifth, the deference exhibited by the constitution to the existing state constitutions; and sixth, the security that the proposed constitution would provide in support of good government, liberty, and prosperity.[32]

To the Antifederalist mind, each of the points listed meant little without explicit guarantees of individual freedom. Though written in a much less structured fashion than the Federalist Papers, the Antifederalists wrote more of a collection of essays from several sources that were placed in a compendium in which each essay was meant to be a response to the 85 essays of the Federalist Papers.[33] The Antifederalist papers were, in some cases, a direct rebuttal of points made in the Federalist Papers and a reinterpretation of Federalist argument in the case of others.[34] What is incontrovertible, however, is that the Antifederalists viewed the lack of an explicit Bill of Rights in the Constitution as an issue that would sink the ratification of the proposed document. Freedom-loving Americans who had just sacrificed blood and sinew on behalf of more explicit freedoms would not stand idly by while being assured that such rights were explicit in the social contract or found in state constitutions, which was the argument being put forth by the Federalists.

Thus, in the Federalist–Antifederalist debate over the Constitution, both sides could rightly claim ownership of the "patriot" label. Federalists who were, in actuality, representatives of the nationalists who constructed the bulk of the proposed Constitution were fulfilling their patriotic duty and vision of forging a new nation unlike any other before it in history. The Federalist "patriots" were striving to construct a new country while being true to the principles of the revolution. While the nature of this patriotism was evolutionary, inasmuch as the country that was envisioned existed only on paper, the sentiment of patriotism was ever present in the creation of a country that would be representative of all the cultures and traditions that then defined the American experience. Antifederalists, on the other hand, were the "patriots" who were defending the newfound freedoms that had so long been denied under the British Crown. Antifederalists were the "patriots" who, by their insistence upon a Bill of Rights, were protecting the people against the future abuses of an inevitably expanding government. In essence, in this debate, patriotism was in the eyes of the beholder.

CITIZEN JEFFERSON AND THE CULT OF THE CONSTITUTION

The patriot and militia movements of today can point to two central threads that seem to be woven into the fabric of the notion of a "patriot" in the 21st century. The first is an affinity for the philosophies and ideas of Thomas Jefferson, third president of the United States. Today's patriots hold up Jefferson as the quintessential supporter of their cause. At the core of Jefferson's belief was the notion of a republican form of government. Though republicanism has meant many things down through the ages, it is generally believed today to denote a government in which the representatives of the people are selected through some other manner than heredity, generally through means of popular election. A republic is one in which there is "rule by the people" and "rule by law," as opposed to the arbitrary and capricious rule by monarchs, autocrats, tyrants, or oligarchies.[35]

Jefferson said of republicanism:

A just & solid republican government maintained here [the United States], will be a standing monument & example for the aim & limitation of the people of other countries; and I join with you in the hope and belief that they will see from our example that a free government is of all others the most energetic; that the inquiry which has been excited among the mass of mankind by our revolution & its consequences will ameliorate the condition of man over a great portion of the globe. (To John Dickinson, Washington, March 6, 1801)[36]

To George Washington in 1788, Jefferson wrote:

I was much an enemy of monarchy before I came to Europe. I am ten thousand times more so since I have seen what they are. There is scarcely an evil known in these countries which may not be traced to their King as its source, nor a good which is not derived from the small fibres [sic] of republicanism exiting among them.[37]

Finally, Jefferson noted:

> But with all the defects of our constitutions, whether general or
> particular, the comparison of our governments with those of
> Europe are like a comparison of heaven & hell. England, like the
> earth, may be allowed to take the intermediate station. And yet, I
> hear there are people among you who think the experience of our
> governments has already proved the republican government will
> not answer. Send those gentry here to count the blessings of the
> monarchy. (To Joseph Jones, Paris, August 14, 1787)[38]

Jefferson firmly believed that republican government would foster a
virtuous and moral citizenry as long as it was supported by two fundamental principles: a strict interpretation of the Constitution and the
protection of states' rights in the face of governmental power.

The first principle—strict Constitutional constructionism—provided
the bulwark of limited government that Jefferson believed was necessary for the protection of the republic. As Jefferson saw it, "the sum
of good government [is] a wise and frugal government, which shall
restrain men from injuring one another, which shall leave them otherwise free to regulate their own pursuits of industry and improvement,
and shall not take from the mouth of labor the bread it has earned."[39] As
Washington's Secretary of State, Jefferson would write:

> I consider the foundation of the Constitution laid on this ground:
> that "all powers not delegated to the United States by the
> Constitution, nor prohibited by it to the States, are reserved to the
> States or to the people." To take a single step beyond the boundar-
> ies thus especially drawn around the powers of Congress, is to take
> possession of a boundless field of power, no longer susceptible of
> any definition.[40]

Thus, Jefferson's notion of strict Constitutional constructionism
went hand-in-hand with his affinity for states' rights.[41] As stated explicitly in the 10th Amendment to the Constitution, all powers not delegated to the federal government were reserved by the states or by the
people. In Jefferson's estimation, certain powers had been specifically
delegated to the federal government for the purposes of establishing a
new national government. Yet this government was purposely limited
in size and scope, as evidenced by the balance of powers and the checking mechanisms that had been built in to the Constitution. Jefferson

wrote of the balance between national and state governments that "My general plan would be to make the States one as to everything connected with foreign nations, and several as to everything domestic."[42] Jefferson asserted that any acts undertaken by the central government that went beyond the explicitly stated powers outlined in the Constitution were "unconstitutional, void, and of no force."[43] Since the states had not contracted to create an ultimate arbiter in the Constitution, each state had "an equal right to judge for itself, as well of the infractions as of the mode and measure of redress."[44]

For Jefferson, the states were the best protectors of republicanism. As he stated to Destutt de Tracy at Monticello in 1811, "The true barriers [i.e., protections] of our liberty in this country are our State governments."[45] Though Americans often complain today that we are in constant election cycles,[46] had Thomas Jefferson had his way, there would have been more rather than fewer elections. Jefferson firmly believed that the people should have the opportunity to elect their representatives either semiannually or annually. Such election cycles were already the norm in Connecticut and Rhode Island.[47] In Federalist No. 53, James Madison makes the case for biannual elections. But Jefferson believed that the people should have the frequent ability to comment (by the power of the vote) upon the manner in which they were being represented at both the state and the national level. State representation was superior for Jefferson, as he believed that state governments dealt more directly with the issues that were closest to the interests of the people. As he wrote to Joseph C. Cabell from Monticello in February 1816:

> The way to have good and safe government, is not to trust it all to one; but to divide it among the many, distributing to every one exactly the functions he is competent to. Let the National government be entrusted with the defense of the nation, and its foreign & federal relations; the State governments with the civil rights, laws, police, & administration of what concerns States generally; the Counties with the local concerns of the counties, and each Ward direct the interests within itself. It is by dividing and subdividing these republics from the great National one down thro' [sic] all its subordinations, until it ends in the administration of every man's farm and affairs by himself; by placing under every one what his own eye may superintend, that all will be done for the best. What has destroyed liberty and the rights of man in every government which has ever existed under the sun? The generalizing & concentrating of all powers into one body. . .[48]

Republicanism, strict Constitutional constructionism, and states' rights were all essential to Jefferson's ideals. But these are not the only elements that attract today's patriots to the Jeffersonian notions of government. Many of today's patriot and militia groups tend to be found more prominently in rural areas of the United States. This concentration is consistent with the characteristics of far-right extremist groups that tend to exhibit behavior related to racism, extreme religiosity, lower education, male-dominated groups, and below-average incomes.[49] Today, attitudes toward rural populations in the United States are mixed, with some authors stating that rural America is often seen as "dumb, boorish, and bigoted."[50] Yet Jefferson believed that the real backbone of the republican ideal was (1) the entire body of landholders throughout the United States and (2) the body of laborers, not being landholders, whether in husbanding or the arts. As noted by Drew McCoy, "the abject dependence of the landless or laboring poor rendered them vulnerable to bribery, corruption, and factious dissension, a society with large numbers of these dependents was hardly suited to the Republican form."[51] Land, then, provided its owner with a great measure of personal independence.[52] Such independence, republicans believed, "permitted a citizen to participate responsibly in the political process, for it allowed him to pursue spontaneously the common or public good, rather than the narrow interest of the men—or the government—on whom he depended for his support."[53] In his *Notes on the State of Virginia*, Jefferson commented that "Those who labour [sic] in the earth are the chosen people of God, if ever he had a chosen people, whose breasts he has made his peculiar deposit for substantial and genuine virtue. . . ."[54]

Jefferson would be the quintessential conservative in today's parlance. This no doubt enamors him to the vast majority of patriot and militia adherents who revere his ideas. Consider, for instance, Jefferson's defense of those who labor on the land:

An industrious farmer occupies a more dignified place in the scale of beings, whether moral or political, than a lazy lounger, valuing himself on his family too proud to work, and drawing out a miserable existence by eating on that surplus of other men's labor, which is the sacred fund of the helpless poor. A pitiful annuity will only prevent them from exerting that industry and those talents which would soon lead them to a better fortune.[55]

Even in Jefferson's time, there were those who saw the moral, spiritual, economic, and political decay that accompanied modern life. One commentator at the time suggested that it was the "inevitable lot" of some in society to be poor and "experience a certain degree of dependence and servility."[56]

Yet Jefferson, believing in the triumph of republican ideals, wrote to a pregnant acquaintance in Europe in 1790, noting that

> You may make children there, but this is the country to transplant them to. . . . There is no comparison between the sum of happiness enjoyed here and there. All the distractions of your great Cities are but feathers in the scale against the domestic enjoiments [sic] and rural occupations, and neighborly societies live amidst here.[57]

Another of Jefferson's endearing qualities to today's patriots and militia groups is his (supposed) stance on firearms and the 2nd Amendment. Two quotes on firearms have been attributed to Jefferson:

> "The beauty of the Second Amendment is that it will not be needed until they try to take it." The variation of this quote is: "The people will not understand the importance of the Second Amendment until it is too late."[58]

The second quote attributed to Jefferson is:

> "The strongest reason for the people to retain the right to keep and bear arms is, as a last resort, to protect themselves against tyranny in government."[59]

The preceding quote was first cited by Charley Reese in his article "Founding Fathers Gave Individuals the Right to Bear Arms," published in the *Orlando Sentinel*, June 22, 1989. This quotation appeared in a number of publications in quick succession in the mid-1990s, including in hearings before a U.S. Senate subcommittee investigating the growth of the militia movement in the United States.[60]

Despite what gun advocates would wish, neither of the quotes above can be directly attributed to Thomas Jefferson.[61] It is true that in his draft of the Virginia Constitution, Jefferson wrote, "No freeman shall be debarred the use of arms." But there is no evidence to support that Jefferson was a full-throated supporter of the 2nd Amendment or the unequivocal right of private citizens to keep and bear arms either as a means to secure a well-regulated militia or in the interest of protecting their personal liberties and freedoms. Still, there are those who believe that Jefferson *might* have said these things. One commentator who read a skeptical account of Jefferson's association with gun rights noted,

> I do not know if Jefferson actually ever made such a statement or not, (but) I find it odd that many people attribute it to him if it wasn't true. It's ridiculous in my opinion to propose that since nowhere in his writings there is trace of such a statement, then Jefferson has never said something like that. Jefferson could have come up with those words in any occasion of his public or private life and someone else recorded and then quoted him.[62]

Whether Thomas Jefferson spoke out forcefully for gun rights or not is really beside the point to most patriots and militia group members. Jefferson gave them more than enough ammunition to oppose governmental overreach on his comments on limited government, personal liberties, and the values of state power versus federal power. These sentiments support and sustain these groups to this day.

And like Jefferson, today's patriots hold an affinity for the U.S. Constitution. Almost upon its construction, the Constitution took on a life far beyond the mere parchment upon which it was written. It became not only the outline for government but a document that was inspired by God. This reverence is epitomized in the following quotes:

> The virtue, moderation, and patriotism which marked the steps of the American people in framing, adopting, and thus far carrying into effect our present system of government has excited the admiration of the nations. (George Washington, 1789)

> The example of changing a constitution, by assembling wise men of the state, instead of assembling armies, will be worth as much to the world as the former examples we had given them. The Constitution, too, which was the result of our deliberations, is unquestioningly the wisest ever presented to men. (Thomas Jefferson, 1788)

> We may be tossed upon an ocean where we can see no land—nor, perhaps the sun or stars. But there is a chart and a compass for us to study, to consult, and to obey. That chart is the Constitution. (Daniel Webster, 1847)

Let every American, every lover of liberty, every well-wisher to his posterity, swear by the blood of the Revolution never to violate in the least particular the laws of the country, and never to tolerate their violation by others. As the patriots of seventy-six did to support the Declaration of Independence, so to the support of the Constitution and laws let every American pledge his life, his property, and his sacred honor. Let every man remember that to violate the law is to trample on the blood of his father, and to tear the charter of his own and his children's liberty. Let reverence for the laws, be breathed by every American mother, to the lisping babe, that prattles on her lap. Let it be taught in schools, in seminaries, and in colleges, let it be written in primers, in spelling books, and in almanacs, let it be preached from the pulpit, proclaimed in legislative halls, and enforced in courts of justice. And, in short, let it become the political religion of the Nation, and, in particular, a reverence for the Constitution. (Abraham Lincoln, 1838, Lyceum Address)[63]

In Lincoln's Lyceum Address, he hints at the reverence that should be accorded the Constitution and its place in the American system of laws. This idea would be expanded upon by later commentators, who would elevate the Constitution's place in the narrative of American history from merely a well-written document to an "inspired" document. Indeed, in later years, the U.S. Constitution would be said to be divinely ordained by God:

The hand of Divine Providence was never more plainly visible in the affairs of men than in the framing and the adopting of that instrument [the Constitution]. It is beyond comparison the greatest even in American history, and, indeed, is it not of all events in modern times the most pregnant with consequences for every people on earth? (Andrew Johnson, 1865)

When we look down 100 years and see the origin of our Constitution, when we contemplate all its trials and triumphs, when we realize how completely the principles upon which it is based have met every national need and every national peril, how devoutly should we say with Franklin, "God governs in the affairs of men," and how solemn should be the thought that to us is delivered this ark of the people's covenant, and to us given the duty to shield it from impious hands. It comes to us sealed with the test of a century. It has been found sufficient in the past, and it will be found sufficient in all the years to come, if the American people are true to their sacred trust. (Grover Cleveland, 1887)

The American system was devised by the ablest group of men who ever appeared at the same time in the same country throughout the history of the world. Just as former times produced masterpieces in literature, philosophy, and art, just as our own period is producing masterpieces in science and commercial organization, so the architects of the American plan of self-disciplined liberty produced a masterpiece of free government. (Senator Albert J. Beveridge, 1923)

Our Constitution is not alone the working plan of a great federation of states under representative government. There are embedded in it also the vital principles of the American system of liberty. That system is based upon certain inalienable freedoms and protections which not even the Government may infringe, and which we call the Bill of Rights. They are as clear as the Ten Commandments. Among others, the freedom of worship, freedom of speech and of the press, the right of peaceable assembly, equality before the law, just trial for crime, freedom from unreasonable search, and security from being deprived of life, liberty, or property without due process of law are the principles which distinguish our civilization. Herein are the invisible sentinels which guard the door of every home from invasion of coercion, of intimidation, and fear. Herein is the expression of the spirit of men who would forever be free. (President Herbert Hoover, 1935)

[The Constitution] is a heritage which we Americans must share with the world, for in his noble heritage of freedom for the individual citizen, without distinction because of race, creed or color, lies the world's greatest hope of lasting peace. (President Harry S. Truman, 1947)

Even those not of the United States have written of the Constitution's uniqueness and genius:

As the British Constitution is the most subtle organism which has ever proceeded from the womb and the long gestation of progressive history, so the American Constitution is, so far as I can see, the most wonderful work ever struck off at a given time by the brain and purpose of man. (W. E. Gladstone, 1878)[64]

More contemporary expressions of the divine nature of the Constitution are found all about. In 1987, Ezra Taft Benson, held up by Mormons as "prophet, seer, and revelator," spoke in the Semi-Annual General Conference of the Church of Jesus Christ of Latter-Day Saints. Also addressed as "President," Benson delivered an address in the Mormon Tabernacle on Temple Square in Salt Lake City, Utah. In his remarks, President Benson spoke of the "divine" nature of the Constitution. Quoting from Mormon scripture—the *Doctrine and Covenants*—Benson noted that Jesus Christ himself sanctioned the Constitution of the United States:

> And the law of the land which is constitutional, supporting that principle of freedom in maintaining rights and privileges, belongs to all mankind, and is justifiable before me. Therefore, I, the Lord, justify you, and your brethren of my church, in befriending that law which is the constitutional law of the land.[65]

Governor Mitt Romney, himself a Mormon who ran unsuccessfully for president of the United States in 2012, noted in a campaign event on February 13, 2012, that the U.S. Constitution and the Declaration of Independence are "either inspired by God or written by brilliant people or perhaps a combination of both."[66] The author of this piece further noted that Governor Romney's theology (i.e., Mormonism) states that "the U.S. Constitution was established by God by men whom God raised for that purpose." Quoting again from the Mormon scripture, the *Doctrine and Covenants*, Rogers notes that Mormon adherents believe that divine revelation sanctions the Constitution:

> "And for this purpose have I established the Constitution of this land, by the hands of wise men whom I raised upon unto this very purpose, and redeemed the land by the shedding of blood" (*Doctrine and Covenants* 101:80). Of course, Governor Romney's belief in the divinity of the Constitution is not unique to him or to the Mormon religion. Again, many of the Framers of the Constitution themselves noted the miraculous nature of the document. For instance, James Madison, who many consider the Father of the Constitution, wrote to Jefferson that it was "impossible to consider the degree of concord which ultimately prevailed as less than a miracle" ("Was the Constitution Divinely Inspired," From the Constitution, September 1987). Charles Pinckney of South Carolina echoed Madison's sentiments when he declared, "When

the great work was done and published, I was. . . struck with amazement. Nothing less than that superintending hand of Providence, that so miraculously carried us through the war, . . . could have brought it about so complete, upon the whole" (Ibid.).

Alexander Hamilton also agreed with Madison and Pinckney. When asked about the Constitution, Hamilton said: "For my part, I sincerely esteem it a system which, without the finger of God, never could have been suggested and agreed upon by such a diversity of interests."[67]

George Washington, the president of the Constitutional Convention, who, on more than one occasion, despaired that there would never be consensus upon a new national government, wrote of the Constitution:

I can never trace the . . . causes which led to these events without . . . admiring the goodness of Providence. To that superintending Power alone is our retraction from the brink of ruin to be attributed. A spirit of accommodation was happily infused into the leading characters of the continent, and the minds of the men were gradually prepared . . . for the reception of a good government.[68]

Benjamin Franklin also saw divinity in the Constitution. He wrote:

I have so much faith in the general government of the world of Providence that I can hardly conceive a transaction of such momentous importance to the welfare of millions now existing, and to exist in the posterity of a great nation, should be suffered to pass without being in some degree influenced, guided, and governed by that omnipotent, omnipresent, and beneficent Ruler in whom all inferior spirts live and move and have their being."[69]

Thus, in 2014, the "cult of the constitution" hardly lies entirely in the hands of patriots or militia groups. Nor does it lie only in the hands of the Tea Party and its like-minded allies. What the "over-the-top" affinity for a nearly 230-year-old parchment does reveal, however, is that the principles of limited government, strict constructionism, states' rights versus federal power, and the limits of each of the three branches has not changed constitutionally since the Constitution was written. What has changed, as almost all would agree, is the nature, size, and complexity of government that has risen to meet the challenges of a modern age. But if the genius of the Constitution, as noted by its Framers, was divinely inspired, shouldn't there have been further inspiration to change the Constitution in order to keep pace with modernity? In other words, if the Constitution was the best that could be achieved nearly 230 years ago, why hasn't society worked to change or amend the Constitution to meet these new challenges? What has happened, in the minds of many groups, is that the federal (national) government has simply acquired more power over the years as it saw the need. Such power came in the form of a strengthened and more powerful Congress, an executive branch and president with nearly unlimited power to radically effect change upon Americans, and a Supreme Court that, although unelected, has significantly changed many of the most hallowed doctrines that once were the hallmarks of American civilization and society. The result of watching this evolution, or perhaps devolution, has been frustration, anger, resentment, and a feeling of helplessness. As individuals feel such things, experience teaches that they turn to violence and aggression.[70] Thus, the introduction to the new patriots of the 21st century—those who wish to return to another point in time when life was more clear cut.

AFTER THE FIGHT: WILL THE REAL PATRIOT PLEASE STAND UP?

The fight for the ratification of the Constitution did not stop the conflict among those vying to claim the title of "patriot." With the establishment of a new country, the federalists held sway that nationalism was the best path forward. That is, the new nation—forged from the remains of colonial government and built upon the ruins of the Articles of Confederation—was the best hope to bring together 13 disparate governments that previously had been in almost continuous conflict with one another. The solidification of an "American" identity was the highest form of patriotism that could be achieved.

Yet to the antifederalists, patriotism still lay in allegiance to one's state. The Constitution was a matter of convenience, a document to create the economic and social conditions under which the individual states and their people could thrive. It was not a document that could assume any powers other than those that had been delegated to it. To the antifederalist mind, government was to be strictly limited to the actual text found in the Constitution. There could be no variation to the left or to the right. Straying from the text of the Constitution would lend itself to an ever-growing and ever-expansive government. The true patriot, therefore, was one who loved his state, saw in it his happiness, and vowed to keep the limits of national power within the strict confines of the text of the Constitution.

THE WHISKEY REBELLION

Though Shays' Rebellion had occurred when a weak national government was unable to quell the unrest of farmers who expressed grievances against government, the Whiskey Rebellion of 1794 occurred when the new government, as established by the Constitution, was fully operative. This rebellion occurred when citizens of western Pennsylvania took up arms to prevent the collection of taxes that the federal government had imposed upon the sale and distribution of whiskey.

As the new nation struggled to find its financial footing, the making, selling, and distribution of whiskey was an economic boon to farmers who found themselves with excess grain on their hands. Whiskey provided much-needed revenue in times when a few dollars might have meant the difference between a family's survival and its economic ruin.

But the presidential administration of George Washington saw an excise tax upon whiskey as an easy way to raise money for the fledgling country. Washington and his secretary of the treasury, Alexander Hamilton, knew that a tax on whiskey would generate protests. They knew that whiskey was an important source of revenue for farmers in western Pennsylvania and for others as well, as it served as a source of barter and was, in fact, a medium of exchange. Yet in 1791, "they convinced Congress to enact it [an excise tax on whiskey] as a way to raise money needed to support federal programs and to show that the national government had the authority and will to collect such a levy."[71]

Supporters of Thomas Jefferson and James Madison, then calling themselves "Republicans," denounced the tax and spoke out against it. As noted by Neil A. Hamilton, "the battle over the excise tax became larger than money—it became an issue of the common people versus the elite."[72] The supporters of the Republican cause said:

The fate of the excise law will determine whether the powers of the government of the United States are held by an aristocratic junto or by the people. The free citizens of America will not quietly suffer the *well born few* to trample them under foot [emphasis in original].[73]

In July 1793, about 500 individuals attacked and destroyed the home of a collector of the excise tax. At the beginning of 1794, those protesting the tax forced revenue collectors to renounce their offices, sometimes at gunpoint. Secretary of the Treasury Hamilton, who wished to make it known that federal control trumped state or local control, antagonized the protestors by demanding that distillers appear in Philadelphia—far from most of their homes—although a law soon to go in effect would have prohibited such actions. It was apparent "that Hamilton wanted to foment armed rebellion; he *wanted* an excuse to use the military so he could show the government's power" [emphasis in original].[74]

For his part, Washington saw the protests as a threat to law and order and opined that if they were allowed to continue, it would bring an end to the Constitution. A militia of some 12,000 men was raised to quell the "rebellion," but when Hamilton led the troops into western Pennsylvania, the protestors had scattered and there was little evidence of the violence that Washington and Hamilton believed might signal the end of the country.

Hamilton was derided in the press for his overzealousness and his desire to impose governmental power upon the frontier. He later defended himself and said that his actions "had shown that the government could restore order and maintain a republican political system against disloyal rabble."[75] But those who rebelled most likely believed that their resort to arms defended the principles of individual liberties and checked the power of a government that wished to extend itself beyond the wishes of the citizenry.

As noted by author Neil A. Hamilton,

On its surface, the Whiskey Rebellion seemed to be a limited complaint by a few people against a specific tax. But the rebellion was a manifestation of a deeper distrust of the national government, part of citizens' desires to protect individual rights against encroachment. Over the years, Americans have expressed ambivalent feelings about their country. On the one hand, they have exhibited intense nationalism, a pride in the United States and what it has accomplished. On the other, they have frequently complained about the power and reach of the national government.

Protests against centralized power have ranged from peaceful proposals pursued in Congress and through other legitimate political channels to armed uprisings. The formation of the Democratic Party in the 1820s was in part a reaction against plans by the ruling party to expand national government programs; so too was the conservatism of Ronald Reagan's Republican Party crusade in the 1980s. . . .[76]

Thus, the Whiskey Rebellion was but a foreshadowing of the patriot/ militia movements that would arise in the latter half of the 20th century and continue into the 21st century. After all, it is the desire of these groups to hold government accountable to its original intent—to "form a more perfect Union, establish Justice, insure domestic Tranquility, provide for the common defence [sic], promote the general Welfare, and secure the Blessings of Liberty to ourselves and our Posterity." Beyond these vagueries and the specific powers granted to the national government, patriots want government to leave them alone to "pursue happiness."

THE JAY TREATY

Not long after the events of the Whiskey Rebellion, the specter of national government overreach again began to manifest itself. The Jay Treaty, negotiated between the new government of the United States and the British Crown, was meant to dispose of lingering conflicts left over between the former colonies and their former colonial master. The Jay Treaty is generally credited with stabilizing relations with Great Britain in a time of great vulnerability and transition for the United States while simultaneously providing a space of ten years of peaceful trade between the two nations. However, being promulgated as it was in the midst of the French Revolutionary Wars, it was seen by some in the U.S. as a deferential nod to Great Britain in opposition to the stated policy of neutrality (a policy that would guide America's interactions with the world for more than 100 years). Further, being the handiwork of Alexander Hamilton, the Jay Treaty was held up by Antifederalists (now calling themselves Jeffersonians) as an overextension of national power and evidence of the inevitable march of centralized government power at the expense of the states.

The treaty was hotly contested by those opposing federal power in each state, but it was eventually ratified by the Senate in June 1795, thus leading to the first party system in the United States— the Federalists favoring Britain and the Jeffersonian Democratic-Republicans favoring France. John Rutledge, who became the second Chief Justice of the United States Supreme Court upon the resignation of Chief Justice John Jay—a strong supporter of the Federalist cause—assumed office in July 1795 as a recess appointment. Rutledge (a former governor of South Carolina) was suspicious of the power of the central government. Upon his appointment, he gave a speech in which he denounced the Jay Treaty, stating "that he had rather the President should die than sign that puerile instrument"—and that he "preferred war to an adoption of it."[77] Rutledge's speech angered many federalist senators, who would subsequently vote to deny Rutledge the permanent position of Chief Justice of the Supreme Court. In fact, Rutledge served only six months as Chief Justice, whereupon he was replaced by arguably the most avid proponent of federalism, Chief Justice John Marshall.

WHO WERE THE PATRIOTS?

Who could really lay claim to the title of "patriot" near the end of the 18th century? In the collective American consciousness, patriots were those who had sacrificed to bring about the revolution with Great Britain. The images of the Sons of Liberty striking a blow for freedom by dumping chests of English tea overboard in Boston Harbor epitomized how most Americans felt then, and perhaps now, about patriots and the spirit of patriotism. In this version, the patriot was "one whose ruling passion is the love of his country" and "a factious disturber of government." The Sons of Liberty were most definitely "factious disturbers of government." Their intent was to disrupt the British government to bring it to the negotiation table or to bring it in to conflict with the colonies. Either way, these patriots were fighting for a cause. Yet it can be rightly said that they were also expressing a "ruling passion" for the love of country, even though that country—the United States of America—did not yet at that time exist except as an idealized abstraction.

With the ratification of the Constitution, the term "patriot" becomes much less of a cut-and-dried term. Some saw patriots as those who supported the new ideas of a federal government whose powers were centralized in order to bring about greater freedom, prosperity, and security than had been possible during the colonial period or the period of governance under the Articles of Confederation. These patriots supported the idea of an "American nation"[78] wherein citizens would sacrifice to defend the idea of one people and not many people.

Contrary to this point of view were those who saw the highest order of patriot and patriotism as protectors of the notion of limited government. They believed in the ideas of Locke (i.e., limited-government theorists) and others who believed that government is a construction of the people and derives only those powers that are granted to it by the people. These patriots also believe that one's allegiance is best given first to one's state and then to a larger, national government. After all, if government is expressed by its proximity to the people (as Jefferson believed), then state governments were a much better arbiter of the freedoms and the liberties of the people than was a centralized government far removed from the people.

At the end of the Revolutionary period, then, a patriot could rightly be said to be either a supporter or a detractor of centralized power. Both notions could rightly lay claim to the legacy of the Sons of Liberty and others who were considered "true patriots."

NOTES

1. Online Etymology Dictionary. 2001–2004. http://www.etymonline.com/index.php?term=patriot. (Accessed April 15, 2013).

2. Ibid.

3. Bailyn, Bernard. 1965. *The Origins of American Politics*. Vintage Books, p. 143.

4. Ibid., at p. 143, footnotes 27 and 28.

5. Ibid., footnote 27.

6. Ibid., at p. 144, footnote 28.

7. Ibid., p. 144.

8. Abanes, Richard. "The Patriot Movement." http://www.equip.org/articles/the-patriot-movement/. (Accessed March 20, 2013).

9. Whaley, Monte. 2013. "51st State Question Answered 'No' in 6 of 11 Counties Contemplating Secession." *The Denver Post*. (November 5). http://www.denverpost.com/breakingnews/ci_24461077/11-counties-weigh-secession-from-colorado-formation-51st. (Accessed November 5, 2013).

10. Ibid.

11. https://tenthamendmentcenter.com/the-10th-amendment-movement/#.Ugk2Qm1dBvU.

12. See Terbush, Jon. 2013. "The Nullification Movement: How States Aim to Ignore Federal Gun Laws." (August 29). http://theweek.com/article/index/248902/the-nullification-movement-how-states-aim-to-ignore-federal-gun-laws. (Accessed May 22, 2014).

See also Tonso, William R. 1985. "Gun Control: White Man's Law." (December). http://www.guncite.com/journals/gun_control_wtr8512.html. (Accessed May 22, 2014).

13. Parenti, Michael. 2004. http://www.michaelparenti.org/super-patriotism.html. (Accessed August 12, 2013).

14. Gill, N. S. "3 Branches of Government in the Roman Republic." http://ancienthistory.about.com/cs/rome/p/blromerepgovt.htm. (Accessed September 23, 2013).

15. Locke, John. 1689. "Republican Government: Second Treatise." *The Founders Constitution.* http://press-pubs.uchicago.edu/founders/documents/v1ch4s1.html. (Accessed September 23, 2013).

16. Buel, Richard Jr. 1972. *Securing the Revolution: Ideology in American Politics, 1789–1815.* Cornell University Press, p. 104.

17. Szatmary, David P. 1980. *Shays's Rebellion: The Making of an Agrarian Insurrection.* University of Massachusetts Press, pp. 29–34.

18. Morse, Anson. 2009. *The Federalist Party in Massachusetts to the Year 1800–1909.* Princeton University Press, p. 208; see also Szatmary, David P. 1980, pp. 79–80.

19. Zinn, Howard. 2005. *A People's History of the United States.* HarperCollins, p. 93.

20. Szatmary, David P. 1980, pp. 94, 97.

21. Manuel, Frank Edward, and Fritzie Prigohzy Manuel. 2003. *James Bowdoin and the Patriot Philosophers.* American Philosophical Society.

22. Szatmary, David P. 1980, pp. 92–93.

23. Ibid., pp. 84–86.

24. Ibid.

25. Zinn, Howard. 2005, p. 95.

26. Richards, Leonard L. 2002. *Shays's Rebellion: The American Revolution's Final Battle.* University of Pennsylvania Press, p. 117.

27. Ibid., p. 95.

28. Gross, Robert A. 1993. "The Uninvited Guest: Daniel Shays and the Constitution." In Gross, Robert A., ed., *In Debt to Shays: The Bicentennial of an Agrarian Rebellion.* University Press of Virginia, p. 2.

29. https://www.facebook.com/usconstitutionalpatriots/info. (Accessed January 10, 2014). See also http://patriotcoalition.com/ and http://theconstitutionalpatriots.com/.

30. Ketchum, Ralph, ed. 2003. *The Anti-Federalist Papers and the Constitutional Convention Debates.* Penguin.

31. Ibid.

32. This scheme of division is adapted from Charles K. Kesler's introduction to *The Federalist Papers* (Signet Classic, 1999), pp. 15–17. A similar division is indicated by Albert Furtwangler, *American Silhouettes: Rhetorical Identities of the Founders* (Yale University Press, 1989), pp. 57–58.

33. The most frequently cited modern collection, *The Complete Anti-Federalist* (University of Chicago Press, 1981), was produced by Herbert Storing and, at seven volumes, is considered the authoritative compendium on the publications.

34. http://www.thefederalistpapers.org/anti-federalist-papers. (Accessed May 2, 2014).

35. Sellers, Mortimer N. S. 1994. *American Republicanism: Romany Ideology in the United States Constitution*. New York University Press, p. 7.

36. Kaminski, John P., 2006, p. 16.

37. Ibid., p. 153.

38. Ibid., pp. 157–158.

39. Brodie, Fawn. 1974. *Thomas Jefferson: An Intimate History*. W. W. Norton & Company, p. 337.

40. Fried, Albert. 1963. *The Essential Jefferson*. Collier Books, p. 298.

41. Balleck, Barry. 1992. "When the Ends Justify the Means: Thomas Jefferson and the Louisiana Purchase," *Presidential Studies Quarterly*, 22 (4), pp. 679–696.

42. Fried, Albert. 1963, p. 261.

43. Peterson, Merrill D. 1970. *Thomas Jefferson and the New Nation*. Oxford University Press, p. 613.

44. Balleck, 1992, p. 681; and Peterson, 1970, p. 613.

45. Kaminski, 2006, p. 122.

46. See Boateng, Ekuna. 2008. "America has Voting Fatigue" (April 30). http://www.fairvote.org/research-and-analysis/blog/america-has-voting-fatigue/; and Corlett, Richard. 2014. "Election Fatigue: Why Talk of 2016 Needs to Stop." http://foreignaffairsreview.co.uk/2014/05/election-fatigue/. (May 5). (Accessed May 10, 2014).

47. http://www.teaparty911.com/info/federalist-papers-summaries/no_53.htm.

48. Kaminski, 2006, pp. 141–142.

49. http://www.publiceye.org/lnk_antidem.html; See also Kimmel, Michael. 2013. "America's Angriest White Men: Up Close with Racism, Rage and Southern Supremacy." *Salon*. (November 17) at http://www.salon.com/2013/11/17/americas_angriest_white_men_up_close_with_racism_rage_and_southern_supremacy/). (Accessed December 9, 2013).

50. Frank, Thomas. 2004. *What's the Matter with Kansas: How Conservatives Won the Heart of America*. Metropolitan Books. See also Gimpel, James G. and Kimberly A. Karnes. 2006. "The Rural Side of the Urban-Rural Gap." *PS: Political Science & Politics*. American Political

Science Association. July 2006, 39 (3), pp. 467–472. PDF online version at http://www.apsanet.org/imgtest/PSJuly06GimpelKarnes.pdf.

51. McCoy, Drew. 1980. *The Elusive Republic: Political Economy in Jeffersonian America*. Little Brown, p. 131.

52. Balleck, 1992, p. 68.

53. Ibid.

54. Brodie, 1974, p. 156.

55. http://famguardian.org/Subjects/Politics/thomasjefferson/jeff1320 .htm. (Accessed May 1, 2013).

56. McCoy, 1980, p. 119.

57. Brodie, 1974, p. 253.

58. http://www.monticello.org/site/jefferson/beauty-second-amendment-quotation.

59. http://www.monticello.org/site/jefferson/strongest-reason-people-to-retain-right-to-keep-and-bear-arms-quotation.

60. Ibid.

61. This is according to the authoritative source on Jefferson, http://www.monticello.org/.

62. Saidi, Nicole. 2013. "Did Jefferson Really Say That? Why Bogus Quotations Matter in Gun Debate." CNN (January 11). http://www.cnn.com/2013/01/11/opinion/jefferson-fake-gun-quotation/. (Accessed March 20, 2013).

63. U.S. Senate, 80th Congress, 2nd Session, Document No. 210—"The United States Constitution."

64. Ibid.

65. *Doctrine and Covenants* 98: 5–6. Church of Jesus Christ of Latter-Day Saints.

66. Rogers, James R. 2012. "Mitt Romney's Constitutional Theology." (February 15). http://www.firstthings.com/web-exclusives/2012/02/mitt-romneys-constitutional-theology. (Accessed March 1, 2014).

67. Ibid.

68. Ibid.

69. Ibid.

70. Brinton, Crane. 1965. *The Anatomy of Revolution*. Vintage. See also Kalyvas, Stathis N., 2006. *The Logic of Violence in Civil War*. Cambridge University Press, and Wienstein, Jeremy M. 2006. *Inside Rebellion: The Politics of Insurgent Violence*. Cambridge University Press.

71. Hamilton, Neil A. 2002. *Rebels and Renegades: A Chronology of Social and Political Dissent in the United States*. Routledge, p. 61.

72. Ibid.

73. Ibid.

74. Ibid.

75. Ibid., p. 62.

76. Ibid., p. 61.

77. *Independent Chronicle* (Boston). (August 13, 1795). Reprinted in Marcus, Maeva and James R. Perry, eds. 2006. *The Documentary History of the Supreme Court of the United States, 1789–1800.* 2 vols. Columbia University Press.

78. McCullough, David. 2002. *John Adams.* Simon & Schuster. (Quote from "John Adams," HBO special *John Adams*, 2008.)

CHAPTER 2

Sowing the Seeds of Discontent

THE SUPREME COURT AND THE EXPANSION OF FEDERAL POWER

The new Constitution established new institutions that lent themselves to a powerful central government. The new bicameral Congress had the power to tax and spend, raise armies, and conduct foreign relations for and on behalf of the United States. The creation of the "executive branch," headed by a president, established powers that would, in time, be seen as "inherent" and "implied." These powers would ebb and flow over the course of American history but would become firmly established as the United States fought global wars and grappled with international economic problems. Indeed, the president would eventually be the catalyst to enact policies that would fundamentally change the political landscape of the country.

Yet the establishment of the judicial branch may have done more to sow the seeds of patriot discontent than either of the other two branches of government. The creation of a federal judiciary, existing alongside state judicial systems, caused antifederalists to question the wisdom of appointing judges for life who would be insulated from standing for regular elections. Such a position, it was thought, could lead to an enormous abuse of power without more stringent checking mechanisms than were provided for in the Constitution. Alexander Hamilton, writing for the Federalist point of view, explicated in Federalist No. 78 that the judicial branch was actually the most innocuous branch of the new central government because it had power over neither "sword nor purse."

As antifederalists feared, the overreach of federal power that began to manifest itself near the end of the 18th century became a full-fledged assault during the chief justiceship of John Marshall, fourth Chief Justice of the United States Supreme Court. It was under Marshall that the U.S. Supreme Court became a branch viewed as coequal with both the legislative and executive branches of government.[1] Once seen as the least dangerous of the three branches of government, the rendering of *Marbury v. Madison* in 1803 established the principle of judicial review and allowed the Supreme Court to "check" the power of both the legislative and executive branches in a manner not envisioned by the Founders.[2] Though the issues and facts surrounding the case are numerous, the essence of the decision revolved around whether Marbury, an appointee of the Federalist Adams administration, had the right to petition the Court for relief when his commission was refused by the Democratic-Republican administration of Thomas Jefferson. In making its ruling, the Marshall Court determined that Marbury did not, in fact, warrant his commission. But Marbury was not denied his petition because of governmental irregularities or because he did not have standing in the case. Rather, Marshall ruled that Congress, in creating the Federal Judiciary Act of 1789, had allowed for petitions such as Marbury's to be directed to the Supreme Court, thus providing "original jurisdiction" for the Court in the case of such circumstances. Yet the Constitution did not allow for the Supreme Court to act in an "original" manner except in the case of disputes between states or disputes involving other countries, particularly as they related to ambassadors and other ministers and consuls. Thus, according to Marshall, Congress had acted contrary to the Constitution in allowing Marbury's case to come directly to the Supreme Court. Marbury's Writ of Mandamus was therefore denied as the petition was ruled unconstitutional based upon Article VI—that is, that the Constitution is the supreme law of the land.

Though the Jefferson administration was pleased with the ruling that denied Marbury his commission, it was not pleased with the intimation that the Supreme Court had the right to review, and indeed overturn, actions of the Congress and, by extension, the president. Nevertheless, the principle of "judicial review" became firmly ensconced and would never be relinquished. Subsequent rulings by the Marshall Court would seem to substantiate fears by those fearing an overexpansive government, particularly those who leaned toward an antifederalist philosophy (of which the Democratic-Republicans were part). In his subsequent actions as chief justice, Marshall exhibited behavior that contributed further to the overreach of federal power. In the rulings of *McCulloch v. Maryland* (1819) and *Gibbons v. Ogden* (1823), the Marshall Court ruled in favor of federal power over state power.[3] In the case of *McCulloch*, the Marshall Court ruled that the state of Maryland had no inherent right to tax the Bank of the United States, a creation of the federal government. Thus, in the battle over states' rights and an interpretation of the 10th Amendment to the Constitution, the states lost in their head-to-head showdown with the national government. In *Gibbons*, the Marshall Court interpreted the Commerce Clause of the U.S. Constitution, ruling that Congress had the power (pursuant to the Commerce Clause) to regulate any commerce between states and any form of transportation upon which such commerce was conducted. These rulings in deference to federal power came at a time when sectional rivalries began to emerge concerning slavery and its continuation in the states where it had not existed before. States' rights advocates were intent upon preserving the status quo in the United States and checking or perhaps even rolling back the deference to federal power that the Marshall Court had been granting to national issues.

THE MISSOURI COMPROMISE OF 1820

The sectional rivalries that began to emerge were immediately punctuated by the Missouri Compromise of 1820. For decades, the expansion of slavery into new territories caused strife and rivalry between slave and nonslave states. Inasmuch as slavery had been institutionalized in the U.S. Constitution, its presence in the original 13 colonies was tolerated by most northern and mid-Atlantic states, while in the South slavery was seen as cultural and a necessary component of the ability of the Southern states to compete with the increasing industrialization of the North. The conflicts that arose over slavery came to a boiling point in Congress in 1820.

As the country began to move west, Southern states were determined to maintain the balance of slave and free states that then existed in the Union. Of the 22 states that constituted the Union in 1820, eleven were considered "free" and eleven were considered "slave" (Alabama had been admitted as the 22nd state in December 1819, bringing the number of slave and free states back into balance.) The proposed admission of Missouri would upset this balance. To those of the North, it was unthinkable that a new state would be added to the Union and that slavery would be legalized there. To Southerners, there was the acute realization that if Missouri was not added as a slave state, the legislative balance that then existed in Congress would be upset and would quickly turn against the southern slave-holding states.

An initial bill to settle the question of Missouri's admittance was offered in 1819, with an amendment offered by James Tallmadge of New York. The Tallmadge Amendment forbade the extension of slavery into Missouri and stated that any child born of slave parents would be considered free at age 25.[4]

However, the next year the bill was again offered, this time with no qualifications such as those that had previously been offered by the Tallmadge Amendment. The possibility of the admission of Missouri as a slave state was as unpalatable to the antislavery North as the possibility of a nonslave Missouri was to the proslavery South. Moreover, a bill to admit Maine as a free state was also before Congress, meaning that the admission of Missouri as anything but a slave state would seriously alter the tenuous balance between slave and free states that then existed in the Union.

The Missouri Compromise of 1820 authorized the admission of Missouri as a slave state. To balance the number of slave and free states, Maine was also added to the Union as a free state. Thus, upon the admission of Missouri, there were 12 free states and 12 slave states. The Missouri Compromise allowed slavery to be legal in Missouri but stated that in the future, slavery could not be extended north of 36°30′ (the southern boundary of Missouri). Though votes in both the House and the Senate were extremely close (24–20 in the Senate and 90–87 in the House), the Compromise passed.[5] The North breathed a sigh of relief in that sectional strife that seemed almost a foregone conclusion had been averted, and the South was content that the possibility of additional slave states could be added as long as they fell below the compromise boundary.

With the promulgation of the Missouri Compromise, the sectional divide between north and south in the United States was muted for a time. However, it was apparent to many that the question of slavery, the question of federal versus state power, and the question of states' rights would continue to plague the young nation. Until now, those who called themselves Americans could rightly lay claim to that moniker while maintaining their fidelity and allegiance to the state of their birth. Americanism became synonymous with the principles of republicanism—meaning limited government, representative democracy, and a national government that was kept "at arms' length." It was still possible, therefore, to be a patriot and pledge one's allegiance to the American nation. Yet it was apparent to most that a system of admitting one slave state for each free state could not possibly be sustained. Eventually, the American Union would have to resolve itself to be completely free or tolerate the existence of slavery in a country that touted the "equality" of all men. A patriot could still be rightly construed as one who supported the United States of America but also one who supported his state against the growing intrusiveness of the national government.

ENTER JOHN C. CALHOUN: DEFENDER OR DISTURBER?

This new spirit of patriotism and antigovernment sentiment was nowhere more clearly embodied than in the person of John C. Calhoun. Having served in a variety of U.S. government positions—including the U.S. House of Representatives, the U.S. Senate, and vice president of the United States—John C. Calhoun was an avid supporter of states' rights and of minimalist government. Curiously, he began his political career as an ardent nationalist, pushing for protective tariffs, a national bank, and internal improvements (such as roads and ports) in order to bolster the strength of the United States. Elected twice to the vice presidency, first under John Quincy Adams and then under Andrew Jackson, Calhoun was noted by some to be the most powerful voice in the U.S. House of Representatives.[6] Yet it was Calhoun's support of the doctrine of nullification and the concept of concurrent majority that kept alive the antigovernment patriotic spirit that began to grow in the decades leading up to the U.S. Civil War.

Near the end of his term as John Quincy Adams's vice president, John C. Calhoun would later echo Andrew Jackson's—the seventh U.S. president's—sentiments toward government power and the rights of the several states to preserve their rights vis-a-vis the national government. Born in Tennessee, Andrew Jackson was the first president of the United States not born into a privileged position. Jackson was a strong supporter of states' rights and of minimal intrusion by the central government into the affairs of the states. Jackson's veto of the bill that would have rechartered the Second Bank of the United States secured his place as an advocate of minimalist government. However, Jackson also is given credit for having expanded the powers of the presidency.[7]

Calhoun's break with Jackson came over the Tariff Act of 1828. Known to Southerners as the "tariff of abominations," the Tariff Act of

1828 was passed by Congress in order to protect the nascent industrial infrastructure that was then emerging in the United States. Because American-produced goods were more expensive than low-priced imported goods from Great Britain, the Tariff of 1828 placed duties on all imported goods in order to foster the growth of American industry. Though this strategy did have the effect of making American goods competitive with British goods, southern economic interests hated the tariff because it caused British goods, which were a staple in the region because of the amount of trade between the two areas, to be more expensive to southern consumers. Moreover, by effectively reducing the amount of British goods in the United States, the tariff made it much more difficult for the British to pay for the cotton that they normally bought from the Southern states.[8] Before the U.S. Civil War, southern cotton accounted for 77 percent of the 800 million pounds of cotton used in Great Britain.[9] A reduction in the amount of cotton purchased from the southern planters was thus a devastating economic blow.

Calhoun believed that the Tariff Act of 1828 was unconstitutional because it favored one section of the country over another. In this case, southern agricultural interests were sacrificed in order to support northern industrial interests. Serving as vice president under John Quincy Adams, Calhoun authored in late 1828 what became known as the "South Carolina Exposition and Protest" document. In his exposition, Calhoun threatened that if the Tariff Act of 1828 was not repealed, South Carolina would have no choice but to secede from the Union. The "Exposition" also stated Calhoun's "doctrine of nullification," or the idea that any state has the right to reject, or nullify, any federal law it believed to be inconsistent with the best interests of the state. This doctrine was first posited by Thomas Jefferson and James Madison in their Kentucky and Virginia Resolutions.[10] Essentially, Calhoun argued that the U.S. government could only impose a tariff in order to generate revenue. Yet the effect of the Tariff Act of 1828 was not to raise revenue but to provide protection for American industries from foreign competition. In this sense, Calhoun held that the several American states, having retained their right to effectively "veto" any act of the national government deemed unconstitutional, could exercise this right at any time of their own choosing.[11] As explained by Calhoun, the "veto" was the core principle of the doctrine of nullification:

> If it be conceded, as it must be by every one who is the least conversant with our institutions, that the sovereign powers delegated are divided between the General and State Governments, and that

the latter hold their portion by the same tenure as the former, it would seem impossible to deny to the States the right of deciding on the infractions of their powers, and the proper remedy to be applied for their correction. The right of judging, in such cases, is an essential attribute of sovereignty, of which the States cannot be divested without losing their sovereignty itself, and being reduced to a subordinate corporate condition. In fact, to divide power, and to give to one of the parties the exclusive right of judging of the portion allotted to each, is, in reality, not to divide it at all; and to reserve such exclusive right to the General Government (it matters not by what department) to be exercised, is to convert it, in fact, into a great consolidated government, with unlimited powers, and to divest the States, in reality, of all their rights, It is impossible to understand the force of terms, and to deny so plain a conclusion.[12]

With the inauguration of President Andrew Jackson in 1829, Calhoun believed that he had found an ally in the fight against the "tariff of abomination." After all, Jackson was a fellow southerner who also strongly believed in states' rights. Yet Jackson was an astute politician, and he noted the winds of change then occurring in the young United States. Though Jackson would later veto the bill to recharter the Second Bank of the United States—much to the delight of his fellow states' rights supporters—Jackson acted very slowly to repeal the Tariff Act of 1828. When he finally did take action with the revised Tariff Act of 1832, Calhoun was bitterly disappointed that Jackson had not secured a repeal of the original act of 1828. In protest of Jackson's intent to sign the revised tariff bill, Calhoun resigned as vice president of the United States to run for the United States Senate, where he could more effectively champion the rights of South Carolina. Calhoun's subsequent action became known as the "nullification crisis."

Espousing the doctrine of "concurrent majority" wherein the tyrannical power of majorities can be suppressed by minority groups possessing veto power, Calhoun set about to make clear that South Carolina—in fact, any state—had the sovereign right to ignore or nullify any act of the national government that was contrary to the interests of the state. The changes in the 1828 Tariff Act brought about by the 1832 Act were too few for South Carolina. As a result, in November 1832, a state convention in South Carolina declared both the 1828 and 1832 Tariff Acts null and void in South Carolina. The acts were deemed unconstitutional and unenforceable in South Carolina. South Carolina's threat to secede was met by a personal admonition from President Andrew Jackson to remember the Union and its purposes. In what would become known as a "Proclamation to the People of South Carolina," in December 1832 Jackson stated:

> Seduced as you have been, my fellow countrymen by the delusion theories and misrepresentation of ambitious, deluded & designing men, I call upon you in the language of truth, and with the feelings of a Father to retrace your steps. As you value liberty and the blessings of peace blot out from the page of your history a record so fatal to their security as this ordinance will become if it be obeyed. Rally again under the banners of the union whose obligations you in common with all your countrymen have, with an appeal to heaven, sworn to support, and which must be indissoluble as long as we are capable of enjoying freedom. Recollect that the first act of resistance to the laws which have been denounced as void by those who abuse your confidence and falsify your hopes is Treason, and subjects you to all the pains and penalties that are provided for the highest offence against your country. Can (you). . . consent to become Traitors? Forbid it Heaven![13]

By early February 1833, South Carolina began military preparations to counter an anticipated action by the federal government. In late February 1833, a "Force Bill" was passed by Congress at the urging of President Andrew Jackson. As in the case of the several Supreme Court cases mentioned earlier, the Force Bill was meant to exert federal control over the actions of states. Relevant sections of the Force Bill included (1) authorizing the president to use armed force to protect customs officers as well as untaxed vessels and cargo in any port or harbor (section 1); (2) expanding the jurisdiction of the federal courts to hear cases arising from revenue collection (section 2); (3) authorizing the president to use whatever force he deemed necessary to suppress insurrection; and, (4) authorizing U.S. Marshals to jail persons imprisoned under federal law.[14]

The threat of federal forces descending upon South Carolina halted the nullification movement, and South Carolina repealed its Nullification Ordinance after another Tariff Bill was negotiated in 1833 that was far more palatable to the people. Yet the meaning of the Force Bill had become clear. As in the case of the several Supreme Court cases that had institutionalized federal power as being superior to state power, the Force Bill portended the force that would later be used by Abraham

Lincoln to justify the use of federal forces against "states in rebellion" at the outset of the Civil War. Jackson himself said:

> "the power to annul a law of the United States, assumed by one State, [is] incompatible with the existence of the Union, contradicted expressly by the letter of the Constitution, unauthorized by its spirit, inconsistent with every principle on which it was founded, and destructive of the great object for which it was formed. . . ." The Constitution. . . forms a government not a league. . . . To say that any State may at pleasure secede from the Union is to say that the United States is not a nation.[15]

Of the seditious nature of South Carolina's actions, Andrew Jackson would write in May 1833 that "the tariff was only the pretext, and disunion and southern confederacy the real object. The next pretext will be the Negro, or slavery question."[16] Upon leaving office, Jackson would quip that among his biggest regrets was that he was unable to "hang John C. Calhoun."[17]

For his part, John C. Calhoun's break with Andrew Jackson was complete after the nullification crisis. He and other "nullifiers," as well as Jackson's opponents, would eventually found the Whig Party, which would eventually be the party of four presidents (William Henry Harrison, Zachary Taylor, John Tyler, and Millard Fillmore). Calhoun later broke with the Whig Party over the issue of abolition. Calhoun, a major supporter of slavery, was one of the key architects of the Fugitive Slave Law of 1850, a piece of legislation that would exacerbate the divisions between those who were proslavery and those who were abolitionists.

Calhoun's patriotism and antigovernment rhetoric were rooted in his firm belief that the Constitution established a clear demarcation between the individual states and the central government. His father had taught him of the virtues of popular self-government and that slave-holding was the mark of a truly civilized world.[18] Calhoun's firm belief in the supremacy of the white race, his deference to states' rights over federal government power, and his lingering doubt over the notion of natural rights characterize him as one worthy to be called a patriot in the 21st century. His commitment to limited government, states' rights, and the idea that states had the right to nullify acts of the federal government with which states did not agree have found their way into the lexicon of modern patriot and militia groups. As shall be discussed later, nullification, once thought to only be a remnant of the pre–Civil War

American experience, has roared back to life today as those fed up with federal overreach once again have made appeals to the notion of nullification to rein in a federal government that has lost its way.

FROM NULLIFICATION TO THE CIVIL WAR

Of course, Calhoun and his part in the nullification crisis of the 1830s was not the end of those who fought against the perceived expansion of federal powers on the part of the national government. Throughout the remainder of the 19th century, there were various armed clashes and other incidents of political violence related to the exercise of federal power.

The Dorr Rebellion of 1841 to 1842 was a reaction to what was seen as the undemocratic principles of the state of Rhode Island. Rhode Island used as the basis for its state constitution statutes that had been promulgated in 1663. These statutes required that for a man to be able to vote, he must own at least $134 in property. Yet the growth of cities due to the effects of industrialization meant that those in the cities were severely underrepresented in the state legislature, as those who voted were primarily concentrated in the rural areas of the state.

Thomas Wilson Dorr, himself a Harvard-educated individual of means, organized the disenfranchised to demand changes to the Rhode Island constitution. In early 1842, Dorr organized militia to demand changes of the governor of Rhode Island, who, once a supporter, had now become intransigent to the Dorrite cause. When the governor—Samuel Ward King—declared martial law and asked for federal troops to help quell the rebellion then fomenting, President Zachary Taylor demurred, believing the threat to be "daily diminishing." Yet Taylor added that "If resistance is made to the execution of the laws of Rhode-Island, by such force as the civil peace shall be unable to overcome, it will be the duty of this Government to enforce the constitutional guarantee—a guarantee given and adopted mutually by all the original States."[19]

In May 1842, the Dorries led an unsuccessful attack against an arms arsenal in Providence, Rhode Island. Defending the arsenal were Charterites, supporters of the original charter that was the basis for the Rhode Island constitution. When a cannon the Dorries had deployed failed to fire upon the arsenal, the action quickly fell apart, and the rebels present with Dorr quickly scattered. Dorr would eventually be convicted of treason against the state and would be sentenced in 1844 to hard labor for life. However, due to criticism surrounding the case, Dorr was released in 1845.

Author George M. Dennison (1976) wrote of the Dorr Rebellion "as a legitimate expression of Republicanism in the United States."[20] Dennison would also note that the same court that convicted Dorr of treason in 1844 would ten years later write "that the charter had improperly authorized a despotic, nonrepublican, un-American form of government."[21]

The Compromise of 1850 would foreshadow many of the events that would culminate in the U.S. Civil War, among these a strengthening of the Fugitive Slave Act. This law, hated by many in the North, particularly abolitionists, stated that any slave who escaped to free territory must be returned to his or her master upon capture. The most galling portion of the act to abolitionists was the provision that citizens of free states were required by law to assist in the repatriation of these individuals to their former condition of servitude.

When the Fugitive Slave Act was finally challenged in the case of *Dred Scott v. Sandford* (1857), the decision angered almost everyone involved. Dred Scott, an African-American slave who had been taken by his owner to a free state, sued in federal court that because he was in a free state, he could not be forced to return to his condition of servitude. The U.S. Supreme Court, in what modern scholars have termed the "worst decision ever rendered by the Supreme Court,"[22] ruled that African Americans, whether free or slave, could not be considered American citizens and therefore had no standing in the Court. Upon the announcement of the 7–2 decision, condemnation was almost universal from voices in the North. Some in the South condemned the ruling, too, but for a different reason. "They argued that if hostile territorial governments could obstruct their right to bring their slaves into a territory by refusing to protect that right, then Congress must intervene to pass a federal slave code for all the territories. They often coupled this position with threats to secede if Congress did not comply."[23] Yet Southern proponents of slavery claimed that the decision was essential to the balance of power in the Union and the preservation of states' rights. As the *Richmond Enquirer* stated:

Thus has a politico-legal question, involving others of deep import, been decided emphatically in favor of the advocates and supporters of the Constitution and the Union, the equality of the States and the rights of the South, in contradistinction to and in repudiation of the diabolical doctrines inculcated by factionists and fanatics;

and that too by a tribunal of jurists, as learned, impartial and un-prejudiced as perhaps the world has ever seen. A prize, for which the athletes of the nation have often wrestled in the halls of Congress, has been awarded at last, by the proper umpire, to those who have justly won it. The *"nation"* has achieved a triumph, *"sectionalism"* has been rebuked, and abolitionism has been staggered and stunned. Another supporting pillar has been added to our institutions; the assailants of the South and enemies of the Union have been driven from their *point d'appui*; a patriotic principle has been pronounced; a great, national, conservative, union saving sentiment has been proclaimed.[24]

For southerners, who believed that the federal government was continuing its quest to bring the states into subjugation once and for all, *Dred Scott* brought a temporary respite from the threats of federal government meddling in state affairs. This relief would not last long, however, as the Civil War was less than four years away.

Still other actions by the federal government against the people at this time involved the activities surrounding the Utah War (1856–1857) and the Raid on Harper's Ferry by John Brown and his followers (1859). Federal troops were dispatched to Utah in 1857 upon reports of Mormon insurrection and the intent on the part of the Mormon leader, Brigham Young, to break away from the United States. For their part, the Mormons were convinced that the federal government was being sent to crush them. In their brief history, Mormons had been driven from both the states of Missouri and Illinois, with Missouri's governor issuing an "extermination order" to kill Mormons wherever they were found.[25] In May 1857, U.S. President James Buchanan declared Utah to be in open rebellion and sent more than 2,500 troops to Utah in a show of federal power. The Mormons formed militias and scorched the earth ahead of the troops so that they would have little food or forage for their animals. Some Mormons panicked and burned their homes and farms, expecting to be killed or imprisoned by the federal government for their beliefs. In the end, the "Mormon War" was no war at all, but it did illustrate the anxiety experienced by a people who felt that there was no protection against the might of the federal government.

John Brown had declared as early as 1837 that he would dedicate his life to the abolition of slavery. When five of his sons moved to Kansas Territory in the 1850s, the battle between proslavery and antislavery groups was painfully evident as the territory struggled to define itself in the midst of the sectional strife that was then gripping the country. A letter from one of Brown's sons, John Brown Jr., in 1855 depicted the situation:

> The storm every day thickens; its near approach is hourly more clearly seen by all. . . . The great drama will open here, when will be presented the great struggle in arms, of Freedom and Despotism in America. Give us the arms, and we are ready for the contest.[26]

An attack on antislavery forces in Lawrence, Kansas, in the spring of 1856 spurred Brown to action. According to affidavits filed by relatives of Brown's victims, John Brown, his five sons, and others "hauled four men into the dirt as the wives and children of the victims trembled in fear, they hacked the men to death with broadswords; they killed one of them by gashing open his head and cutting off his arms."[27] Neither Brown nor any of his followers was prosecuted for the crime.

Early in 1857, Brown began to plan to invade the South. He sent his son, John Jr., to reconnoiter Harper's Ferry—a federal arsenal—in the western mountains of Virginia. In October 1859, Brown and his followers attempted to gain control of the arsenal by cutting telegraph wires and gaining control of the bridges leading to the area. Brown and his men were trapped in the armory engine house by Virginia militia, which were joined by a marine detachment under the command of Colonel Robert E. Lee. When Brown refused to surrender, he was severely wounded by one of the marines.

The state of Virginia put Brown on trial for conspiracy and first-degree murder. He offered no defense and was found guilty of his crimes. He was hanged on December 2, 1859. Prior to the execution of his sentence, he had slipped a note to his jailor that read, "I John Brown am now quite certain that the crimes of this guilty land will never be purged away, but with Blood."[28]

As noted of John Brown and others of his time who were disturbed by the seeming inaction of government as it pertained to social issues:

> The radicals of the mid-1800s exhibited a mix of the old and the new that was the basis for their movements. Time and again radicals reached back to the American Revolution for ideas and inspiration. The belief that "all men are created equal," as asserted in 1776, found expression among abolitionists, who argued that slavery violated natural rights. Women's rights advocates extended the concept beyond the noun *men* and argued that all *men and women* were created equal. . . .

Radicals reached back as well to the moral content of Puritanism with emphasis on building a better society. They were influenced by the evangelical spirit of reform found among Congregationalists and Baptists, a sense that every person could be improved and society could be cleansed of sin.

Radicals were also heavily influenced by the new individualism found in the democratic spirit emanating from the Jacksonian era and in the philosophical movement of transcendentalism. Many no longer felt they had to rely on the elite to show them what to do or to lead the way. Whether it was Sojourner Truth speaking out or John Brown firing rifles, many radicals expressed a democratic spirit.[29]

THE U.S. CIVIL WAR AND ITS AFTERMATH

With the raid on Harper's Ferry, rumors circulated that Brown had constructed a map that indicated that South Carolina was the next target to have been attacked. Southern secessionists, known as "fire eaters," wanted South Carolina out of the Union. They stated:

Men of the South! Think of your threatened firesides, your menaced wives and daughters, and beware of this useless strife. . . . We believe [southern civilization] to be the best ever devised. But it has enemies by the thousands and hundreds all over Christendom. . . .

The election of [Abraham Lincoln] will be a virtual subversion of the constitution of the United States, and . . . submission to such a result must end in the destruction of our property and the ruin of our land.[30]

Perhaps no other single event in American history better illustrates the juxtaposition of the notion of a patriot than the Civil War. For Northerners, the secession of the South was treasonous, as it disregarded the Union that had been established by the Founders and sought to bring about the destruction and downfall of the federal government. When Abraham Lincoln called for 75,000 volunteers to protect the Union in early 1861, that many and more stepped forward to preserve and protect the government they firmly believed was the best to govern the variety of states then in the Union.

For their part, Southerners believed it their patriotic duty to stand against an oppressive government and declare their intention to create their own system of politics and practices relative to their culture. In much the same way as the American revolutionaries had, Southern secessionists believed that they were following the credo of the Declaration of Independence, written, as it was, by Thomas Jefferson, a southerner from Virginia:

> That whenever any Form of Government becomes destructive of these ends, it is the Right of the People to alter or to abolish it, and to institute new Government, laying its foundation on such principles and organizing its powers in such form, as to them shall seem most likely to effect their Safety and Happiness. Prudence, indeed, will dictate that Governments long established should not be changed for light and transient causes; and accordingly all experience hath shewn, that mankind are more disposed to suffer, while evils are sufferable, than to right themselves by abolishing the forms to which they are accustomed. But when a long train of abuses and usurpations, pursuing invariably the same Object evinces a design to reduce them under absolute Despotism, it is their right, it is their duty, to throw off such Government, and to provide new Guards for their future security. . . .[31]

For the states that would follow South Carolina into secession, there was the firm belief and commitment that they were doing nothing that was not sanctioned by the Constitution. After all, the various states had voluntarily joined the Union. There was no sense that they could not just as easily dissolve their allegiances to it as well. Moreover, many in the South, who tended to be Constitutional literalists—they strictly interpreted the Constitution as being complete and felt reinterpretations of the Constitution were illegitimate—believed that they were well within their rights as citizens to accuse the federal government of having slipped into despotism, and it was their right to "alter or abolish" such government. For secessionists, they intended neither to revise the Constitutional government nor to overthrow it. Rather, they simply wanted to leave the Union they had voluntarily joined and begin their own system of government. It wasn't until the federal government, under Lincoln, decided to force the South to remain loyal to the Union that the patriots of the South became "factious disturbers of government."

Though the causes and consequences of the American Civil War are far too numerous and convoluted to be dealt with in the current study, for the purposes of answering the question "Who were the patriots of the American Civil War?" the answer could undoubtedly be answered "both factions." Those who rallied to the cause of the Union were supporting and defending their government and the principles enshrined in the Constitution. On the other side, the Confederates believed that they, too, were being patriotic in their defense of their homes, their land, and their civilization. As noted previously, the southern states had always considered their culture separate and distinct from the rest of the country. When the actions of the federal government meant to force southern states to remain in the Union, these "patriots" opted to initiate their own form of government "as to them shall seem most likely to effect their safety and happiness."

In an article titled "From the Lost Cause to the New South: A Brief History of Southern Heritage," author Steven K. Monk explicates the notion of the southern patriot:

From 1861 until 1865, the Southern states of what we today call the United States of America existed as a sovereign nation known as the Confederate States of America. Because of differences in culture, economics and religion which the South felt were irreconcilable, they had seceded from their alliance with the Northern states. This was an act which, under the terms which they had ratified the Constitution, they had the right to do (they had in fact entered that union as sovereign states under contract with the other sovereign states and a federal entity known as the United States or federal government).

All would have been well and good had the federal government simply let the Southern states go their way. We had no hatred for the Northern people ["Yankees"], we simply wanted to be left alone. But empires are not built through pacifism and so federal forces acting under the dictatorial authority of Abraham Lincoln invaded our homeland with a vehemence that was unprecedented in the history of mankind. In the single most costly war in American history brother was often times pitted against brother in a conflict that took more American lives than have all the wars that she has ever fought in combined.

Although we lost the War for Southern Independence, the cause for which we fought still lives on in the hearts of our fellow Southern patriots, or Southrons, as they are more properly termed. It will always live on so long as men desire to be free—free to live their lives in the way they see fit without the constraints and infringements of government. Government without the consent of the people is tyranny and, as such, has no legitimacy (please refer to the quote at the top of this page entitled "Why We Fought the Civil War"). Patriots fought against tyranny in 1776 and they fought against it again in 1861. Man's desire to be free does not sleep nor will it die. It is an inalienable right granted by God and not by any governmental institution created by men. . . .

The war ended in 1865 with the peace to which Robert E. Lee agreed, but the hostilities continue. It has been 138 years since the last shots of the War for Southern Independence were fired, but still, Yankee troops remain on our soil and their Washington based government continues to rule us with an iron hand. We are living under an occupational government. The Yankee Empire has replaced our constitutional form of government with a bureaucracy, backed by a non-elected judiciary of unprecedented power. Its open-door policy on illegal aliens is daily destroying our unique Southern culture with government-enforced multiculturalism and "political correctness." This same wave of political correctness has incited the removal of many of our monuments and memorials from public display. The removal of still others is a constant threat. Even our cherished banners—symbols of Southern Pride—have been banned from public display and from schools in many areas of our beloved Southland. I can remember a time when the playing of "Dixie" at a school football game would bring the crowd to its feet with wildly exuberant cheers and Rebel Yells. Now it too has been banned from school grounds and alumni events, right along with prayer. . . .[32]

At the same site as the quote above is a section dedicated to Lieutenant General Nathan Bedford Forrest, first Grand Wizard of the Ku Klux Klan (KKK). Under the direction of Forrest, the KKK manifested itself as an organization to protect southern culture from the heavy hand of federal troops that were occupying the former confederate states as part of reconstruction. Meant to frighten supporters of the Union, the KKK aimed to preserve a past that had been largely destroyed by the Civil War. When it began to degenerate into an organization of hatred and violence, Forrest resigned his membership. A link in the section referenced directs one to a book titled *Nathan Bedford Forrest: Southern Hero, American Patriot*.[33] From the title of this book, it is apparent what has often been said of terrorists: "One man's terrorist is another man's freedom fighter." This euphemism applies to patriots as well, inasmuch as one man's patriot may be another's terrorist, or freedom fighter. It really is a matter of perspective.

From the end of the Civil War to the Great Depression, political life in America was an ebb and flow between state and federal power. Though federal power continued to expand as the national government dealt with the increasing complexity of modern life and the United States's place in this new world, state and local governments continued to hold sway, as evidenced by the policies known as "Jim Crow" and Supreme Court decisions such as *Plessy v. Ferguson* (1896), which upheld as constitutional the rights of states to impose racial segregation in public facilities. The growth of groups such as the KKK during this time epitomized the sentiments of many who were becoming suspicious of the factors then at work that were slowly but surely transforming the country. Thus, like the KKK, many groups in the United States began to take on characteristics that were overtly nationalistic—particularly as they pertained to white, Anglo-Saxon culture—anti-immigration, and even anti-communist. Though these forces machinated largely in the shadows in various localities, it was the explosion of government in response to the conditions of the Great Depression that brought them into the light.

ROOSEVELT AND THE NEW DEAL

For patriots, Franklin Delano Roosevelt's New Deal fundamentally changed the nature of government and its relationship to the people. Despite efforts that strengthened the central government vis-a-vis state governments, most of the Founding Fathers recognized the fundamental "federal" nature of the governmental system that had been constructed under the Constitution. Separation of powers and checks and balances were both meant to prevent the rise of tyrannical government, but the third principle of the Constitution—federalism—was meant to preserve the essential characteristic of the systems of government that predated the Constitution—the states. The Founders had also constructed an economic system based on the principles of Adam Smith and the notion of "laissez faire." Minimal government intrusion into economic matters was considered the best way to ensure the growth and maintenance of the economic system. Such was the case for nearly 150 years of economic history.

This philosophy changed with the advent of the Great Depression. Government *inaction* was the standard method by which economic downturns had been handled in the past, and there was no reason to believe that such a policy would not lift the country out of the economic doldrums upon the crash of the stock market in October 1929. However,

as the Great Depression continued unabated, increased calls for government *action* went unheeded by the presidential administration of
Herbert Hoover. Minimalism in government action had held sway in
economic matters for decades, and Hoover was content to let the
Depression run its course while the markets corrected themselves,
which would eventually bring a return to prosperity.

As the Great Depression drug on, it became evident that standard
government policy was not an option. Citizens began to demand change.
At this time, socialist democracies were nearly the norm in many parts
of the world—democracies wherein a great number of social and other
services were paid for and provided by the state. Yet America's antipathy for all things socialist (which was thought to go hand in hand with
communism at the time) prevented the Hoover administration from
taking more aggressive actions to correct the most devastating effects of
the Great Depression.

Franklin Delano Roosevelt, a Democrat, ran for the presidency in
1932 on the platform of proposing a "New Deal" with the American
people. Roosevelt promised to heal the nation's economic wounds and
to put people back to work. Through the New Deal, "FDR's administration forever changed the relationship between the government and
the people, and between the president and Congress. The American
people began to want and expect more from their government (especially social welfare), and similarly, the power of the president in relation to Congress increased."[34] Through the institution of such programs
as the Tennessee Valley Authority (TVA), Civilian Conservation Corps
(CCC), Agricultural Adjustment Act (AAA), Federal Deposit Insurance
Corporation (FDIC), Supplemental Social Income (SSI) Act, and many
others, Roosevelt not only put Americans back to work, but he established the mechanisms for the protection of deposited money and the
protection of individuals in their old age.[35]

The New Deal would have a profound effect on the future of the
patriot movement for three fundamental reasons. First, the New Deal
established liberalism as an ideology that favored the expansion of government to build government agencies and programs aimed at protecting various categories of citizens—workers, farmers, and others—from
the power of business and large corporations.[36] Second, the provision of
social welfare made Americans dependent upon the government,
thereby pacifying them to be more deferential to the exercise of government power. Indeed, as the old adage proclaims, "One does not bite the
hand that feeds it." Finally, the power and influence of the Democratic
Party was strengthened. As noted by one author:

The New Deal produced a new political coalition that sustained the Democratic Party as the majority party in national politics for more than a generation after its own end. Historians generally agree that during Roosevelt's 12 years in office, there was a dramatic increase in the power of the federal government as a whole. Roosevelt also established the presidency as the prominent center of authority within the federal government. Roosevelt created a large array of agencies protecting various groups of citizens—workers, farmers, and others—who suffered from the crisis, and thus enabled them to challenge the powers of the corporations. The power of labor unions similarly increased during this time, and the New Deal also led to increased federal regulation of the economy. In this way, the Roosevelt Administration generated a set of political ideas—known as New Deal liberalism—that remained a source of inspiration and controversy for decades and helped shape the next great experiment in liberal reform, the Great Society of the 1960s.[37]

Thus, the New Deal laid the foundation for all things antithetical to patriots—expansive government power, social welfare, liberal policies that teach and promote change, tolerance, social evolution, and the like. That these ideas would be further articulated by the policies of successive Democratic presidents—Harry Truman's decision to integrate American troops, John Kennedy's "New Frontier," and Lyndon Johnson's "Great Society"—was evidence of the challenges the patriot would have to confront in the second half of the 20th century.

NOTES

1. http://www.pbs.org/wnet/supremecourt/democracy/landmark_marbury.html.

2. As noted by the website, http://www.uscourts.gov/educational-resources/get-informed/supreme-court/landmark-supreme-court-cases.aspx, "Landmark Supreme Court Cases," *Marbury v. Madison* (1803) established the doctrine of judicial review. In the Judiciary Act of 1789, Congress gave the Supreme Court the authority to issue certain judicial writs. The Constitution did not give the Court this power. Because the Constitution is the supreme law of the land, the Court held that any contradictory congressional act is without force. The ability of federal

courts to declare legislative and executive actions unconstitutional is known as judicial review.

3. As noted by the website, http://www.uscourts.gov/educational-resources/get-informed/supreme-court/landmark-supreme-court-cases.aspx, "Landmark Supreme Court Cases," *McCulloch v. Maryland* (1819) confirmed that the Constitution gives the federal government certain implied powers. The state of Maryland imposed a tax on the Bank of the United States and questioned the federal government's ability to grant charters without explicit constitutional sanction. The Supreme Court held that the tax unconstitutionally interfered with federal supremacy and ruled that the Constitution gives the federal government certain implied powers. As noted by Alex McBride at http://www.pbs.org/wnet/supremecourt/antebellum/landmark_gibbons.html, *Gibbons v. Ogden* (1823) held that Congressional power to regulate interstate commerce does not "stop at the external boundary line of each State, but may be introduced into the interior." *Gibbons v. Ogden* set the stage for future expansion of congressional power over commercial activity and a vast range of other activities once thought to come within the jurisdiction of the states. After *Gibbons*, Congress had preemptive authority over the states to regulate any aspect of commerce crossing state lines. Thus, any state law regulating in-state commercial activities (e.g., workers' minimum wages in an in-state factory) could potentially be overturned by Congress if that activity was somehow connected to interstate commerce (e.g., that factory's goods were sold across state lines). Indeed, more than any other case, *Gibbons* set the stage for the federal government's overwhelming growth in power into the 20th century.

4. Dixon, Mrs. Archibald and Susan Built Dixon. 1899. *The True History of the Missouri Compromise and Its Repeal*. Reprinted in 2012 by HardPress Publishing, pp. 49–51. The Senate refused to vote on the bill and it died quietly in 1819.

5. http://www.loc.gov/rr/program/bib/ourdocs/Missouri.html.

6. Meigs, William Montgomery. 1917. *The Life of John Caldwell Calhoun*. Reprinted by BiblioBazaar, 2009, p. 221.

7. Finkelman, Paul. 2006. "Jackson, Andrew (1767–1845)." *Encyclopedia of American Civil Liberties*, 3 vols., Routledge, vol. 2 (G–Q), pp. 832–833.

8. https://www.princeton.edu/~achaney/tmve/wiki100k/docs/Tariff_of_1828.html.

9. Dattel, Eugene R. "Cotton and the Civil War." http://mshistorynow.mdah.state.ms.us/articles/291/cotton-and-the-civil-war. (Accessed March 10, 2014).

10. Willis, John C. "South Carolina, 'Exposition.'" *America's Civil War*. http://www.sewanee.edu/faculty/willis/Civil_War/documents/SC Exposition.html. (Accessed May 25, 2014).

11. Ratcliffe, Donald. 2003. "South Carolina Exposition and Protest." *Dictionary of American History*. http://www.encyclopedia.com/doc/1G2-3401803952.html. (Accessed May 27, 2014).

12. Calhoun, John C. 1828. "South Carolina Exposition and Protest." This work, published before January 1, 1923, is in the public domain worldwide because the author died at least 100 years ago.

13. Remini, Robert V. 2001. *The Life of Andrew Jackson*. Perennial, an imprint of HarperCollins Publishers, p. 241.

14. "Force Bill." https://www.princeton.edu/~achaney/tmve/wiki100k/docs/Force_Bill.html. (Accessed May 27, 2014).

15. Syrett, Harold C. 1953. *Andrew Jackson: His Contribution to the American Tradition*. Bobbs-Merrill, p. 36.

16. Meacham, Jon. 2009. *American Lion: Andrew Jackson in the White House*. Random House Trade Paperbacks, p. 247. See also "Correspondence of Andrew Jackson," Vol. V, p. 72. Bassett, John Spencer, and Daniel M. Matteson, eds. *Correspondence of Andrew Jackson*. 7 vols. Washington, DC: Carnegie Institution of Washington, pp. 1926–1935.

17. Bargeman, Walter R. 2009. *Polk: The Man Who Transformed the Presidency and America*. Random House Trade Paperbacks, p. 36.

18. Bartlett, Irving H. 1994. *John C. Calhoun: A Biography*. W. W. Norton and Company.

19. Rae, John B. 1936. "Democrats and the Dorr Rebellion," *New England Quarterly* 9 (3): 476–483.

20. Dennison, George M. 1979. "The Dorr War and Political Questions," *Supreme Court Historical Society Yearbook*, pp. 45–62.

21. Ibid., p. 196.

22. Finkelman, Paul. 2007. "*Scott v. Sandford*: The Court's Most Dreadful Case and How it Changed History" (PDF) http://scholarship.kentlaw.iit.edu/cgi/viewcontent.cgi?article=3570&context=cklawreview. *Chicago-Kent Law Review* 82 (3): 3–48.

23. Wallace, Gregory J. 2006. "Dred Scott." *Civil War Times Magazine* (March/April). See also http://www.historynet.com/dred-scott.

24. Finkleman, Paul. 1997. *Dred Scott vs. Sandford: A Brief History with Documents*. Palgrave Macmillan, p. 5.

25. Cook, Lyndon W., and Donald Q. Cannon, eds. *The Exodus and Beyond: Essays in Mormon History*. Hawkes Publishing.

26. Hamilton, Neil A. 2002. *Rebels and Renegades: A Chronology of Social and Political Dissent in the United States*. Routledge, p. 117.

27. Ibid.

28. Oates, Stephen B. 1970. *To Purge This Land with Blood: A Biography of John Brown*. Harper & Row.

29. Hamiltòn, 2002, p. 118.

30. Ibid., p. 119.

31. http://www.archives.gov/exhibits/charters/declaration_transcript .html. (Accessed January 21, 2014).

32. Monk, Steven K. "From the Lost Cause to the New South: A Brief History of Southern Heritage." http://www.confederateamerican pride.com/. (Accessed May 1, 2014).

33. Seabrook, Lochlainn. 2009. *Nathan Bedford Forrest: Southern Hero, American Patriot*. 2nd ed. Sea Raven Press.

34. "The Legacy of the New Deal." https://www.boundless.com /u-s-history/the-new-deal-1933-1940/the-legacy-of-the-new-deal/the -legacy-of-the-new-deal/. (Accessed May 15, 2014).

35. "The New Deal or Radical Change." http://www.austincc.edu/ lpatrick/his1302/deal.html. (Accessed May 15, 2014).

36. "The Legacy of the New Deal." http://www.boundless.com /u-s-history/the-new-deal-1933-1940/the-legacy-of-the-new-deal/the -legacy-of-the-new-deal/. (Accessed May 15, 2014).

37. Ibid.

CHAPTER 3

The Creation of the Contemporary Patriot

THE 1950S: EXPANSIVE GOVERNMENT AND THE THREAT OF COMMUNISM

Of course, American political violence has not always been initiated by patriots and their desire to support and protect government or elicit some "retro" notion of what government should be—an idealized version of a government and its responsibilities and limitations. As noted earlier, Thomas Jefferson believed that the American Republic was destined to decay and that government would become abusive of its powers not unlike every other government in history to this time. The Louisiana Purchase was meant to forestall this inevitable decay for some 150 years. To Jefferson's thinking, then, the vast frontier of the Louisiana Purchase would forestall the revolution and political violence that comes when a citizenry becomes disaffected with its government. If this is to be believed, the 1950s would roughly serve as the decade when the American political system began to decay.

To many "purists," the 1950s were the last decade of innocence for the American people. In fact, public opinion polls have demonstrated that a plurality of Americans believe the 1950s to be the greatest American decade.[1] Beginning in the mid-1950s, the delicate balance between state and national power began to be upset. Though the Civil War was believed by many to have answered the federalist dilemma of state versus national power and which reigned supreme, the post–Civil War era of Jim Crow laws institutionalized segregation and once again made states (particularly Southern states) nearly "supreme" within their own boundaries. *Brown v. Board of Education* (1954) began to change this notion. With one monumental decision, the United States Supreme Court once again reasserted national authority by striking down segregationist laws around the country, thereby signaling that national authority was indeed supreme. This "activist" decision by a Court that had hitherto been somewhat deferential to state power brought about an era of great Court activity that resonates to this day.[2] Indeed, there are many within the United States and particularly in modern patriot movements that see an "activist" Supreme Court as tantamount to a hijacking of the United States Constitution. After all, unlike the U.S. Congress and the president, which are both elected by the people, the Supreme Court is appointed. Each member of the Court is Constitutionally protected from expulsion from the chamber by unhappy or disgruntled constituents. Members of the Supreme Court do not stand for election, and they can only leave office in one of three ways: (1) voluntary retirement; (2) impeachment (being subjected to many of the same "high crimes and misdemeanors" as the president); or (3) death (Article III, U.S. Constitution). Individuals with power such as that possessed by members of the Supreme Court constitute the epitome of danger to a limited and principled government.

Yet beginning with *Brown v. Board of Education* (1954), the balance once again began to shift toward the national government. Throughout the remainder of the 1950s, the United States dedicated itself to the building of a great standing army, a phenomenon heretofore unknown in the American experience. Up until the end of World War II, the United States had largely relied upon a small standing army and a navy that could protect its maritime borders but little else. With the end of World War II, however, the United States for the first time found itself standing on the edge of history as the only remaining great state that had not been fundamentally wrecked by the ravages of the war. Quite the contrary: the United States emerged from World War II as a superpower, and it embarked upon a program to defend itself and its postwar allies from the looming threat posed by global communism.

With the elucidation of National Security Council Report 68 (NSC-68) in 1950, the United States committed itself to a post–World War II strategy containing global communism. Prior to World War II, U.S. defense spending had been only in the tens of millions of dollars per year. This figure jumped enormously during World War II, but the demobilization of U.S. military forces after World War II brought spending levels back in line with pre–World War II levels. However, with the detonation of a Soviet atomic bomb in 1949 and the loss of China in the same year, American military planners believed that the next war would be a war with some element of the global communist conspiracy. NSC-68, with its recommendations to "contain" global communism with U.S. military might, necessitated an enormous buildup of U.S. military force—so much so that U.S. defense spending in 1953 approached $500 billion per year where this amount had only been $12.5 billion five years before.[3] The term "military-industrial complex"—to denote the collaboration between defense contractors, the Department of Defense, and the congressional districts that benefitted from large military contracts and other military associations—became part of the American lexicon at this time to such an extent that upon leaving office in 1961, President Dwight D. Eisenhower would remark:

> Our military organization today bears little relation to that known by any of my predecessors in peacetime, or indeed by the fighting men of World War II or Korea.
>
> Until the latest of our world conflicts, the United States had no armaments industry. American makers of plowshares could, with time and as required, make swords as well. But now we can no longer risk emergency improvisation of national defense; we have been compelled to create a permanent armaments industry of vast proportions. Added to this, three and a half million men and women are directly engaged in the defense establishment. We annually spend on military security more than the net income of all United States corporations.
>
> This conjunction of an immense military establishment and a large arms industry is new in the American experience. The total influence—economic, political, even spiritual—is felt in every city, every State house, every office of the Federal government. We recognize the imperative need for this development. Yet we must not fail to comprehend its grave implications. Our toil, resources and livelihood are all involved; so is the very structure of our society. In the councils of government, we must guard against the acquisition of unwarranted influence, whether sought or unsought, by the military-industrial complex. The potential for the disastrous rise of misplaced power exists and will persist.
>
> We must never let the weight of this combination endanger our liberties or democratic processes. We should take nothing for granted. Only an alert and knowledgeable citizenry can compel the proper meshing of the huge industrial and military machinery of

defense with our peaceful methods and goals, so that security and liberty may prosper together.[4]

Eisenhower's warning came on top of an expanding federal government that only three decades earlier had radically reoriented the American idea away from laissez-faire capitalism and individualism. With Roosevelt's New Deal had come a rapidly expanding government that was antithetical to anything that had been experienced before. Those who now saw an overbearing and omnipresent government began to fear that a fundamental reorientation of American politics was taking place. The fear that drove the change in the American military establishment—the threat of global communism—began to be manifested within public in a hyperactive and sinister way. The first of these was the efforts shepherded by Senator Joseph McCarthy (R-WI). Beginning in 1951, Senator McCarthy orchestrated a campaign against all those in the United States who would be disloyal to its tenets or adherents of another political ideology—in this case, communism. Senator McCarthy couched the battle he was waging as a battle of ideologies—on the one hand the ideology of Christianity and the purity of the American system and on the other the godlessness and moral neutrality of communism. His comments about this battle set the stage for those who would later make the battle against Christian ideals their rallying cry:

> . . .Today we are engaged in a final, all-out battle between communistic atheism and Christianity. The modern champions of communism have selected this as the time, and ladies and gentlemen, the chips are down—they are truly down.[5]
> . . . As you know, very recently the secretary of state proclaimed his loyalty to a man guilty of what has always been considered as the most abominable of all crimes—of being a traitor to the people who gave him a position of great trust. The secretary of state, in attempting to justify his continued devotion to the man who sold out the Christian world to the atheistic world, referred to Christ's Sermon on the Mount as a justification and reason therefore, and the reaction of the American people to this would have made the heart of Abraham Lincoln happy. When this pompous diplomat in striped pants, with a phony British accent, proclaimed to the American people that Christ on the Mount endorsed communism, high treason, and betrayal of a sacred trust, the blasphemy was so great that it awakened the dormant indignation of the American people. He has lighted the spark which is resulting in a moral

uprising and will end only when the whole sorry mess of twisted warped thinkers are swept from the national scene so that we may have a new birth of national honesty and decency in government.[6]

In his quest to find the communist conspirators in the American government, Joseph McCarthy was unwittingly giving voice to the sentiments of those who felt besieged by the realities of the new world that had emerged as a result of the end of World War II. No longer was the United States a country that could hide behind its ocean barriers and remain disengaged from the affairs of the world. Nearly 150 years of isolationism had come crashing down, and the results were disconcerting to many who saw conspiracies everywhere and of every kind. McCarthy simply was providing the public voice to such fears.

Yet there were those who were extremely critical of McCarthy and his "witch hunt." Senator J. William Fulbright (D-AR) said of McCarthy that "[t]he junior senator from Wisconsin, by his reckless charges, has so preyed upon the fears and hatreds and prejudices of the American people that he has started a prairie fire that neither he nor anyone else may be able to control."[7]

But McCarthy had his supporters as well, one in the form of former President Herbert Hoover. Indeed, it was said that "Hoover knew that Joe wasn't the best guy in the world to be doing this job. We all did . . . But his attitude was, 'Thank God somebody's doing it.' They were fighting the same enemy, you know."[8]

Though Senator McCarthy would ultimately fail in his attempts to draw out communism, his efforts did not go unnoticed and gave rise to other conservative groups hoping to preserve the essence of the American ideal. Among such groups was the John Birch Society. Founded in 1958, the John Birch Society gave voice to every fear of the increasing reach of federal power and the noticeably left-leaning agenda of U.S. domestic policy. The core beliefs of the organization—limited government, anti-communism, antisocialism, constitutionalism, and opposition to wealth distribution or economic interventionism—epitomize many of the same beliefs espoused by today's self-styled patriot groups. The John Birch Society was a reaction to the final remnant of Jefferson's extended republic. With the dwindling amount of land available to the American public to escape from the overreach of governmental power, the opposition to such power began to manifest itself in opposition to the forces then seen to be at work in the United States government. However, while many saw these forces as being anti-American in their scope and function, there were other groups that began to emerge in the 1960s that would signal a new wave of American political violence. This violence would not be predicated upon the protection or survival of the American system, however. It would, in fact, be based upon the notion of a country and government that had lost their way and were ripe for overthrow. Such were the sentiments of the rise of leftist groups in the 1960s.

THE 1960S: A "NEW FRONTIER" FOR SOCIAL AND POLITICAL CHANGE

As the 1960s dawned, it was clear to most that the United States was on a different path. The election of John F. Kennedy in 1960 led to a new sense of optimism among some and a growing sense of dread among others.[9] Kennedy's "New Frontier" and race to space would galvanize liberal America as it had not been even in the days of Franklin Roosevelt. Liberals saw an America that was moving forward and addressing the repression and discrimination of the past. Yet to the conservative elements in the United States—those who wished to preserve the essence of the past—the 1960s were the beginning of a long decline in political, moral, and religious values that continues to this day.[10]

The moral decline began almost immediately with the introduction of the first oral birth control pill for women in 1961. It is widely believed that widespread availability and acceptance of "the pill" ushered in what would be called the "sexual revolution" of the 1960s and the 1970s. With the pill, women no longer had to rely upon their male partners for birth control. Though other methods for preventing conception were available to women before this time, the fact that the pill was small, discreet, could be taken daily, and could provide almost 100 percent protection against unwanted pregnancy made it the perfect vehicle for women to express their sexual independence. It was no longer necessary for a woman to fear sexual intimacy; she could be as indiscreet as a man in choosing her sexual partners. This attitude gave rise to decades-long fears of promiscuous and sexually ravenous women unleashed on society. For many of a conservative nature, these fears were realized with the full realization of the sexual revolution.

An increasingly activist Supreme Court (one that increasingly began to clarify the rights of perpetrators as opposed to victims), coupled with two liberal presidents who dedicated themselves to the notion of civil rights and an end to the "genteel" arrangements of past society, came to be viewed by conservatives as an all-out assault on basic American freedoms. The rise of extremely radical leftist groups of the late 1960s confirmed the fears of many conservative Americans. As one conservative commentator, George Will, has pointed out, in September 1964, President Lyndon Johnson made a speech in which he proclaimed: "We're in favor of a lot of things and we're against mighty few." Will notes that in that same year—1964—76 percent of Americans trusted government to do the right thing "just about always or most of the time." Today, 19 percent do. According to Will, "the former number is one reason Johnson did so much; the latter is one consequence of his doing so."[11]

Though the end of the 1960s would see the emergence of several radical groups dedicated to changing the American system of government, there were still defenders of the government, not necessarily as it was but as it had been in the past.

BARRY GOLDWATER, JOHN BIRCH, AND THE MINUTEMEN

America's turn to the left did not go unnoticed by politicians or the public as the 1960s dawned. The ultraconservative John Birch Society had already been founded in 1958 in reaction to the perception that the United States was under duress from communist influences and was surrendering its traditional values to those of liberalism. The society's principles read as follows:

> We believe that the Communists seek to drive their slaves and themselves along exactly the opposite and downward direction, to the Satanic debasement of both man and his universe. We believe that communism is as utterly incompatible with all religion as it is contemptuous of all morality and destructive to all freedom. It is intrinsically evil. It must be opposed, therefore, with equal firmness, on religious grounds, moral grounds, and political grounds. We believe that the continued coexistence of communism and a Christian-style civilization on one planet is impossible. The struggle between them must end with one completely triumphant and the other completely destroyed. We intend to do our part, therefore, to halt, weaken, rout, and eventually to bury, the whole international Communist conspiracy.
>
> One of our most immediate objectives . . . is to get the United States out of the United Nations, and the United Nations out of the United States. We seek thus to save our country from the gradual and piecemeal surrender of its sovereignty to this

Communist-controlled supergovernment, and to stop giving our support to the steady enslavement of other people through the machinations of the Communist agency.

We believe that a constitutional republic, such as our founding fathers gave us, is probably the best of all forms of government. We believe that a democracy, which they tried hard to obviate, and into which the liberals have been trying for fifty years to convert our republic, is one of the worst of all forms of government.[12]

The principles of the John Birch Society would portend rhetoric used by patriot and militia groups as they rose in the 1980s and 1990s. But the more immediate effect of the presence of the John Birch Society was a type of renaissance of the conservative cause that, for nearly 30 years, had largely been discredited by the rise of liberalism in the United States. The spokesperson for this renaissance came in the form of one Barry Goldwater, senator from Arizona. Goldwater is the politician most often given credit for sparking a revival of the American conservative movement in the 1960s.[13] In 1964, he unsuccessfully ran for the U.S. presidency against Lyndon Johnson but was defeated in one of the largest electoral landslides in U.S. history. Though his defeat also took with it many older conservatives, it paved the way for younger conservatives that would eventually rally to the conservative causes of Ronald Reagan. For many conservative followers in the 1960s, Goldwater was the hope and future of American conservatism. His 1960 book, *The Conscience of a Conservative*, became an important book in conservative circles and inspired many political conservatives who were then rising within the American political system.

But it was Goldwater's fights against the legacies of the New Deal, his avowed opposition to communism and the Soviet Union, and his opposition to the unchecked influence of labor unions and the spread of the American welfare state that won over most conservatives of his time. Goldwater became famous for his reactionary rhetoric, stating upon his acceptance of the 1964 Republican nomination for president that "extremism in the defense of liberty is no vice. . . and that moderation in the pursuit of justice is no virtue." Such rhetoric, while standing Goldwater in good stead among fellow conservatives, was distrusted by many in the American public. At a time when the Soviet Union was pursuing nuclear parity with the United States, there were many who believed that Goldwater might not hesitate to use nuclear weapons against the Soviets if he were elected president. The Johnson campaign took advantage of this perception and crafted what became known as the "daisy ad." This television spot, though aired only once, did more to define Barry Goldwater in the minds of most Americans than perhaps anything else said during the 1964 presidential campaign.[14]

Goldwater's rise coincided with another important event that would foreshadow the rise of the contemporary patriot and militia movements in the United States. In 1961, Robert Boliver DePugh founded the Minutemen, using for the name of his organization the groups made famous for their rapid defense of American interests during the 18th century. Like their founder, the Minutemen became known for their avowed anticommunism. They became convinced that communism would soon take over the United States. Thus, the Minutemen "armed themselves [and prepared] to take back the country from the 'subversives.'" The Minutemen organized themselves into small cells and stockpiled weapons for an anticipated counterrevolution."[15] DePugh, himself a member of the John Birch Society, published a pamphlet on guerilla warfare in 1961[16] and helped develop a long-lasting food system for human consumption known as "Minutemen Survival Tabs."[17]

The rise of reactionary groups in American politics in the post–World War II period should not be of any great surprise. As noted by one source:

> Researchers need only look at the immediate post–World War II era to find the roots of today's militia movement. It was a time of distrust and competition for international supremacy between America and the Soviet Union. For Americans, Cold War extremism—the intense fear of communism that characterized this period—along with the rapid economic and social development, and sharp disagreement over racial equality, foreign wars, the United Nations, and McCarthyism provided a seedbed for political extremism—shaping it, encouraging it, propelling it.[18]

By the end of the 1960s, though not in total disrepute, the forces that had contributed to the rise of political extremism in the United States had somewhat abated. Though the Soviet Union was still very much the adversary it had always been, Americans had grown tired of the long and exhausting process of fighting Soviet incursions on every front. Particularly in Vietnam, where the longest war in U.S. history to that time was still raging, Americans began to be disillusioned and skeptical of the worldwide communist conspiracy. This skepticism was expressed in Stanley Kubrick's 1964 film, *Dr. Strangelove or: How I Learned to Stop Worrying and Love the Bomb*. Moreover, that revelations about the conduct of the war began to demonstrate the futile nature of its goals began to turn American public opinion away from a full-scale prosecution of the war and more toward a negotiated settlement.[19] This position was strengthened by those veterans of the war who returned home and began to speak out against the policies of the United States in Southeast Asia.[20] Moreover, as the decade of the 1960s closed, the civil rights movement had made large strides in securing its goals with the passage of such legislation as the Civil Rights Act of 1964 and the Voting Rights Act of 1965. The segregationist policies of the 1950s and the 1960s were waning, and states were slowly coming to the realization of the new reality in American politics. An evolutionary social change was taking place on the American political landscape, though decades later, the exact form of this change is still unclear. Nevertheless, the muting of conservative forces near the end of the 1960s was palpable.

THE 1970S: THE RISE OF THE POLITICAL LEFT– PATRIOTS IN THE EXTREME

In place of conservative ideals, there arose the politics of the "extreme left" as the 1960s gave way to the 1970s. Though they could hardly be called patriots in the conventional sense of the word, the leftist groups of the 1960s and the 1970s directly challenged the long-held values of American exceptionalism. Whereas the increasing military prowess of the United States was seen as a source of pride for many Americans—in fact, in many quarters patriotism became a hallowed concept—to others, the United States had strayed from the path of originalism. Whereas the United States was founded upon the principles of limited government, liberty, equality, and justice, the "new" America was one that had military bases around the world and was acting like the imperial powers of the early 20th century. Moreover, the United States was increasingly interjecting itself into the foreign relations of other states. The notion that such interventions were intent on preserving the American way of life rallied many to its cause.

(This researcher could find no published example of the groups of the late 1960s and early 1970s referring to themselves as "patriots." Indeed, in their public statements, these groups seem to go out of their way to disassociate themselves from traditional American narratives. Nevertheless, the fact that these groups, perhaps more than others of later years, engaged in political violence makes their inclusion in this study pertinent.)

The decade of the 1970s was a time of great revolutionary upheaval in the world. Political violence from the left was inspired by socialism movements that were then occurring throughout the world. For instance, in Colombia, the Revolutionary Armed Forces of Colombia (FARC) was fomenting rebellion by raising a peasant army in the name of agrarianism, anti-imperialism, and Marxist-Leninism. In Peru, the Shining Path was advocating communism and Marxism-Leninism together with Maoism. Both of these Latin American movements were finding fuel for their socialist revolutions through the political movement of "liberation theology," a term coined in 1971 by Peruvian priest Gustavo Gutierrez.[21] Liberation theology was a movement that interpreted the teachings of Jesus Christ to justify liberation from "unjust economic, political, or social conditions."[22] Detractors referred to it as "Christianized Marxism."[23]

Other revolutionary groups of the time—Japanese Red Army and the Baader-Meinhof Gang (a.k.a. Red Army Faction)—were also intent on fomenting Marxist-Leninist–style revolutions throughout the industrialized world. As the 1970s began, the pace of urbanization and modernization was increasing throughout the world. The flood of oil money that was then beginning to be felt throughout the world was fundamentally changing some societies, particularly those in the Middle East. As the gaps between rich and poor became more pronounced, groups organized on behalf of the poor, dispossessed, and economically downtrodden. Though the effects of these groups were much more pronounced in areas such as Europe, Asia, and the Middle East, the United States was not immune from the spreading dissatisfaction of the imperial nature of the global economic order, particularly as it was being manifested in the United States.

THE SYMBIONESE LIBERATION ARMY

The Symbionese Liberation Army (SLA) was a left-wing revolutionary organization active in the United States from 1973 until 1975. It is most famous for its kidnaping of newspaper heiress Patty Hearst in 1974. The de facto founder and leader of the SLA, Donald DeFreeze, a.k.a. "General Field Marshal Cinque," gathered together a small band of ex-convicts and UC–Berkeley students.[24] The name DeFreeze chose to begin his revolution—Cinque—was the name of the rebellion leader aboard the slave ship *Amistad* in 1839.[25]

The "symbionese" portion of the group's name came from the term "symbiosis," wherein different types of organisms come together to live

in harmony and partnership for the good of the whole. For DeFreeze,
"symbionese" was in reference to different types of people—black and
white, young and old, male and female—living in harmony.[26] As did
most groups of the time, upon founding the SLA, DeFreeze issued a
manifesto and declaration of war. Titled "The Symbionese Federation
& Symbionese Liberation Army Declaration of Revolutionary War &
the Symbionese Program," the manifesto declared:

> The Symbionese Federation and The Symbionese Liberation
> Army is a united and federated grouping of members of different
> races and people and socialistic political parties of the oppressed
> people of The Fascist United States of America, who have under
> black and minority leadership formed and joined The Symbionese
> Federated Republic and have agreed to struggle together in behalf
> of all their people and races and political parties' interest in the
> gaining of Freedom and Self Determination and Independence for
> all their people and races.
>
> The Symbionese Federation is not a government, but rather it is
> a united and federated formation of members of different races and
> people and political parties who have agreed to struggle in a united
> front for the independence and self determination of each of their
> races and people and The Liquidation of the Common Enemy. . . .
>
> We of the Symbionese Federation and The S.L.A. define our-
> selves by this name because it states that we are no longer willing
> to allow the enemy of all our people and children to murder, op-
> press and exploit us nor define us by color and thereby maintain
> division among us, but rather have joined together under black and
> minority leadership in behalf of all our different races and people
> to build a better and new world for our children and people's
> future. We are a United Front and Federated Coalition of members
> from the Asian, Black, Brown, Indian, White, Women, Grey and
> Gay Liberation Movements.
>
> Who have all come to see and understand that only if we unite
> and build our new world and future, will there really be a future
> for our children and people. We of the People and not the ruling
> capitalist class, will build a new world and system. Where there is
> really freedom and a true meaning to justice and equality for all
> women and men of all races and people, and an end to the murder
> and oppression, exploitation of all people. . . .
>
> We are of many colors, but yet of one mind, for we all in histo-
> ry's time on this earth have become part of each other in suffering

and in mind, and have agreed that the murder, oppression and exploitation of our children and people must end now, for we have all seen the murder, oppression and exploitation of our people for too long under the hand of the same enemy and class of people and under the same system.

Knowing this, the Symbionese Federation and The S.L.A. know that our often murderous alienation from each other aids and is one of the fundamental strengths behind the capitalist class's ability to murder and oppress us all. By not allowing them to define us by color, and also recognizing that by refusing ourselves to also internalize this false division definition, knowing that in mind and body we are facing the same enemy and that we are all comrades of one people, the murdered and oppressed, we are now able to become a united people under the Symbionese Federation and make true the words of our codes of unity that to die a race, and be borne a nation, is to become free.

Therefore, we of the Symbionese Federation and The S.L.A. do not under the rights of human beings submit to the murder, oppression and exploitation of our children and people and do under the rights granted to the people under The Declaration of Independence of The United States, do now by the rights of our children and people and by Force of Arms and with every drop of our blood, Declare Revolutionary War against The Fascist Capitalist Class, and all their agents of murder, oppression and exploitation. We support by Force of Arms the just struggle of all oppressed people for self determination and independence within the United States and The World. And hereby offer to all liberation movements, revolutionary workers groups, and peoples organizations our total aid and support for the struggle for freedom and justice for all people and races. We call upon all revolutionary black and other oppressed people within the Fascist United States to come together and join The Symbionese Federation and fight in the forces of The Symbionese Liberation Army.[27]

Members of the SLA murdered the superintendent of the Oakland school system, Marcus Foster, in 1973. Foster was targeted by the SLA for his support of the issuance of identification cards into the Oakland school system, having been called a "fascist" by DeFreeze. Foster's deputy was badly wounded in the attack. Later attacks included bank robberies and the placement of bombs under police vehicles. In April 1975, members of the SLA shot and killed a mother of four during a bank robbery. When later asked to reflect on the murder, the shooter, Emily Harris, said: "Oh, she's dead, but it doesn't really matter. She was a bourgeois pig anyway. Her husband is a doctor."[28]

The most infamous act of the SLA was the kidnaping of newspaper heiress Patricia Hearst in February 1974. Upon her abduction, the SLA demanded that Hearst's father, *San Francisco Examiner* managing director Randolph Hearst, distribute food to the hungry of the San Francisco Bay area. Initially, the SLA demanded that $4 million worth of free food be distributed in return for Patty Hearst's return. This amount later grew to $400 million. Though some food was distributed, the program was discontinued when thousands of people showed up for the food giveaways.[29]

Thirteen days after her capture, the SLA released an audiotape in which Patty Hearst is heard espousing SLA ideology. After this initial communiqué, Hearst announced that she had joined the SLA and had taken on the name of "Tania." A mere 10 weeks after her abduction, Patty Hearst was filmed robbing the Hibernia bank in San Francisco. She later opened fire on a department store after a botched shoplifting attempt by SLA members and may have been the getaway driver in other robbery attempts.[30]

On May 16, 1974, several members of the SLA, including Donald DeFreeze, were killed in a shootout with the FBI in Los Angeles. Remaining members of the SLA found their way back to the San Francisco Bay area, where they committed several more robberies. Finally, on September 18, 1975, Patty Hearst was captured. She was convicted of the Hibernia Bank robbery, though her defense team argued that she was the victim of Stockholm syndrome, wherein a hostage exhibits loyalty to her or his abductor. Hearst was convicted, though she served only 21 months of a 7-year prison term after being pardoned by President Jimmy Carter. Other members of the SLA who escaped lived "above ground" until all were eventually captured and imprisoned.

The short and turbulent existence of the Symbionese Liberation Army demonstrates the depth and breadth of commitment that members of this organization had to their cause of bringing about a social revolution within the United States. Though it was determined to bring about political change in the United States through violent means, the SLA never attracted enough support to be a viable revolutionary force. In fact, had it not been for the kidnapping of Patty Hearst, it is quite possible that the SLA would be a mere footnote in the history of political violence in the United States.

THE BLACK PANTHERS

The Black Panther Party (or Black Panthers) was an ostensibly black socialist revolutionary organization founded at the height of the civil rights movement in the United States. It was active from its founding in 1966 to its official disbandment in 1982. The original goal of the Black Panthers was to provide a protective force for black neighborhoods from police brutality during the unrest of the civil rights movement. Later, the philosophy and objectives of the Black Panthers would evolve to include demands relating to the place of blacks within American society and the American political system.

Soon after its founding in 1966, the Blank Panthers published the "Ten-Point Program," also known as "The Black Panther Party for Self-Defense Ten-Point Platform and Program." The program became the guiding manifesto by which all Black Panther Party members were encouraged to live. The Ten-Point Program comprised two sections, titled "What We Want Now!" and "What We Believe." The program was a statement about what the Black Panthers believe was the inherent right of every Black American:

What We Want Now!

1. We want freedom. We want power to determine the destiny of our Black Community.
2. We want full employment for our people.
3. We want an end to the robbery by the white men of our Black Community.
4. We want decent housing, fit for shelter of human beings.
5. We want education for our people that exposes the true nature of this decadent American society. We want education that teaches us our true history and our role in the present day society.
6. We want all Black men to be exempt from military service.
7. We want an immediate end to POLICE BRUTALITY and MURDER of Black people.
8. We want freedom for all Black men held in federal, state, county and city prisons and jails.
9. We want all Black people when brought to trial to be tried in court by a jury of their peer group or people from their Black Communities, as defined by the Constitution of the United States.

10. We want land, bread, housing, education, clothing, justice and peace.

What We Believe:

1. We believe that Black People will not be free until we are able to determine our own destiny.

2. We believe that the federal government is responsible and obligated to give every man employment or a guaranteed income. We believe that if the White American businessmen will not give full employment, the means of production should be taken from the businessmen and placed in the community so that the people of the community can organize and employ all of its people and give a high standard of living.

3. We believe that this racist government has robbed us and now we are demanding the overdue debt of forty acres and two mules. Forty acres and two mules was promised 100 years ago as redistribution for slave labor and mass murder of Black people. We will accept the payment in currency which will be distributed to our many communities: the Germans are now aiding the Jews in Israel for genocide of the Jewish people. The Germans murdered 6,000,000 Jews. The American racist has taken part in the slaughter of over 50,000,000 Black people; therefore, we feel that this is a modest demand that we make.

4. We believe that if the White landlords will not give decent housing to our Black community, then the housing and the land should be made into cooperatives so that our community, with government aid, can build and make a decent housing for its people.

5. We believe in an educational system that will give our people a knowledge of self. If a man does not have knowledge of himself and his position in society and the world, then he has little chance to relate to anything else.

6. We believe that Black people should not be forced to fight in the military service to defend a racist government that does not protect us. We will not fight and kill other people of color in the world who, like Black people, are being victimized by the White racist government of America. We will protect ourselves from the force and violence of the racist police and the racist military, by whatever means necessary.

7. We believe we can end police brutality in our Black community by organizing Black self-defense groups that are dedicated to defending our Black community from racist police oppression and brutality. The second Amendment of the Constitution of the United States gives us the right to bear arms. We therefore believe that all Black people should arm themselves for self-defense.

8. We believe that all Black people should be released from the many jails and prisons because they have not received a fair and impartial trial.

9. We believe that the courts should follow the United States Constitution so that Black people will receive fair trials. The 14th Amendment of the U.S. Constitution gives a man a right to be tried by his peers. A peer is a person from a similar economic, social, religious, geographical, environmental, historical, and racial background. To do this the court will be forced to select a jury from the Black community from which the Black defendant came. We have been, and are being tried by all White juries that have no understanding of "the average reasoning man" of the Black community.

10. When in the course of human events, it becomes necessary for one people to dissolve the political bonds which have connected them with another, and to assume among the powers of the earth, the separate and equal station to which the laws of nature and nature's god entitle them, a decent respect to the opinions of mankind requires that they should declare the causes which impel them to separation. We hold these truths to be self-evident, and that all men are created equal that among these are life, liberty, and the pursuit of happiness. That to secure these rights, governments are instituted among men, deriving their just powers from the consent of the governed,—that whenever any form of government becomes destructive of these ends, it is the right of the people to alter or abolish it, and to institute new government, laying its foundation on such principles and organizing its power in a such a form as to them shall seem most likely to effect their safety and happiness. Prudence, indeed, will dictate that governments long established should not be changed for light and transient causes; and accordingly all experience hath shewn, that mankind are more disposed to suffer, while evils are sufferable, than to right themselves by abolishing the forms to which they are accused. But

when a long train of abuses and usurpations, pursuing invariably the same object, evinces a design to reduce them under absolute despotism, it is their right, and their duty, to throw off such government, and to provide new guards of their future security.[31]

Though considered socialist or even Marxist in its overtones, the Ten-Point Program nevertheless expressed many of the ideals of the Founding Fathers, who simply wanted proper recognition from the political elements that governed them. Two points of particular note were the notion of monetary reparations for the centuries of slavery under which Black Americans had been forced to labor (Point 3—What We Believe) and the end of conscription for black soldiers who, as the Program noted, are "forced to fight in the military service to defend a racist government that does not protect us" (Point 6—What We Believe). Of the Black Panthers, author Jam Laser wrote:

As inheritors of the discipline, pride, and calm self-assurance preached by Malcolm X, the Panthers became national heroes in black communities by infusing abstract nationalism with street toughness—by joining the rhythms of black working-class youth culture to the interracial élan and effervescence of Bay Area New Left politics . . . . In 1966, the Panthers defined Oakland's ghetto as a territory, the police as interlopers, and the Panther mission as the defense of community. The Panthers' famous "policing the police" drew attention to the spatial remove that White Americans enjoyed from the police brutality that had come to characterize life in black urban communities.[32]

Throughout the early part of their existence, the Black Panthers were known for their militancy and their violent tactics against police.[33] On May 2, 1967, members of the Black Panthers appeared at a hearing of the California State Assembly in Sacramento. The group was in attendance to protest contemplated changes to the Mulford Act, which allowed California residents to carry firearms as long as they were openly displayed and not pointed at anyone. By this time, the public display of guns had become a significant symbol for the Black Panthers. Portraying themselves as a self-defense movement against the brutality of predominantly white police forces, the Black Panthers openly displayed weapons both in private and in public. Moreover, they would regularly make open threats against police officers, chanting slogans such as "The revolution has come, it's time to pick up the gun. Off the pigs!"[34] Author

Linda Lumsden contends that such displays "reclaimed black masculinity and traditional gender roles."[35] Indeed, several authors consider the Black Panthers' policy of armed resistance a reaffirmation of black masculinity, "with the use of guns and violence affirming proof of manhood."[36] Many female Black Panther Party members also were participants in the self-defense movement, often photographed playing with their children with guns noticeably displayed—thereby serving as protectors of the home, the family, and the community.[37] This visual would play in stark contrast to many patriot/militia groups of later years that made it a point never to include women in their organizations.

Thus, when the Black Panthers entered the California State Assembly in May 1967, they may have firmly believed that they were exercising their rights under California law and under the protections of the United States Constitution to keep and bear arms. However, the reaction to their presence in a legislative body was anything but cordial. All of the members who entered the chamber, including Bobby Seale, a cofounder of the movement, were arrested on misdemeanor charges. As one newspaper of the time noted,

> In May 1967, the Panthers invaded the State Assembly Chamber in Sacramento, guns in hand, in what appears to have been a publicity stunt. Still, they scared a lot of important people that day. At the time, the Panthers had almost no following. Now, (a year later) however, their leaders speak on invitation almost anywhere radicals gather, and many whites wear "Honkeys for Huey" buttons, supporting the fight to free Newton, who has been in jail since last Oct. 28 (1967) on the charge that he killed a policeman.[38]

The quoted account references an incident in which Huey Newton, who together with Seale founded the Black Panther Party, became involved in an altercation with Oakland police officer John Frey after a traffic stop. Frey was killed and his backup officer was wounded, as was Newton. Newton was arrested and charged with murder that sparked a "Free Huey" campaign both in California and around the world.[39]

In February 1968, at a Free Huey rally, several Black Panther leaders spoke, one even declaring: "Huey Newton is our only living revolutionary in this country today . . . He has paid his dues. He has paid his dues. How many white folks did you kill today?"[40] As the mostly black audience in attendance erupted into applause, another Black Panther arose and said:

We must serve notice on our oppressors that we as a people are not going to be frightened by the attempted assassination of our leaders. For my assassination—and I'm the low man on the totem pole—I want 30 police stations blown up, one southern governor, two mayors, and 500 cops, dead. If they assassinate Brother Carmichael, Brother Brown . . . Brother Seale, this price is tripled. And if Huey is not set free and dies, the sky is the limit![41]

After three years in prison, Huey Newton was released from prison on appeal. He would later boast to sociobiologist Robert Trivers (one of the few white people to ever be a member of the Black Panthers) that he had, in fact, murdered officer John Frey.[42]

A mere two months after the February 1968 gathering in Oakland, the Reverend Martin Luther King Jr. would be assassinated in Memphis, Tennessee. Two days later, Eldridge Cleaver, the Black Panther Party Minister of Information, was joined by 17-year-old Bobby Hutton on what Cleaver later admitted was an "ambush" on Oakland police officers.[43] In the ensuing shootout, Bobby Hutton was killed and two Oakland police officers were wounded. Cleaver himself was wounded as well. Though the Black Panthers would contend that Hutton and Cleaver were ambushed by the police, Cleaver would admit that it was, in fact, a provocation on his part to exacerbate the raw feelings between the black and white communities over the King assassination. In fact, author Kate Coleman, who interviewed Eldridge Cleaver in *New West Magazine* in 1980, noted that Cleaver's admission of guilt was startling given that "[t]he Panthers had steadfastly maintained that they had never attacked first, that they armed only in self-defense"[44] "But," as noted by Coleman, "even the formidable array of weaponry recovered near the scene of the shootout—from repeating pump-action shotguns and M-16s to high caliber pistols—hardly seemed the stuff of self-defense."[45]

In the months following the Seale and Newton incidents, 9 police officers were killed and 56 were wounded. Ten Black Panther members also died during this time, and many sustained injuries. In 1969, 348 Black Panthers were arrested for a variety of crimes.[46] Perhaps the most galvanizing of the events in 1969 was the death of Fred Hampton, deputy chairman of the Black Panther Party in Illinois. Closely surveilled by the Federal Bureau of Investigation (FBI) since 1967, Hampton's activities were infiltrated by an FBI informant who had agreed to get close to Hampton in exchange for the dropping of felony charges against him. When the FBI informant—William O'Neal—reported that the Black Panthers were merely feeding breakfast to inner-city children, J. Edgar

Hoover, the long-time director of the FBI, wrote a scathing memo to O'Neal reminding him that his future aspirations depended upon supplying evidence to Hoover in support of his (Hoover's) belief that the Black Panthers were "a violence-prone organization seeking to overthrow the Government [of the United States] by revolutionary means."[47] On December 3, 1969, a raid of Hampton's apartment organized by the Cook County office of the state's attorney resulted in Fred Hampton's death. Postmortem analysis revealed the presence of barbiturates in Fred Hampton's bloodstream, though he was known not to be a drug user. Many believed that O'Neal had slipped the barbiturates to Hampton in an effort to keep him from reacting to the police raid. Hampton was shot twice in the head.[48] Though a federal grand jury was convened in the matter of Hampton's death, no one associated with the raid was ever prosecuted.[49]

As the 1970s dawned, the killing of Black Panther Party members by individuals internal to the organization began the disaffection that many members of the party had begun to feel. Coupled with ideological differences over whether the Party should continue its armed confrontation or whether it should focus on community service coupled with self-defense led to an irreparable split in the Black Panther movement. By 1980, membership in the Black Panthers was only 27, whereas it had been nearly 10,000 at the end of the 1960s.[50]

As was the case with most leftist American groups of the late 1960s and early 1970s, the Black Panthers disappeared under the weight of their own contradictions. The Black Panthers, along with the Symbionese Liberation Army, had attempted to foment socialist/Marxist rebellions in a country that had very little stomach for such ideologies. Indeed, the ideologies of individualism, self-sufficiency, limited government, and rule of law had trumped the uncertainty of the ideas being put forth by the Black Panthers and others. And yet, the Black Panthers had espoused many of the same principles as the early (and later) patriots. They had, in fact, believed wholeheartedly in a self-defense practice based upon the 2nd Amendment principle of private gun ownership. Moreover, they had demanded only that which had been promised to every American citizen—that the promises of the Founders, as articulated in the Declaration of Independence and the United States Constitution, apply equally across the board to any American regardless of their skin color, gender, ethnicity, religion, or sexual orientation. Though they never referred to themselves as patriots, the Black Panthers certainly epitomized many of the same principles that many contemporary groups espouse, particularly in regard to holding their government to account as the guardians of the principles of the Founding Fathers. As such, the Black Panthers had as much of a claim to the term "patriot" as many of the other groups that this study examines.

THE WEATHER UNDERGROUND

The Weather Underground was organized in 1969 on the campus of the University of Michigan. More commonly referred to as the Weathermen, the group was a leftist organization with sympathies to the Black Power movement of the late 1960s and was distinguished by its violent actions in opposition to the Vietnam War. The group was a faction of Students for a Democratic Society (SDS), whose primary intent was to form a clandestine revolutionary organization that would be capable of overthrowing the U.S. government.[51] The Weathermen grew from a faction of the SDS—the Revolutionary Youth Movement (RYM)—taking its name from a Bob Dylan song whose lyrics included, "You don't need to be a weatherman to know which way the wind blows." This phrase inspired what would become the founding document of the Weathermen. It was distributed to SDS and RYM members at the SDS convention that was held in Chicago on June 18, 1969—the same city that only a year before had been the scene of the Democratic National Convention that saw four days of intense violence grip the city. The Weathermen "position paper" called for "a 'white fighting force' to be allied with the 'Black Liberation Movement' and other radical movements to achieve 'the destruction of US imperialism and achieve a classless world: world communism.'"[52]

The unifying force behind the Weathermen was their opposition to U.S. global policies, particularly the U.S. presence in Vietnam. Like other leftist movements of the late 1960s and early 1970s, the Weathermen grew out of the social and political turmoil elicited by the civil rights movement in the United States as well as the U.S. policy of global confrontation with communism. The Revolutionary Youth Movement (RYM), which had inspired the formation of the Weathermen, believed that America's youth possessed the wherewithal to create a revolutionary force that would overthrow and destroy capitalism.[53] As author Ron Briley noted:

> . . . The milieu of the late 1960s. With a growing protest movement in the United States and the global struggle in which anti-imperialist forces were on the march in Vietnam, Algeria, and Angola, the

Weathermen believed they were on the winning side of history—creating new communities free from capitalist exploitation and embracing the Che Guevara prediction that numerous Vietnam-type conflicts would topple the American regime.[54]

The Weathermen strongly identified with the Black Panther Party (BPP), and the killing of Fred Hampton in late 1969 galvanized the resolve of the organization so much that the Weathermen issued a declaration of war against the United States Government in July 1970:

****

Declaration of a State of War

Transcription originally posted at http://www.lib.berkeley.edu/MRC/pacificaviet/scheertranscript.html.

From The Berkeley Tribe, July 31, 1970.

Hello. This is Bernardine Dohrn.

I'm going to read A DECLARATION OF A STATE OF WAR.

This is the first communication from the Weatherman underground.

All over the world, people fighting Amerikan imperialism look to Amerika's youth to use our strategic position behind enemy lines to join forces in the destruction of the empire.

Black people have been fighting almost alone for years. We've known that our job is to lead white kids into armed revolution. We never intended to spend the next five or twenty-five years of our lives in jail. Ever since SDS became revolutionary, we've been trying to show how it is possible to overcome the frustration and impotence that comes from trying to reform this system. Kids know the lines are drawn revolution is touching all of our lives. Tens of thousands have learned that protest and marches don't do it. Revolutionary violence is the only way.

Now we are adapting the classic guerrilla strategy of the Viet Cong and the urban guerrilla strategy of the Tupamaros to our own situation here in the most technically advanced country in the world.

Ché taught us that "revolutionaries move like fish in the sea." The alienation and contempt that young people have for this country has created the ocean for this revolution.

The hundreds and thousands of young people who demonstrated in the Sixties against the war and for civil rights grew to hundreds of thousands in the past few weeks actively fighting Nixon's invasion of Cambodia and the attempted genocide against black people. The insanity of Amerikan "justice" has added to its list of atrocities six blacks killed in Augusta, two in Jackson and four white Kent State students, making thousands more into revolutionaries.

The parents of "privileged" kids have been saying for years that the revolution was a game for us. But the war and the racism of this society show that it is too fucked-up. We will never live peaceably under this system.

This was totally true of those who died in the New York townhouse explosion. The third person who was killed there was Terry Robbins, who led the first rebellion at Kent State less than two years ago.

The twelve Weathermen who were indicted for leading last October's riots in Chicago have never left the country. Terry is dead, Linda was captured by a pig informer, but the rest of us move freely in and out of every city and youth scene in this country. We're not hiding out but we're invisible.

There are several hundred members of the Weathermen underground and some of us face more years in jail than the fifty thousand deserters and draft dodgers now in Canada. Already many of them are coming back to join us in the underground or to return to the Man's army and tear it up from inside along with those who never left.

We fight in many ways. Dope is one of our weapons. The laws against marijuana mean that millions of us are outlaws long before we actually split. Guns and grass are united in the youth underground.

Freaks are revolutionaries and revolutionaries are freaks. If you want to find us, this is where we are. In every tribe, commune, dormitory, farmhouse, barracks and townhouse where kids are making love, smoking dope and loading guns—fugitives from Amerikan justice are free to go.

For Diana Oughton, Ted Gold and Terry Robbins, and for all the revolutionaries who are still on the move here, there has been no question for a long time now—we will never go back.

Within the next fourteen days we will attack a symbol or institution of Amerikan injustice. This is the way we celebrate the example of Eldridge Cleaver and H. Rap Brown and all black revolutionaries who first inspired us by their fight behind enemy lines for the liberation of their people.

Never again will they fight alone.
May 21, 1970[55]
****

As Weathermen member David Gilbert has said:

> We petitioned, we demonstrated, we sat in. I was willing to get hit
> over the head, I did; I was willing to go to prison, I did. To me, it
> was a question of what had to be done to stop the much greater vio-
> lence that was going on.[56]

The Weathermen believed that the primary global struggle taking
place in the 1960s and 1970s was the reality of U.S. imperialism and the
various national liberation struggles around the world that were confronting it.[57] The Weathermen drew their inspiration from Vladimir
Lenin's 1916 work, "Imperialism, the Highest Stage of Capitalism," in
which Lenin argues that the forces of capitalism perpetuate generations
of "oppressed people" who are actually the creators of the wealth that
capitalism enjoys, as the products bought and sold in the marketplace
are the results of their labor. The goal of the revolutionary struggle
against capitalism, then, had to be to seize wealth in the name of the oppressed peoples and achieve a classless world, a world of communism.
In their goals, the Weathermen strove to make the point that their ideas
were both anti-imperialist and antiracist, as they believed in a classless
society where all of the world's workers would share equally in the
wealth that they created.[58] To this end, Weathermen member Bernardine
Dohrn said:

> We've known that our job is to lead white kids into armed revolu-
> tion. We never intended to spend the next five to twenty-five years
> of our lives in jail. Ever since SDS became revolutionary, we've
> been trying to show how it is possible to overcome frustration and
> impotence that comes from trying to reform this system. Kids
> know the lines are drawn: revolution is touching all of our lives.
> Tens of thousands have learned that protest and marches don't do
> it. Revolutionary violence is the only way.[59]

The efforts at "organizing whites against their own perceived
oppression" were "attempts by whites to carve out even more privilege
than they already derive from the imperialist nexus."[60] This idea,
which came to be known as "white privilege," raised the question

of "what does it mean to be a white person opposing racism and imperialism?"[61]

The Weathermen staged their first act of public violence at a rally in Chicago on October 8, 1969. Known as the Days of Rage, the days were a series of direct actions from October 8 through 11 staged in opposition to the Vietnam War with "Bring the War Home" as their rallying cry.[62] Members gathered in Grant Park in Chicago and listened to fiery speeches by SDS leaders about the world revolution and the activities of such revolutionaries as Che Guevara. When the rally spilled into the streets of Chicago, participants "vandalized businesses, smashed car windows and blew up a statue of a policeman known as the Haymarket statue."[63] The Days of Rage would cost the city of Chicago nearly $250,000 in payroll, damages, and medical expenses.[64] The Weather Underground Organization would pay out more than $243,000 to cover the bail of those Weathermen arrested during the days.[65] Fred Hampton, the Black Panther Party (BPP) leader in Chicago, denounced the Weathermen's actions, fearing the potential police reprisals against the Black Panthers.[66] He was supposed to have said of the Weathermen's actions that "We believe that the Weather [Underground Organization's] action was anarchistic, opportunistic, individualistic, chauvinistic, [and] Custeristic. . . . It's nothing but child's play—it's folly."[67] A mere nine months later, the Weathermen would declare war on the United States government, in part for Fred Hampton's shooting death at the hands of Cook County police officers.

Before issuing its declaration of war against the United States, the Weathermen issued a communiqué in May 1970 in which it taunted the FBI and challenged the organization to find its members. On June 9, 1970, a bomb composed of 10 sticks of dynamite exploded at the New York City police headquarters. The explosion was preceded by a warning about the bombing as well as the claim of Weathermen responsibility. After the declaration of war in July 1970, subsequent bombings by the Weathermen occurred on March 1, 1971, at the U.S. Capitol Building, May 19, 1972, at the Pentagon, and January 29, 1975, at the U.S. Department of State. In each of these cases, a communiqué issued prior to the bombings warned occupants of the buildings to evacuate so that no injuries or deaths occurred, though property damage was extensive.[68] The Weathermen claimed that all three bombings were in response to an escalation of events in Vietnam and U.S. involvement in these escalations. Of course, by 1975, the United States had largely withdrawn from Vietnam, but according to the Weathermen, its policies were still contributing to the deaths of tens of thousands of Vietnamese.

In other instances of planned or perpetrated acts of political violence against the U.S. government, three members of the Weathermen were killed in March 1970 when a nail bomb planned for a Fort Dix, New Jersey, noncommissioned officer (NCO) dance exploded prematurely in the group's Greenwich Village safehouse. Earlier in February, a nail bomb attack had been perpetrated upon the Park police substation in San Francisco. In the attack, police Sergeant Brian McDonnell was killed and a second officer, Robert Fogarty, was partially blinded by the bomb's shrapnel. Though the Weathermen were suspected, they had not claimed responsibility for the attack, as would become their signature. In 2001 and 2009, grand juries convened in an attempt to tie Weathermen members Bill Ayers, Bernardine Dohrn, Howie Machtinger, and others to the bombing.[69] Though not directly involved, it was concluded by these grand jury investigations that the Black Liberation Army—a group with whom the Weather Underground affiliated—was responsible for the Park police bombing as well as others in the San Francisco area.

On February 21, 1970, three gasoline-filled Molotov cocktails were thrown at the home of New York Supreme Court Justice John M. Mustagh, who was presiding over the pretrial hearings of the "Panther 21"—members of the Black Panther Party who had been accused of plots to bomb New York City landmarks and department stores.[70] Though the damage to the justice's home was relatively light, suspicion soon fell upon the Weathermen. Indeed, prior to the attack, an anonymous phone call placed to the police had reported prowlers in the area, prompting a strong police presence in the neighborhood. Earlier in the evening, Molotov cocktails had been thrown at the Columbia University Law Library and at a police car parked at a police station in the West Village in Manhattan. Similar devices were also thrown at the Army and Navy recruiting booths near Brooklyn College.[71] Bernadine Dohrn—who would within months issue the Weathermen's Declaration of War against the United States—was quoted in a fellow Weather Underground member's 2007 memoir as saying the fire bombings carried out on the evening of February 21, 1970, were carried about by members of the cell that was decimated by the Greenwich Village townhouse explosion two weeks later.[72, 73]

As the Vietnam War drew to a close for the United States, members of the Weathermen sought to more closely align their philosophies with Marxist-Leninist ideology. Bill Ayers, Bernardine Dohrn, Jeff Jones, and Celia Sojourn would all collaborate on a published manifesto titled "Prairie Fire: The Politics of Revolutionary Anti-Imperialism."[74] The name of the manifesto came from a quote by Mao Tse Tung that stated

that "a single spark can set a prairie fire." Among other things, the manifesto urged the violent overthrow of the U.S. government and the establishment of a dictatorship of the proletariat—a Marxist term meant to
denote control of political power by the proletariat, or working classes.
"Prairie Fire" was meant to outline the Weathermen's new way forward
in light of the end of the Vietnam War and the spirit of detente that was
then taking place between the United States and the Soviet Union. In
light of these new realities:

> The only path to the final defeat of imperialism and the building of
> socialism is revolutionary war. . . . Socialism is the violent over-
> throw of the bourgeoisie, the establishment of the dictatorship of
> the proletariat, and the eradication of the social system based on
> profit. . . . Revolutionary war will be complicated and pro-
> tracted. . . . It includes mass struggle and clandestine struggle,
> peaceful and violent, political and economic, cultural and military,
> where all forms are developed in harmony with the armed strug-
> gle. Without mass struggle there can be no revolution. Without
> armed struggle there can be no victory.[75]

As the Weathermen struggled to find a new identity, they were accused by some groups of having abandoned their original ideologies in
favor of a less racially inclusive message.[76] Several members of the organization turned themselves in under the terms of President Jimmy
Carter's amnesty for draft dodgers, while still others left their revolutionary rhetoric behind and tried to lead normal lives.[77] Bill Ayers and
Bernardine Dohrn would surrender themselves in December 1980.
Charges against Ayers were dropped, while Dohrn received three years'
probation and was fined $15,000.[78]

During its time and afterward, the Weathermen would be referred to
as a terrorist organization.[79] Yet Bill Ayers, undoubtedly the most recognized of the former members of the Weathermen because of his con-
nections to President Barack Obama, wrote a book—*Fugitive Days*—in
which he stated that "[t]errorists terrorize, they kill innocent civilians,
while we organized and agitated. Terrorists destroy randomly, while
our actions bore, we hoped, the precise stamp of a cut diamond.
Terrorists intimidate, while we aimed only to educate. No, we're not
terrorists."[80] Ayers would later say:

> We did carry out symbolic acts of extreme vandalism directed at
> monuments to war and racism, and the attacks on property, never

on people, were meant to respect human life and convey outrage and determination to end the Vietnam war. . . . The responsibility for the risks we posed to others in some of our most extreme actions in those underground years never leaves my thoughts for long. The antiwar movement in all its commitment, all its sacrifice and determination, could not stop the violence unleashed against Vietnam. And therein lies cause for real regret.[81]

Other Weathermen have expressed similar ambivalence toward their violent actions. Brian Flanagan, for instance, has stated that "When you feel that you have right on your side, you can do some pretty horrific things."[82] Mark Rudd has echoed similar sentiments that express "mixed feelings" and "feelings of guilt and shame":

These are things I am not proud of, and I find it hard to speak publicly about them and to tease out what was right from what was wrong. I think that part of the Weatherman phenomenon that was right was our understanding of what the position of the United States is in the world. It was this knowledge that we just couldn't handle; it was too big. We didn't know what to do. In a way I still don't know what to do with this knowledge. I don't know what needs to be done now, and it's still eating away at me just as it did 30 years ago.[83]

Notwithstanding that the original Weathermen are now mostly dead or have been integrated back in to society, a faction of the Weathermen still exists today in the form of the Prairie Fire Organizing Committee. Their official site touts their goals:

Prairie Fire Organizing Committee is a grassroots activist organization that has worked for social change since 1975. We want to live in a world which has a just distribution of resources and a political system based on empowerment, participation and responsibility.

To achieve this goal requires building a strong movement. It is a long-term endeavor that demands organization, commitment and a collective process. For us, educational forums, street demonstrations and a range of creative actions are all part of developing a powerful and collective mass movement. We invite you to read this brochure and learn more about us.

We oppose oppression in all its forms including racism, sexism, homophobia, classism and imperialism. We demand liberation and justice for all peoples. We recognize that we live in a capitalist system that favors a select few and oppresses the majority. This system cannot be reformed or voted out of office because reforms and elections do not challenge the fundamental causes of injustice.[84]

Thus, though the revolutionary leftist groups of the 1960s and 1970s have largely faded into the background, their legacy of political violence still checkers the American political landscape and haunts the memories of their victims.

THE REASONS FOR POLITICAL VIOLENCE

The reasons for the political violence perpetrated by the groups are well documented by researchers and by the groups themselves. That this violence came from the left of the political spectrum, as opposed to the right that is the focus of this study, is of little consequence. One explanation for such violence that should be considered, however, is the lack of political representation that extremist groups have in a two-party system such as that in the United States. It is well documented that the two-party system in the United States does not cater to extremist elements on either the right or the left. Although these voices may be within the respective political parties of the United States—Democrats and Republicans—they are largely marginalized as to their influence in the parties. For instance, a common complaint heard about the United States's political system today is that it does not adequately represent those whose interests lie outside of the interests of the main political parties. The recent Tea Party may prove to be an exception to this, but it must be kept in mind that the Tea Party is not a separate or third party. Rather, it is a more conservative faction of the long-standing Republican Party. Though it has been successful in recent years in having adherents elected to the U.S. Congress and elsewhere, it does not stand as an independent voice for all of those who share its values. Indeed, the Tea Party must continue to work within the two-party system currently in place if it hopes to have any chance of influencing politics.

While the phenomenon of the Tea Party is not new within American politics, it does bring into clear relief one of the major problems associated with representation in a democratic system such as that of the United States. Most elective offices at the national level are contended for by either the Democratic or the Republican Party. If one wishes to run as a Republican representative in a particular state, that person generally must run in a primary in order to determine a candidate for the general election. In a "politically safe" Republican district, candidates will vie for votes by taking positions that they know will cater to those who generally vote in primaries. These individuals tend to be the most ideological members of their parties who have very definitive ideas about public policy goals and the manner in which the country should be governed. Thus, a primary voter must often attract votes from primary voters that may or may not reflect his/her own political positions. If a candidate is successful in winning a primary challenge, they may have to ameliorate their primary campaign rhetoric to appeal to the broader interests of the public that will vote in the general election. In this instance, the candidate that primary voters thought they were electing turns out to be a somewhat different candidate in the general election. Of course, this is not always the case, but such a scenario does often stifle voter turnout, as those who would vote determine that no candidate represents their views either in part or in total. "Fringe elements" of either political party in the United States are generally marginalized so that their interests are subsumed to the more "middle-of-the-road" voter that will be evident in a general election.[85] This dilemma is nowhere more evident than in the case of presidential elections. For instance, Mitt Romney, who had governed Massachusetts (often considered one of the most liberal states in the United States), was forced to move to the right of the political spectrum in order to secure the 2012 Republican presidential nomination. By the time of the general election, Romney, who had championed health care reform in Massachusetts not unlike that put forth by the Obama administration in the Affordable Care Act, could no longer garner the support of moderates. This did not appeal to the conservative base of the Republican Party whose banner he held. Yet by undertaking this position, Romney no doubt alienated voters who may have otherwise voted for him.

   True third parties in the United States have generally played the role of "spoiler" in national elections. In 1992, for example, Ross Perot's third-party challenge siphoned votes from Republican George H. W. Bush that led to the election of Bill Clinton. In 2000, Ralph Nader's run as the Green Party candidate siphoned votes away from the Democratic presidential nominee, Al Gore. Were the candidacies of Ross Perot and Ralph Nader partially responsible for the defeats of George H. W. Bush and Al Gore, respectively? Consider that in a plurality voting system such as that of the United States ("first past the post"), Bill Clinton won 43 percent of the popular vote, while George H. W. Bush garnered 37 percent and Ross Perot garnered 19 percent (other candidates account for remaining 1 percent). Did Perot's candidacy cost George H. W. Bush votes? Most likely it did. As did the candidacy of Ralph Nader who, in 2000, received 97,421 votes in Florida. In this case, the Democratic candidate, Al Gore, lost to the Republican candidate, George W. Bush, by a mere 537 votes. Certainly, had Nader not been in the race, Al Gore would have won Florida, thereby providing him with enough electoral votes to claim the presidency. Other examples of third parties acting as spoilers can be found in the elections of 1968 and 1912.

Whether it is a major factor or not, one should not discount the representation factor when considering political violence. In the first post-Soviet election in the Russian Federation in 1994, more than 40 political parties vied for seats in the Russian Duma, or parliament.[86] Of these, five political parties garnered enough votes to be represented in the Duma. This number was possible due to a Russian law requiring proportional representation that necessitates that if a political party receives enough votes to push it past a particular agreed-upon threshold, generally 5 percent, then that party shall receive a representative voice. Other states have similar procedures. Israel, for instance, currently has 12 political parties represented in the Israeli Knesset, or parliament. The parties have ideologies that range from the conservative on the right to the liberal on the left, religious parties, secular parties (such as the current Likud Party), and parties that support the independence of Palestine. Each of these political parties provides an outlet for unfulfilled expressions of political frustration by politicians and citizens alike. If the United States had a multiparty political system, would there be political violence in this country as we see it today?[87]

NOTES

1. Harper, Jennifer. 2013. "What Other Decade Would You Live In? Most Americans Choose the 1950s." *The Washington Times*. (August 16). http://www.washingtontimes.com/blog/watercooler/2013/aug/16/what-other-decade-would-you-live-most-americans-ch/. (Accessed February 10, 2014).

2. Schiller, Reuel, E. 2007. "The Era of Deference: Courts, Expertise, and the Emergence of New Deal Administrative Law." *Michigan Law Review*. (December). http://www.michiganlawreview.org/assets/pdfs/106/3/schiller.pdf. (Accessed February 10, 2014).

3. http://www.cfr.org/defense-budget/trends-us-military-spending/p28855; see also http://www.usgovernmentspending.com/defense_spending and http://www.usgovernmentspending.com/past_spending.

4. "Dwight D. Eisenhower." 1961. *Public Papers of the Presidents*, pp. 1035–1040.

5. McCarthy, Joseph. 1950. "Speech in Wheeling, West Virginia." *History Matters*. (February 9).

6. McCarthy, Joseph. 1950. "Speech in Wheeling, West Virginia" *Civics Online*. (February 9). http://www.civics-online.org/library/formatted/texts/mccarthy.html.

7. Fulbright, Senator J. William (D-Arkansas), as quoted in Arthur Vivian Watkins. 1969. *Enough Rope: The Inside Story of the Censure of Senator Joe McCarthy by His Colleagues, the Controversial Hearings that Signaled the End of a Turbulent. . . and a Fearsome Era in American Public Life.* Prentice-Hall.

8. Morris, Robert J., as quoted in David M. Oshinksky. 2005. *A Conspiracy So Immense: The World of Joe McCarthy*. Oxford University Press, p. 258.

9. Young, John. 2013. "Why the Hate of John F. Kennedy?" *Abilene Reporter News*. (November 17). http://www.reporternews.com/news/john-young-why-the-hate-of-john-f-kennedy. (Accessed August 8, 2014).

10. Ibid.

11. Will, George F. 2013. "The Slow Decline of America Since LBJ Launched the Great Society." *The Washington Post*. (May 16). http://www.washingtonpost.com/opinions/george-f-will-the-slow-decline-of-america-since-lbj-launched-the-great-society/2014/05/16/21f70a8c-dc5c-11e3-b745-87d39690c5c0_story.html. (Accessed May 20, 2014).

12. Van Doren, Charles Lincoln, and Robert McHenry, eds. 1971. *Webster's Guide to American History: A Chronological, Geographical, and Biographical Survey and Compendium*. Merriam Webster, p. 576.

13. Poole, Robert. 1998. (August–Sept 1998), "In Memoriam: Barry Goldwater." Obituary. *Reason Magazine*. (August/September).

14. http://www.livingroomcandidate.org/commercials/1964/peace-little-girl-daisy. (Accessed March 21, 2014).

15. http://gdc.gale.com/archivesunbound/archives-unbound-the-minutemen-part-i/. (Accessed March 21, 2014).

16. Barth, Alan. 1961. "Report on the 'Rampageous Right:' Today's Tensions Have Led to a Proliferation of 'Conservative Extremists.'" *New York Times*. (November 26).

17. http://www.survivaltabs.com/. These tabs are still reportedly in use by survivalist groups today.

18.   http://gdc.gale.com/archivesunbound/archives-unbound-the
-minutemen-part-i/.

19. Schlussel, Debbie. 2009. "Buh-Bye, Walter Cronkite: He Lost
the Vietnam War for the U.S. on TV, Had American Blood on His
Hands." (July 17). http://www.debbieschlussel.com/5426/buh-bye-
walter-cronkite-he-lost-the-vietnam-war-for-u-s-on-tv-had-american-
blood-on-his-hands/comment-page-1/. (Accessed April 3, 2014).

20. See Kovic, Ron. 2005. *Born on the Fourth of July*. Akashic Books.
See also Caputo, Philip. 1996. *A Rumor of War*. Holt Paperbacks.

21. Berryman, Phillip. 1987. *Liberation Theology*. Temple University
Press.

22. Boff, Leonardo, and Clodovis Boff. 1987. "A Concise History of
Liberation Theology." Reprinted from *Introducing Liberation Theology*.
Orbis Books. http://www.landreform.org/boff2.htm. (Accessed April 2,
2014).

23. Shaffer, Robert. 2007. "Acceptable Bounds of Academic
Discourse," *Organization of American Historians* Newsletter 35.
(November). Shaffer asserts that "David Horowitz first describes liberation theology as 'a form of Marxised Christianity,' which has validity
despite the awkward phrasing, but then he calls it a form of 'Marxist–
Leninist ideology,' which is simply not true for most liberation
theology. . . ."

24. "Symbionese Liberation Army." http://www.discoverthenet-
works.org/printgroupProfile.asp?grpid=6466. (Accessed March 3, 2014).

25. "Cinque." http://law2.umkc.edu/faculty/projects/ftrials/amistad
/ami_bcin.htm. (Accessed March 3, 2014).

26. "Symbionese Liberation Army." http://www.discoverthenet-
works.org/printgroupProfile.asp?grpid. (Accessed March 3, 2014).

27. DeFreeze, Donald (aka Cinque). 1973. "The Symbionese
Federation and the Symbionese Liberation Army Declaration of Revolutionary War and the Symbionese Program" (August). http://www.feastof
hateandfear.com/archives/sla.html. (Accessed March 3, 2014).

28. "Symbionese Liberation Army." http://www.discoverthenet-
works.org/groupProfile.asp?grpid=6466. (Accessed March 3, 2014).

29. Welsh, Calvin. 1974. "The Legacy of the SLA." *Foundsf.org*.
(March 25). http://foundsf.org/index.php?title=The_Legacy_of_the_
SLA. (Accessed March 12, 2014.)

30. Brown, Sarah. 2002. "America's Hippy Extremists." *BBC*.
(January 17). Brown states that "[Hearst] claimed to have been sitting
in the getaway car when at some point during the robbery an SLA
member blasted mother-of-four Myrna Opsahl with a shotgun as she

stood depositing church receipts, killing her instantly." http://news.bbc
.co.uk/2/hi/americas/1765993.stm. (Accessed March 4, 2014).

31. Bloom, Joshua, and Waldo E. Martin. 2014. *Black Against Empire: The History and Politics of the Black Panther Party*. University of California Press, pp. 71–72. See also http://blackpanther.org/TenPoint.html. (Accessed February 28, 2014).

32. Laser, Jam, and Ahura R. Williams. 2006. *In Search of the Black Panther Party: New Perspectives on a Revolutionary Movement*. Duke University Press.

33. Pearson, Hugh. 1994. *In the Shadow of the Panther: Huey Newton and the Price of Black Power in America*. Perseus Books, p. 152. See also Austin, Curtis. 2008. *Up Against the Wall: Violence in the Making and Unmaking of the Black Panther Party*. University of Arkansas Press, 2006, pp. 89–94; and Westneat, Danny. 2005. "Reunion of Black Panthers Stirs Memories of Aggression, Activism." *The Seattle Times*. http://seattletimes.com/html/localnews/2002270461_danny11.html. (Accessed March 7, 2014).

34. Farber, David. 1994. *The Age of Great Dreams: America in the 1960s*. Hill and Wang, p. 207.

35. Lumsden, Linda. 2009. "Good Mothers With Guns: Framing Black Womanhood in the Black Panther, 1968–1980." *J & MC Quarterly*, 86 (4), pp. 900–922.

36. Williams, Jakobi. 2012. "'Don't No Woman Have to Do Nothing She Don't Want to Do': Gender, Activism, and the Illinois Black Panther Party." *Black Women, Gender Families* 6/2 (Fall 2012), pp. 29–54.

37. Lumsden, Linda. 2009.

38. "Black Panthers: A Taut, Violent Drama." 1968. *St. Petersburg Times* (July 21). Special to the *St. Petersburg Times* from the *New York Times*.

39. Bloom and Martin, p. 313.

40. Pearson, p. 152.

41. Ibid.

42. Ibid., pp. 3–4, 283–291.

43. Coleman, Kate. 1980. "Souled Out: Eldridge Cleaver Admits He Ambushed Those Cops." *New West Magazine*. http://colemantruth.net/kate4.pdf. (Accessed March 8, 2014). A discussion of the event can be found in Epstein, Edward Jay. 1971. "The Black Panthers and the Police: A Pattern of Genocide?" *The New Yorker*. (February 13), p. 4.

44. Coleman, Kate. 1980.

45. Ibid.

46. Pearson, p. 206. Pearson discusses many of these events, including a partial list of those arrested from the summer of 1968 through the end of 1970.

47. Smitha, Frank. 1998. "Ruin for the Black Panther Party, 1968–89." *Macrohistory and World Timeline*. http://www.fsmitha.com/h2/ch28B-5.htm. (Accessed May 25, 2014).

48. Churchill, Ward, and Jim Vander Wall. 1988. *Agents of Repression: The FBI's Secret Wars Against the Black Panther Party and the American Indian Movement*. South End Press, pp. 69–70.

49. Bennett, Hans. 1999. "The Black Panthers and the Assassination of Fred Hampton." *Philadelphia Independent Media Center*. Originally published at www.TowardFreedom.com. Found at http://towardfreedom.com/31-archives/americas/1676-book-review-the-black-panthers-and-the-assassination-of-fred-hampton. (Accessed March 23, 2014).

50. Perkins, Margo V. 2000. *Autobiography as Activism: Three Black Women of the Sixties*. University Press of Mississippi, p. 5. Also see Pearson, p. 299.

51. *The Weather Underground*. 1975. U.S. Government Printing Office, pp. 1–2, 11–13.

52. Berger, Dan. 2006. *Outlaws of America: The Weather Underground and the Politics of Solidarity*. AK Press, p. 95. See also Revolutionary Youth Movement. Karen Asbley et al., 1969. "You Don't Need a Weatherman to Know Which Way the Wind Blows." (June 18). *New Left Notes*. Found at https://archive.org/stream/YouDontNeedAWeathermanToKnowWhichWayTheWindBlows_925/weather_djvu.txt.

53. "Toward a Revolutionary Youth Movement." 1968. Found within "Debate Within SDS. RYM II vs. Weatherman." *Encyclopedia of Anti-Revisionism On-Line*. https://www.marxists.org/history/erol/ncm-1/debate-sds/rym.htm. (Accessed March 14, 2014).

54. Briley, Ron. 2009. "Bringing the War Home: The Weather Underground at Forty." *History News Network* (July 20). Found at http://hnn.us/article/93754.

55. Dohrn, Bernardine. 1970. "Weathermen—First Communique, July 31, 1970. A Declaration of War." The Berkeley Tribe. (July 31). http://www.lib.berkeley.edu/MRC/pacificaviet/scheertranscript.html. (Accessed January 10, 2014).

56. *The Weather Underground*. 2003. A DVD documentary produced by Carrie Lozano. Directed by Bill Siegel and Sam Green. *New Video Group*.

57. "You Don't Need a Weatherman to Know Which Way the Wind Blows," p. 40.

58. Jacobs, Harold. 1970. *Weatherman*. Ramparts Press, p. 135.

59. Dohrn. Original at http://www.lib.berkeley.edu/MRC/pacificaviet/scheertranscript.html.

60. Jacobs, p. 135.

61. Berger, p. 272.

62. Wilkerson, C. 2007. *Flying Close to the Sun: My Life and Times As a Weatherman*. Seven Stories Press.

63. See Berger, Dan. 2005. *Outlaws of America: The Weather Underground and the Politics of Solidarity*. AK Press. Also see Jacobs, Ron. 1997. *The Way the Wind Blew: A History of the Weather Underground*. Verso Press; and, Jones, Thai. 2004. *A Radical Line: From the Labor Movement to the Weather Underground, One Family's Century of Conscience*. Free Press.

64. http://vault.fbi.gov/Weather%20Underground%20% 28Weathermen%29.

65. Sale, Kirkpatrick. 1973. *SDS: The Rise and Development of the Students for a Democratic Society*. Vintage Books.

66. Berger, Dan. 2005.

67. Lozano, C. (Producer), B. Siegel, & S. Green. 2003. *The Weather Underground* (motion picture). New Video Group.

68. Berger, 2005, p. 95.

69. Jamison, Peter. 2009. "Time Bomb." *SF Weekly*. (September 14). At SFweekly.com. Also see http://www.sfgate.com/default/article/S-F-police-union-accuses-Ayers-in-1970-bombing-3248056.php. (Accessed September 10, 2013).

70. Cotter, Joseph P., and Lee Dembart. 1970. "Four Bombs at Mustagh Home; Panther Hearing Judge." *New York Post*, p. 1 (February 21). See also Perlmutter, Emanuel. 1970. "Justice Mustagh's Home Target of 3 Fire Bombs." *The New York Times*, p. 1 (February 22). And "Police Investigate Law Firebombing." 1970. *Columbia Daily Spectator*, p. 1. (February 24).

71. "Police Investigate Law Firebombing."

72. Dohrn, Bernardine. 1970. "New Morning—Changing Weather." In Ayers, Bill, Bernardine Dohrn, and Jeff Jones. 2006. *Sing a Battle Song: The Revolutionary Poetry, Statements, and Communiqués of the Weather Underground, 1970–1974*. Seven Stories Press, p. 163.

73. See also Powers, Thomas. 1971. *Diana: The Making of a Terrorist*. Houghton Mifflin, p. 217; Jacobs, Ron. 1997. *The Way the Wind Blew: A History of the Weather Underground*. Verso Press, pp. 98, 125; Berger, Dan. 2006. *Outlaws of America: The Weather Underground and the Politics of Solidarity*. AK Press, p. 340; Barber, David. 2006. "Leading the Vanguard: White New Leftists School the Panthers on Black Revolution." In Laser and Williams, pp. 243, 250; Wilkerson, pp. 324–325.

74. Jacobs. See also https://archive.org/details/PrairieFireThePolitic sOfRevolutionaryAnti-imperialismThePolitical.

75. Ayers, Dohrn, Jones, and Sojourn, pp. 2–3. In online version found at http://www.sds-1960s.org/PrairieFire-reprint.pdf.

76. Varon, Jeremy. 2004. *Bringing the War Home: The Weather Underground, the Red Army Faction and Revolutionary Violence in the Sixties and Seventies*. University of California Press, pp. 296–297.

77. Jacobs,.

78. Ibid.

79. On Jan. 19, 1971, Bernardine Dohrn issued a statement from hiding suggesting that the group was considering tactics "other than bombing and terrorism." See also Powers, and Franks *UPI* feature series and winner of the Pulitzer Prize; September 23, 1970: "Of the 400 people who attended the Flint council [of the Weatherman group], fewer than 100 went underground. For those few, committed to the revolution above all else, it was a matter of logic. Community organizing had failed. Mass demonstrations had failed. Fighting in the streets had failed. Only terror was left." September 17, 1970: "She [Diana Oughton] never lost her gentleness, either, or her sense of morality; but consumed by revolutionary commitment, she became a terrorist, fully prepared to live as outlaw and killer." September 21, 1970: "The group's opponents argued that the Weathermen were repeating the errors of the 'Narodniki' (Russian terrorists) who assassinated the czar in 1881 and set back the cause of reform in Russia for decades." Ayers, Bill. 2006. "Weather Underground Redux," post April 20 (http://billayers. org/2006/04/), "Bill Ayers" blog, retrieved September 21, 2013: "This was a time when I, along with most of my closest friends, were referred to again and again as 'home-grown American terrorists'. That's what *Time* magazine called us in 1970, and the *New York Times*, too, and that was the word hurled in my direction from the halls of Congress." Mehnert, Klaus. 1977. *Twilight of the Young, the Radical Movements of the 1960s and Their Legacy*. Holt, Reinhart and Winston, p. 47: "Within the political youth movement of the late sixties (outside of Latin America), the 'Weathermen' were the first group to reach the front page because of terrorist activities." Martin, Gus. 2012. *Understanding Terrorism: Challenges, Perspectives, and Issues*. 4th ed. Sage Publications. "A number of terrorist groups and cells grew out of this environment. Although the most prominent example was the Weatherman group [. . .]"; Simon, Jeffrey D. 2001. *The Terrorist Trap: America's Experience with Terrorism*, 2nd ed. Indiana University Press, p. 96: "the most active American terrorist group at the end of the 1960s."

80. Ayers, Bill. 2009. *Fugitive Days: Memoirs of an Antiwar Activist*. Beacon Press, p. 263.

81. Ayers, William. 2008. "The Real Bill Ayers." *The New York Times*. (December 5). http://www.nytimes.com/2008/12/06/opinion/06ayers.html?_r=0. (Accessed October 8, 2013).

82. "The Americans Who Declared War on Their Country." 2003. *The Observer* (September 21). http://www.upstatefilms.org/weather/guardobserver.html. (Accessed October 10, 2013).

83. The Weather Underground. 2003; Mark Rudd. 2009. *Truth and Consequences: The Education of Mark Rudd*. Grove Press; Mark Rudd, 2009. *Underground: My Life with SDS and the Weathermen*. William Morrow.

84. http://www.prairiefire.org/about.shtml.

85. Mohan, Vas. 2014. "Vulnerable and Marginalized Populations." *International Foundation for Electoral Systems*. http://www.ifes.org/Content/Topics/Inclusion-and-Empowerment/Vulnerable-and-Marginalized-Populations.aspx. (Accessed May 10, 2014).

86. Among these was the Beer Lovers' Party, whose platform was "the protection of interests of beer lovers regardless of racial, national, or religious affiliation."

87. Countries with multiple political parties include Israel, Lebanon, Brazil, Denmark, Germany, India, Indonesia, Ireland, Italy, Japan, Mexico, Netherlands, New Zealand, Norway, Pakistan, Portugal, Serbia, Spain, Sweden, Taiwan, and the Philippines.

CHAPTER 4

Rise: The Inspiration for the New Patriot of the Late 20th Century and Beyond

THE BREEDING GROUND FOR VIOLENCE

As noted earlier, the post–World War II environment in the United States provided the perfect breeding ground for today's patriot and militia movements. First, there was the over-arching fear of the worldwide communist movement. Prior to the war, communism had been a nuisance, an annoyance confined to the Soviet Union and localized radical groups wishing to impose Marxist ideology upon democratic/capitalist systems. Yet after the war, the Soviet Union stood alongside the United States as a great power. Though economically wounded, the Soviet Union had amassed the largest army in the world and was entrenched in several Eastern European states, most of which it had no intention of ever leaving. Communism, once almost an afterthought in terms of the great issues of the world, was now front and center and challenging the ideas of individualism and liberty Americans held so dear. The possibility that communism could infiltrate the United States was real, as epitomized by the McCarthy hearings of the early 1950s.

The second major factor that contributed to the growth of right-wing extremist groups was the growing presence of the United States on the world stage. Prior to its involvement in World War I, the United States had never sent troops outside of the western hemisphere. The long-standing admonition of George Washington had been the guiding principle of American foreign policy for more than 120 years—"Don't become involved in European affairs." Even after its involvement in the First World War, the United States had returned to its traditional isolationist stance and had retired from its role as a major global power. The end of World War II, however, ended the luxury that the United States had prior to this catastrophic event. The economic collapse of most of the European powers and the threat that communism would become a reality in the postwar governments of Western Europe prompted the United States to fully engage in global affairs. Aid packages, such as the Marshall Plan, which were meant to rebuild Western Europe, fully tied the United States to the postwar fate of these countries. Moreover, the postwar belligerence and adventurism of the Soviet Union convinced the United States government that it must abandon its traditional isolationist stance, as it was the only major democratic/capitalist country that had not been seriously damaged by the war. As such, the United States embarked on its first-ever peacetime alliance. The formation of the North Atlantic Treaty Organization (NATO) and subsequent regional alliances around the world committed the United States to the defense of countries far from its shores. Part and parcel to the strategy of postwar "containment" entered into by the United States, containment necessitated the waging of "proxy wars" in order to thwart Soviet/communist expansion throughout the world. This meant that the United States would have to maintain a large standing army and significantly increase the amount it spent on defense.

Third, the new strategic direction of the United States necessitated a spirit of engagement and cooperation hitherto unknown in the country. After World War II, the United States joined with other countries to "save succeeding generations from the scourge of war. . ." (United Nations Charter Preamble). By joining the United Nations in 1945, the United States committed itself to internationalist principles that had been eschewed by the government of the United States and its people in the past. Indeed, whereas regional wars had raged for decades on the different continents of the world prior to 1914, the United States had never seen fit to participate in these conflicts. But because World War II had cost nearly 60 million lives, the United States decided that a global organization founded on peace, security, and justice in international affairs was an important piece of the post–World War II strategic environment. After all, by failing to join the League of Nations in 1919, the United States had found itself embroiled in a second world war a mere 23 years after the first had ended. This fact was not lost on the new generation of American leaders who had listened to the prediction of President Woodrow Wilson, who had stated that the failure of the

United States to join the League of Nations would precipitate a new world war within a generation. Sadly, this had come to pass.

A fourth element that contributed to the rise of patriot/militia groups in the United States was the rapid increase in the size, scope, and spending of the federal government. Beginning in the 20th century, government spending in the United States was about 7 percent of total gross domestic product (GDP). However, this number jumped significantly in the years following World War II to where government spending now accounts for almost 40 percent of GDP.[1] In addition to increased defense spending, which became the norm after World War II, much of the spending increase seen during the 20th century "goes for health care, education, pensions, and welfare programs."[2] That so much of the U.S. federal budget is devoted to "entitlement" programs is yet another reason for the rise of patriot/militia groups that tend to be populated by individuals who believe in small government, low taxes, and the real and supposed benefits of the market system. To think that so much of the budget goes to people in entitlements is akin, to many in these groups, to "welfare-state" policies, much like the socialist governments of Europe and elsewhere.

A fifth cause of the rise of patriot/militia groups in the years after World War II can be found in the civil rights movement. Though the U.S. Civil War ostensibly addressed the issue of race relations in the United States through the passage of the 13th, 14th, and 15th Amendments to the U.S. Constitution in the aftermath of that war, race relations continued to be a social and religious issue that divided many in the country. Though there were those who did not mind the presence of minority groups in the United States, they did not want to be told by the government that they had to fight with them, eat with them, shower with them, go to school with them, and the like. Over the course of several decades after World War II, the civil rights movement slowly moved many in the country who were already on the right of the political spectrum farther right because of their refusal to embrace the notion of equality in all its forms. As a consequence, many Americans simply withdrew from public life and failed to participate in any meaningful way, while still others decided to fight back against the social changes that they believed were bringing about social and political decay.

Finally, the evolution of modern life is disquieting to many. Sarup[3] defines modernity as "the progressive economic and administrative rationalization and differentiation of the social world." One of the general characteristics of modernity is "to question the foundations of past knowledge."[4] Boyne and Rattansi note that modernity has two sides:

"the progressive union of scientific objectivity and politico-economic rationality" and "disturbed visions of unalleviated existential despair."[5] It is the second of these meanings that is the most applicable for this study, for it is the "despair" that many patriot/militia adherents feel that defines their attitudes toward modern life. Such despair is not unique to these groups, however. A 2006 Pew study found some support for such attitudes.[6] In a 2013 work, Zafirovksi and Rodeheaver "discover and predict anti-liberalism in the form of conservatism as the main source and force in modern terrorism."[7] Though this study confirms what many already suspected, it was a Muslim scholar—Sayyid Qutb—who, after having visited the United States from 1948 to 1950, wrote the book *The America That I Have Seen*. In this book, Qutb "was critical of things he had observed in the United States: its materialism, individual freedoms, economic system, racism, brutal boxing matches, 'poor' haircuts, superficiality in conversations and friendships, restrictions on divorce, enthusiasm for sports, lack of artistic feeling, 'animal-like' mixing of the sexes (which 'went on even in churches'), and strong support for the new Israeli state."[8] Qutb was particularly critical of the sexuality of American women: "the American girl is well acquainted with her body's seductive capacity. She knows it lies in the face, and in expressive eyes, and thirsty lips. She knows seductiveness lies in the round breasts, the full buttocks, and in the shapely thighs, sleek legs—and she shows all this and does not hide it."[9] Qutb would become an adherent of the Muslim Brotherhood and, as such, greatly influenced the thinking of Osama bin Laden and Ayman al-Zawahiri, the current leader of Al-Qaeda as of this writing.

The factors discussed, then, influence the rise of the patriot/militia movement in the United States. Though they would be expressed in different ways, one of the most powerful influences of the patriot/militia movement is found in the common law court movement. This movement, which disavows the jurisdiction of any federal U.S. court to prosecute U.S. citizens, has inspired many of the groups this study addresses. A brief look at this movement follows.

THE COMMON LAW COURT MOVEMENT

The following story is largely retold from the "Anti-Government Movement Guidebook." To many, the verdict of the county court was predictable. Caught driving without a license or proof of insurance, Sherry Scotka received a $350 fine from the Ken County, Texas, court for each offense. But Scotka, during the summer of 1993, was anything but predictable. Acting as her own lawyer, she appealed the county court's decision, requesting that the Texas Appeals Court transfer her case to the "Common Law Court of the United States of America." Her argument? That as a "sovereign citizen," she was outside the jurisdiction of Texas law or Texas courts.

In the case of Sherry Scotka, the appeals court did not look upon her request with favor, noting that she could not even show that the Common Law Court of the United States of America existed. This was not the first time that the Court of Appeals had faced this sort of peculiar argument. From the Texas hill country had come a rash of such claims, all from strangely similar cases: traffic violations, foreclosures, frivolous suits. Brought to court, the defendants, usually operating *pro se*—that is, defending themselves—would demand that the case in question be removed to the "Common Law Court for the Republic of Texas." Finally, in 1992, the Appeals Court noted officially that there was no such thing. "We hold," said the court, "that the Common Law Court for the Republic of Texas, if it ever existed, has ceased to exist since February 16, 1846"—in other words, when Texas state government was organized. It was then that the defendant changed the transfer reference in her pleading to the "Common Law Court of the United States of America," although interestingly, the address on the legal documents remained the same. What the Texas appeals court was just beginning to perceive was the beginning of a movement created by recalcitrant, self-proclaimed "sovereign citizens" determined to wrest control of their lives back from all forms of government or authority. Appearing first in isolated spots in Texas and Florida, the notion of common law courts soon spread to Kansas and other farm states, then quickly across the nation. The "common law court movement," as it has somewhat clumsily come to be called, now exists in some form in every state in the country. In some states, activity is minimal; in others, common law courts are a serious nuisance; in some, they are a plague on the judicial system.[10]

In 1997, 27 judges, court clerks, court administrators, and prosecutors met in Scottsdale, Arizona, to more closely examine the so-called common law court (CLC) movement. The goal of this group was to "make recommendations for establishing a curriculum for judicial educators to train judges and court officials on how to deal with CLC activities in their own jurisdictions."[11] The preface of the "Anti-American Government Guidebook" stated that the CLC movement was an outgrowth of a phenomenon that had been growing in the United States over the course of three decades:

There is a movement afoot in this country today that is made up of disaffected and often dispossessed Americans who are seeking a better way through a wholesale *return to their view of the past* (emphasis added). This movement has been called many things: the antigovernment movement, the sovereignty movement, and the common law courts movement. Regardless of the name attached to the beliefs and the people who follow them, one common denominator exists: a *feeling of despair* [emphasis added], rooted in personal and pecuniary loss, and manifested in a new, defiant mistrust and spite for the ways of the current government. This guide focuses on the ways in which followers of these movements impact the operation of our state court systems.

While the commentators have discussed these movements from all angles—ranging from ridicule to outrage to fear—most of the mainstream pundits discount the powerful emotion that drives individuals from the fold of our everyday society and into the ranks of the modem patriots. This guide asks that our state courts not take these individuals and their problems and concerns so lightly. In 1928, Justice Brandeis said:

> "Decency, security, and liberty alike demand that government officials shall be subjected to the same rules of conduct that are commands to the citizen. In a government of laws, existence of the government will be imperiled if it fails to observe the law scrupulously. Our government is the potent, the omnipresent teacher. For good or for ill, it teaches the whole people by its example."

The people who make up the movements that we are concerned with consistently speak out to say that our government today does not listen, it no longer serves the American people, it exists to serve its own ends. The merits of that argument are not within the purview of this guide. Rather, the authors wish to urge Justice Brandeis's warning upon those who administer our state courts. That is, while we do not advocate an ultra-sympathetic response at the expense of safety and the efficient operation of the courts, we do implore those charged with running our court system to do two things: learn the history behind the beliefs we are seeing spread across our land, and understand that these are not militia members or "Patriots" or "ultra-conservatives," but rather citizens who come before you seeking the same fair treatment that those without any label attached receive.[12]

THE POSSE COMITATUS

The post–World War II conditions in the United States previously noted in this study gave rise to groups such as the John Birch Society and the Minutemen. However, the rise of the modern patriot/militia movement begins with the group known as the Posse Comitatus ("force [or power] of the county").[13] Founded in 1967 in Oregon by a retired dry cleaner named Henry Lamont "Mike" Beach (a former member of the 1930s pro-Nazi group the Silver Shirts), the Posse Comitatus was a right-wing extremist organization that advocated resistance to the oversight of federal authority of almost every kind, ranging from the payment of taxes to the issuance of drivers' licenses. A similar organization to Posse Comitatus—the United States Christian Posse Association—was founded in California by William Potter Gale about the same time. These and other groups began to proliferate during the 1970s as "average" Americans began to protest what they perceived as the "heavy-handedness" of the U.S. government. By the mid-1970s, there were some 80 or so groups similar to the Posse Comitatus in several states, most notably in the West and Midwest. The primary ideology of all of these groups was that there was no legitimate form of government above that of the county and no higher law enforcement authority than that of the county sheriff.[14] As Brent L. Smith explained, if the sheriff of a county refused to carry out the will of the people, "he shall be removed by the Posse to the most populated intersection of streets in the township and at high noon be hung by the neck, the body remaining until sundown as an example to those who would subvert the law.[15]

As recently as 2012, members of a "new" Posse group were arrested in connection with the deaths of two sheriff's deputies in St. John Parish, Louisiana.[16]

As early as 1974, Posse groups were violently confronting federal officials. In Wisconsin, Thomas Stockheimer, head of the Posse in that state, was convicted on charges of assaulting an agent of the Internal Revenue Service (IRS).[17] Another Posse leader, James Wickstrom, "styled himself the 'national director of counterinsurgency'" of the Posse and liked to conduct paramilitary training established the "Constitutional Township of Tigerton Dells," a "township that consisted of a compound of trailers on a farm lot."[18] Wickstrom "waged a war against local authorities" that eventually resulted in the destruction of the "township" and Wickstrom's arrest. In other states, Posse members clashed with federal authorities and local government officials—resulting in several deaths and injuries.[19]

It was Gordon Kahl who became the first official "martyr" of the Posse cause. Kahl, a violent racist and tax protestor, traveled throughout the Midwest in the early 1980s to protest the worsening conditions of farms and the intrusion of government regulations into the lives of Americans. In 1983, four U.S. Marshals and two local law enforcement officers set up a roadblock in North Dakota to arrest Kahl for violating the terms of his probation. On June 3, a shootout ensued between Kahl and the marshals that resulted in the death of two of the marshals and the wounding of two others. Also wounded was Kahl's 20-year-old son. When Kahl fled the state, a nationwide manhunt—and nationwide publicity—began. Months later, Kahl was tracked down in Arkansas, where he died during another gunfight in which a county sheriff was killed.[20]

The efforts of Kahl and others established the philosophies of the Posse that would come to be self-sufficiency, localism, and antitax revolt. Indeed, most Posse members refused to pay taxes, obtain drivers' licenses, or otherwise comply with any government regulation. Posse Comitatus and similar groups do not believe in "floating exchange rates" for currency, instead believing that the only valid forms of currency are those that can be backed up dollar for dollar by gold. This, they insisted, was a requirement of the Constitution.[21]

Justification for claims and actions of the Posse Comitatus was found in what was known as the "hidden history" of the United States. According to this theory, Posse members believe that the "true history" of the United States and thus the "true laws" of the United States have been hidden from the people by a "massive, long-lasting conspiracy." The Posse believed that:

> the rule for the Judiciary, both State and Federal, has been subtle subversion of the Constitution of these United States. The subversion and contempt for the Constitution by the Judiciary is joined by the Executive and Legislative branches of government. It is apparent that the Judiciary has attempted to alter our form of Government. By unlawful administrative acts and procedures, they have attempted to establish a Dictatorship of the Courts over the citizens of this Republic. The legal profession has, with few exceptions, conspired with the Judiciary for this purpose.[22]

Posse leaders thus developed tales of conspiracy and cover-up that had taken place since the Founding that were designed to subvert liberty. The "true laws" of the United States had been covered up by a vast band of conspirators that included legislators, judges, and lawyers. Posse adherents set about to "find" these laws "through searching through law books and legal codes, the writings of the founders and early legal scholars, the Uniform Commercial Code, the Bible, and other documents."[23]

One of the purported "found" documents was the discovery of what was called the "Missing 13th Amendment." According to a Texas Posse advocate, a draft of the constitutional amendment from the republic's early days had been found together with a copy of the Constitution that listed the draft amendment along with the other amendments that had actually been ratified. Supposedly, the 13th Amendment would have allowed for the denial of citizenship to any American who accepted a title of nobility. To the Posse, lawyers had "titles of nobility" because they often placed the term "esquire" after their names. To the thinking of the Posse, then, lawyers were not legal citizens of the United States and had purposely usurped the inclusion of this amendment into the final copy of the Constitution.[24]

Another example of such "hidden" or "missing" history was put forth by William Potter Gale, founder of the United States Christian Posse Association. According to Gale, the Articles of Confederation—the initial Constitution of the United States—had never been officially repealed and, therefore, remained in force even to this day. Gale noted a clause in the Articles that allowed for Congress to appoint a committee when it was not in session to conduct the general affairs of the country. Gale interpreted this to mean that the states constituted this committee and, as such, had coequal authority with Congress.[25]

The Posse's ideology attracted many of those who were involved in the antitax movement of the time, as these groups firmly believed in different interpretations of the tax code and that the 16th Amendment—the amendment that made constitutional a federal income tax—had never been legitimately ratified.

Another group to which the Posse appealed was Christian Identity. From the beginning, Posse ideology was attractive to Christian Identity and vice versa. Christian Identity, which was inherently anti-Semitic, looked to the Bible as a document inspired by God. Posse members, looking for the source of the "conspiracy" to hide the true history of the country, found justification in Christian Identity ideology that pointed to "international bankers," most of whom were Jews, as the conspirators who had subverted the truth. This Posse/Identity link served both groups well during the farm crisis of the 1980s (see what follows):

...when inflation, falling land values, rising interest rates, and poor lending practices combined to create a financial crisis that threatened to overwhelm farmers of little or moderate means. . . . [t]he Posse offered a culprit—the international (Jewish) banking conspiracy which had destroyed the Constitutional/Biblical monetary system and replaced it with one based on credit designed to suck people dry.[26]

Thus, the Posse's antigovernment stance and Identity's anti-Semitism would serve to galvanize the groups that would come to epitomize the patriot/militia groups of the 1990s and beyond.

Though Posse Comitatus would not survive into the 1990s, its influence would be felt far beyond its brief existence. Indeed, given its various philosophies, a penchant for survivalism would come to epitomize those with Posse sympathies. The CLC movement mentioned previously, as well as the "sovereign citizen movement," are legacies of the Posse Comitatus. The sovereign citizen movement claims "that a U.S. citizen can become a 'sovereign citizen' and thereby be subject only to common law and/or 'constitutional law,' not to statutory law (including most taxes).[27] This sovereign citizen movement gave rise to the "redemption movement" that claims that the U.S. government has enslaved its citizens by using them as "collateral against foreign debt."[28] Those who promote redemption schemes utilize the mechanisms of "false liens"—wherein liens that have no basis in fact are filed against government officials and judges—as a tool of harassment. These methods have been criminalized by the U.S. Congress, and U.S. Sentencing Guidelines state that filing a false lien against a government official is as serious as physically threatening a government official of the United States.[29] Harassment of this type has been dubbed "paper terrorism," which refers to the use of false liens, frivolous lawsuits, bogus letters of credit, and other legal documents that have no basis in fact but are used to intimidate government officials.[30]

Perhaps the most insidious of the Posse Comitatus's legacies, and one that pervades much of the patriot/militia group movement today, is the ideology of Christian Identity (more about this in following sections). This belief, based on anti-Semitism and white supremacy, holds that the U.S. government is illegitimate, as it is in the hands of the Zionist Occupation Government (ZOG), a worldwide Jewish conspiracy to control key countries around the world.[31] In 1985, the "Christian Posse Comitatus Newsletter" commented that "Our nation is now completely under the control of the International Invisible government of the

World Jewry."[32] White supremacists who are members of Posse groups have maintained that African Americans, who only gained legal citizenship after the Civil War and passage of the 14th Amendment, are in reality "14th Amendment citizens" with fewer rights than whites, who are, in fact, "organic citizens."[33] Thus, though the original group is long gone, its legacy of hate, racism, mistrust, and violence endures in the groups that now exist on the American landscape.

SHOCKS TO THE LIBERAL IDEAL: THE RISE OF THE POLITICAL RIGHT

Though groups that espoused political violence from the left and the right would dot the American political landscape in the late 1960s and early 1970s, by the late 1970s, most leftist organizations had largely disappeared because of the end of the Vietnam War. Yet by the end of the 1970s, a general malaise was affecting the post–World War II generation of Americans that hitherto had experienced more than 30 years of U.S. supremacy. A sense that the United States had "lost" the Vietnam War, coupled with the worst political scandal in U.S. history—Watergate—shook Americans to their core. Trust in government plummeted,[34] and the backlash against the Republican Party manifested itself by propelling a relatively unknown Jimmy Carter to the presidency in 1976, as well as the domination by the Democrats of both houses of the U.S. Congress.

Despite what promised to be a "new start" with Vietnam and Watergate behind it, the United States quickly found itself in conditions that caused even the most stout-hearted of Americans to question their country's position in the world. For instance, U.S. support of Israel had fostered a foreign-policy backlash from many Arab and Islamic countries that protested the heavy-handedness of U.S. foreign policy in the Middle East. These "protests" often found voice in the form of terrorism and violent acts against U.S. interests and citizens abroad. The oil embargo of 1973 was the first shock that rocked Americans, followed by a second oil embargo in 1978 that stifled American economic growth and forced American motorists to wait for hours in line for a gallon of gas. The detente that the U.S. had with the Soviet Union during the Nixon years had degenerated into bitter animosity as a second arms-control agreement, the Strategic Arms Limitation Talks II (SALT II), had failed to gain support for ratification in the U.S. Senate. A near nuclear disaster at Three Mile Island in Pennsylvania in 1979 caused

Americans to question whether nuclear power was a safe alternative to the long-forecast and impending energy crises that analysts were predicting. Inflation approached 20 percent and unemployment was more than 10 percent—numbers that were among the worst in modern U.S. history. Crime rates in major U.S. cities soared,[35] and cities themselves began to fall into decay. The American public began to speak quite frankly about "moral decay" as evidence mounted of increasing drug use, sexual promiscuity, and rising divorce rates. As a result, religion turned political in the hopes of "changing directions toward a more innocent time."[36]

Two additional shocks to America's self-identity would have serious ramifications for the future of the patriot/militia movements that would proliferate during the 1980s and the 1990s. The first was the Iranian Revolution that occurred throughout 1979. Beginning with the abdication of Shah Mohammad Reza Pahlavi of Iran in February, extremist Islamic forces—led by the exiled Ayatollah Ruhollah Khomeini—would seize control of Iran, later precipitating an attack on the American embassy in Tehran and the seizure of 52 American hostages who would subsequently be held for 444 days. The change of governments in Iran meant the loss of a key ally of the United States in the ongoing Cold War with the Soviet Union. Iran had been a bulwark of listening posts and other intelligence-gathering activities during the course of the Cold War given its proximity as a border state of the Soviet Union. The more troubling facet of the Iranian Revolution, however, would be the growing presence of Islamic extremism in the Middle East, much of it aimed at the United States and its policies and associations in this key part of the world. Indeed, the Iranian Revolution precipitated a fundamental change in terrorist incidents, as many now became religiously rather than politically motivated. Once thought unthinkable, the seizure of American hostages by Iran in November 1979 convinced Americans that the United States had become weak and was, in fact, "losing" the Cold War with the Soviet Union.

A second event in late 1979 would further shake American confidence in the country's ability to deter its enemies. On December 27, 1979, Soviet forces would invade and occupy Afghanistan. The occupation would last almost 10 years and would see the rise of the mujahideen ("holy warriors"), the emergence of a little-known character by the name of Osama bin Laden, and the establishment of the terror group Al-Qaeda ("the Base") that would combine extremist Islamic radical movements from across the Middle East into a concentrated effort to attack and destabilize the United States over the coming years.

Though the Soviet invasion of Afghanistan was well outside the purview of the U.S. policy of containment of the Soviet Union, the invasion nevertheless signaled to many, and most importantly to Americans, that the United States had become largely impotent in deterring Soviet actions around the world. Much of the dissatisfaction expressed by Americans at this time about the reduced standing of the United States in the world focused on President Jimmy Carter and his foreign policies. Carter had entered office with the pledge of demanding better human rights accountability from U.S. allies. Whether true or not, his policies led to revolutions in Iran and Nicaragua that replaced governments friendly to the United States with antagonistic governments. At least two Hollywood movies of recent years have made mention of the late 1970s as a time of great uncertainty among Americans (e.g., *Miracle* and *Argo*).

As 1980 dawned, Ronald Reagan, the former governor of California and an anticommunist with long conservative credentials, asked Americans, "Are you better off than you were four years ago?" Even supporters of the Democratic Party and those with more liberal views could not answer this question with a resounding "yes!" Reagan, who promised to rebuild America's military strength and confront the Soviet Union at every conflict point, swept to a landslide victory in the 1980 general election. Reagan's emphasis on American exceptionalism seemed to be just what most Americans needed and wanted as the new decade dawned.[37] Reagan had allied himself closely with the most conservative elements of the Republican Party and had enlisted the support of Christian groups, who believed, like him, that the United States had lost its moral center.[38] Reagan's belief and advocacy of smaller government, fewer entitlement programs, more personal responsibility, and a military unmatched by any other in the world appealed to the new brand of "patriot" that was emerging as the millennium was coming to a close.

THE 1980S FARM CRISIS

As a result of the Soviet invasion of Afghanistan, President Carter—together with other actions—instituted an embargo on the sale of grain to the Soviet Union. During most of the 1970s, lowered trade barriers coupled with record purchases of American grain by the Soviet Union led to sharp increases in American agricultural exports. As a result of these conditions:

Farm incomes and commodity prices soared. The removal of restrictions on Federal Land Bank lending, coupled with increased
lending by other entities for farmland purchases in the Seventies,
led to rising land values. Conveniently low interest rates persuaded
many farmers—and would-be farmers—to go deeply into debt on
the assumption that commodity prices and land values would continue to rise. Farm household income had been below the national
average in the 1960s; in the next decade it was higher than the national average for every year except one. But it would return to the
1960s levels in the Eighties. The agricultural "boom" didn't last
long.[39]

By the early 1980s, tightened money supplies and high interest rates
had burst the agricultural bubble that had been based on the speculation of continued good times. The U.S. government estimated that
farmland value dropped nearly 60 percent in some parts of the Midwest
between 1981 and 1985. Many farmers found it impossible to pay down
their debts due to several factors. First, record grain harvests had led to
a glut in farm commodities, driving prices way down from where they
had been in the 1970s. Second, the global economic stagnation of the
late 1970s and early 1980s, coupled with the strong U.S. dollar abroad,
affected purchasing states such that U.S. agricultural exports declined
by more than 20 percent between 1981 and 1983, with real commodity
prices decreasing 21 percent in the same period. (By 1984, an overval-
ued dollar was adding a 32 percent surcharge to all U.S. exports.) In the
1970s, the federal government tried to offset a growing U.S. trade defi-
cit (caused by the OPEC oil embargo) by expanding agricultural sales
overseas. Subsidies to overseas purchasers via loans by the Commodity
Credit Corporation and the extension of credit to foreign governments
by commercial banks contributed to a surge in U.S. farm exports that
went from $8 billion in 1971 to $43.8 billion in 1981. But by the 1980s,
the worldwide financial community realized that debtor nations could
not repay their loans unless they drastically reduced imports, and the
gushing tap of credit largesse was shut off.[40] Third, President Carter's
grain embargo of the Soviet Union prompted the Soviets to look for
other agricultural suppliers. Agricultural price supports, which since
the Great Depression had meant to artificially keep commodity prices
high to ensure the survival of the "American family farm," allowed
farmers in Argentina, Australia, Canada, and Europe to fill the void in
the international marketplace that had been created as a result of the
Soviet grain embargo.[41]

The hardest hit during the farm crisis of the 1980s were "middle-level" farmers—those whose income ranged between $40,000 and $500,000 a year. Farmers making less than $40,000 per year derived the majority of their income from nonfarm sources. Therefore, they had not incurred large amounts of debt. Farmers who made more than $500,000 a year were able to weather the financial hard times.[42] As farm profits declined 36 percent between 1980 and 1988, the mid-level farmer began experiencing financial stress, leading to increases in child abuse rates, divorce rates, and alcohol abuse.[43] By early 1984, farm indebtedness had risen to $215 billion, double what it had been in 1978 and 15 times more than it had been in 1950. For the first time in history, interest payments on farm debt exceed total net farm income.[44]

Though Ronald Reagan had entered office with the support of many of the individuals who were now losing their livelihoods to the crushing debt they had incurred, his administration's policy was laissez-faire— let the marketplace operate according to its nature. One commentator of the time perfectly described the Reagan administration's point of view:

> The primary function of the Government should be to insure small and moderate-size farmers against natural disasters and price fluctuations that have threatened them since the beginning of time. . . . But the Government cannot protect farmers either from themselves or from inevitable changes in technology and the marketplace.[45]

The latter observation was exactly what the federal government had been trying to do for farmers since the days of the New Deal. As Susan DeMarco put it, the "most devastating force at work in the farm belt is America's disastrous agriculture policy," which she described as a "dizzying array of ad-hoc, often conflicting programs devised over decades to serve special interests."[46] Stuart Hardy, manager of food and agricultural policy for the U.S. Chamber of Commerce, claimed that "price support programs and import quotas add several billion dollars annually to retail food prices."[47] According to David Stockman, Reagan's director of the Office of Management and Budget (OMB), the farmers had been "greedy and were suffering the consequences." "Taxpayers," said Stockman, "ought not be required to refinance the bad debt incurred by those farmers." These comments led Senator Tom Harkin (D-IA) to warn Stockman that if he stepped foot in Iowa, he would be lynched.[48] As noted by one commentator, however, "The biggest problem for Reagan and Stockman was the fact that the middle-level farmer-entrepreneur proved to be highly skilled at politicking and publicizing, and was determined not to go quietly."[49]

On March 17, 1986, protestors used tractors and other farm machinery to surround the Farmers Home Administration (FmHA) office in Chillicothe, Missouri. Chanting "Farm aid, not Contra aid" and "Butter, not guns!" the group raised awareness of the terrible conditions that were befalling the traditional institution of the American family farm. This was the beginning of the National Save the Family Farm Coalition, "which called for higher commodity prices, production controls, immediate debt relief, a moratorium on farm foreclosures, and emergency assistance to suffering farm families."[50] Coalition farmers claimed that Reagan administration policies were hurting family farms while benefitting large agribusinesses.[51]

Many of the protests taking place at this time were staged to disrupt or stop the auctioning of foreclosed farms. In March 1985, a gathering in Plattsburg, Missouri, for this purpose turned violent and a number of people were injured. Eight persons were arrested.[52] Many farm aid associations created crisis hotlines to assist distressed farmers, particularly with legal advice. (Some activists were not concerned with the legal ramifications of their advice.) In Worthington, Minnesota, 250 families gathered to hear one such activist assure them that they had "no moral obligation to pay an unjust debt" and that they had the right to use guns to protect their farms from foreclosure.[53] Farmers made alliances with civil rights groups and organized labor. A Farmer-Labor Alliance was also founded in Missouri wherein representatives from both factions pledged to support each other's legislative agendas—"farmers would back a minimum wage increase while unions would support the moratorium on farm foreclosures."[54]

The results of the farm crisis of the 1980s were varied. It produced rage against state and federal government policies in many Midwestern states and elicited sympathies from many extremist elements. Moreover, support for Ronald Reagan eroded among farmers:

> Though a slim majority of farmers supported Reagan in 1980 and again in 1984, his approval rating in the farm community nationwide dropped from 51 percent in 1984 to 39 percent in 1985.[55] In Missouri, three county-level Republican leaders switched to the Democrats in protest of Reagan's farm policy. In Nebraska, three rural Republican legislators also switched. In Minnesota, Reagan's 1984 state campaign coordinator became the Democratic

candidate running against Republican Representative Vin Weber.[56] These were but a few of the defections.[57]

The farm crisis of the 1980s would prove to stoke the fires of discontent that were then being fanned by what was perceived as the runaway nature of big government. This phenomenon would coincide with a rise in religious intolerance and bigotry as expressed by groups that simultaneously held strict religious views—particularly as they pertained to the influences of Judaism in the American system—and views of a federal government that had overstepped its traditional boundaries and was now venturing into the territory of the tyrannical government that the Founding Fathers had feared.

The next section will examine the concomitant rise of extreme religious fanaticism with renewed antigovernment sentiment that was closely tied to both the patriot and militia movements that were beginning to form in the late 1980s.

CHRISTIAN IDENTITY

In the early 1980s, a coalition of loosely affiliated Christian believers and churches began to emerge that echoed many of the sentiments of the Ku Klux Klan (KKK) and other groups. Christian Identity espouses a white supremacist philosophy, justifying its beliefs on specific interpretations of the Bible and influences from elsewhere. Some adherents of Christian Identity (e.g., Aryan Nations) couple a strongly held antigovernment sentiment with their theological beliefs. Christian Identity "theology" consists of several tenets: (1) Adam and Eve were the progenitors of the white race, and all other races are pre-Adamic or beasts that evolved into human form; (2) modern-day Jews are not the true descendants of the tribe of Judah but are descendants of Esau, Isaac's oldest son, who sold his birthright (inherited by Jacob) for a bowl of "pottage," or red stew (Genesis 25:29–34); (3) there will be an "End Times" and the epic battle of Armageddon that will herald the Second Coming of Jesus Christ; (4) interracial marriage, homosexuality, and any "deviant" behavior is not of God and is, therefore, beastly and deserving of eradication; and, (5) a general suspicion of the federal government and, in particularly, anything pertaining to a "new world order."

Christian Identity has its ideological origins in the 1920s and the 1930s in what was known as "British Israelism."[58] This philosophy held that white Europeans were the actual descendants of Israel (Jacob) through the lost Ten Tribes that had been taken into captivity by the armies of Assyria. Modern-day Jews, on the other hand, are descendants of Esau or Satan. Adam and Eve were the parents of the white race, and all other races "predate" Adam and Eve. These "other" races existed prior to the creation of Adam and Eve and evolved to where they became human in form, but they possess no souls and therefore can never earn the blessings that God has promised his children.[59] Though British Israelism was not inherently anti-Semitic, when the idea came to the United States, the idea took "an ugly turn." According to the Anti-Defamation League,

> Once on American shores, British-Israelism began to evolve. Originally, believers viewed contemporary Jews as descendants of those ancient Israelites who had never been "lost." They might be seen critically but, given their significant role in the British-Israel genealogical scheme, not usually with animosity. By the 1930s, however, in the U.S., a strain of anti-Semitism started to permeate the movement (though some maintained traditional beliefs)—and a small number of traditionalists still exist in the U.S.[60]

Christian Identity posits what is known as "two-house theology," which states that the ancient kingdom of Israel was split into two houses—Israel and Judah—about 931 BCE. In approximately 722 BCE, most of those living in the northern portion of what had been the Kingdom of Israel were taken into captivity and scattered about after having been conquered by the Assyrians. The southern part of the Kingdom, including Judah, largely survived to constitute modern-day Jews. However, whereas British Israelism held that Jews were descended from the tribe of Judah, Christian Identity in its American bastardization believed that the true descendants of Judah (and Israel) are instead white Europeans. These were members of the original Lost Ten Tribes that had been "scattered" but that had settled in Scotland, Germany, and other European countries. These "true Israelites" are Anglo-Saxon, Celtic, Germanic, Nordic, and kindred peoples.[61]

In the philosophy of Christian Identity, contemporary Jews are the descendants of Esau (son of Isaac), who sold his God-given birthright for a bowl of pottage (Genesis 25: 29–34). Jacob, his younger brother, who would become Israel (and would have 12 sons), thus became the recipient of the promises made to Abraham and his posterity. The "dual seedliner" strain of Christian Identity thought holds that the Jews are actually the spawn of Satan through Adam and Eve's son Cain. In this belief, Satan seduced Eve and she gave birth to Cain, while Abel, whom Cain would slay, was the "pure" progeny of Adam and Eve. This line of reasoning was fostered by a book by Charles Carroll who, in 1900, wrote a book titled *The Negro: A Beast or in the Image of God?* In his treatise, Carroll concluded that only the white race was the true offspring of Adam and Eve, "while Negros are pre-Adamite beasts and could not possibly have been made in God's image and likeness because they are beastlike, immoral and ugly.[62] Carroll insisted that blacks did not have souls and that the mixing of the races led to the blasphemous ideas of atheism and evolutionism.[63] Variants on these themes have led many Christian Identity adherents to believe fiercely in the separation of the races, with one author denoting the Christian Identity belief that the mixing of the races is a defilement of the white race and that the penalties for this and other "beastly" behaviors (e.g., homosexuality) should be death.[64]

In addition to racism, Christian Identity teaches that there will be an end of times and that the biblically foretold battle of Armageddon, in which the forces of good will battle the forces of evil, will be fought. This "end times" scenario makes Christian Identity members very extremist in their interpretation of events. For instance, adherents view the United Nations as an organization controlled by a Jewish-backed conspiracy that aims itself at overthrowing the United States of America.[65] Jews also play prominently in their control of the world banking system and their control of the "root of all evil"—paper money. As noted by author James Alfred Ago, "The creation of the Federal Reserve System in 1913 shifted control of money from Congress to private institutions and violated the Constitution. The money system encourages the Federal Reserve to take out loans, creating trillions of dollars of government debt and allowing international bankers to control America.[66] Christian identity preacher Sheldon Eery claims, "Most of the owners of the largest banks in America are of Eastern European (Jewish) ancestry and connected with the (Jewish) Rothschild European banks; thus, in Identity doctrine, the global banking conspiracy is led and controlled by Jewish interests."[67]

A leading figure in the cause of Christian Identity was William Potter Gale (1917–1988), a former aide to General Douglas MacArthur. Gale was a leading figure in the antitax and paramilitary movements of the 1970s and 1980s, including the Posse Comitatus, and was an intellectual forefather of contemporary militia movements.[68] Several past and current patriot/militia groups identify with Christian Identity ideas, including the Covenant, Sword, and the Arm of the Lord; the Faience

Priesthood; the Aryan Republican Army; the Church of Jesus Christ, Christian; Church of Israel; and Kingdom Identity Ministries. Perhaps the most "successful" of the groups is Aryan Nations. Aryan Nations adheres to most of the regular tenets of Christian Identity but differs in the zeal with which it professes antigovernment sentiments. The ultimate goal of Aryan Nations is to establish a "whites only" homeland in five northwestern states—Oregon, Idaho, Wyoming, Washington, and Montana. If ceded by the government, these states were to become the base of the "White Power" movement and be known as the "Northwest Territorial Imperative." The headquarters of Aryan Nations was headquartered in Hayden Lake, Idaho, from the late 1970s until the early 2000s. It was founded by Richard Butler, who was inspired by William Potter Gale's association with the Posse Comitatus movement. Butler was a great admirer of Adolph Hitler, and he longed for a whites-only homeland in the Pacific Northwest. In 1981, Butler held the first of many Aryan World Conferences on his Hayden Lake property. These "confabs" would attract

> almost every nationally significant racist leader around. Among them: Tom Metzger, former Klansman and leader of White Aryan Resistance; Louis Beam, another onetime Klansman who promoted the concept of leaderless resistance; Don Black, the former Klansman who created Stormfront, the oldest and largest white nationalist forum on the Web; and Kirk Lyons, a lawyer who has represented several extremists and who was married on the compound by Butler.[69]

Richard Butler died in September 2004, but by this time his legacy had already become bloodied. Butler's most loyal and committed follower was Robert Jay ("Bob") Mathews, who founded the Order.

THE ORDER (INSPIRED BY *THE TURNER DIARIES*)

Robert Jay "Bob" Mathews stunned his middle-class parents when he announced at 11 years old that he had joined the ultraconservative John Birch Society.[70] When he entered high school, he was baptized into the Mormon faith and formed what became known as the Sons of Liberty, an anticommunist militia made up almost entirely of Mormon survivalists.[71] After being arrested for tax fraud (Mathews had claimed 10 dependents on his W-4 form) and serving probation, Bob Mathews's family moved to Washington, where they purchased land for a new home.

From his own experiences and readings, Mathews believed that the white race was in danger of extinction from intermarrying and the challenges being placed upon it by societal forces, all of which were being driven by the American government. Mathews made a concerted attempt to create a whites-only homeland in the Pacific Northwest—the White American Bastion. In 1983, Mathews made a speech before the National Alliance—a white-nationalist, anti-Semitic, and white-separatist group that had been founded by William L. Pierce in 1974. Mathews called upon those assembled at the convention, particularly "the yeoman farmers and independent truckers," to rally to his White American Bastion notion and take back what was rightfully theirs. Reportedly, Mathews received the only standing ovation at the conference.[72] Mathews became an avid reader and a proponent of National Alliance founder William Pierce's fantasy novel *The Turner Diaries*, written in 1978.

The Turner Diaries, written under Pierce's pseudonym Andrew Macdonald, depicts a time of violent revolution in the United States when the American government is overthrown and a race war ensues that leads to the extermination of all groups deemed by the author to be impure—Jews, homosexuals, and nonwhites.[73] The book was called "explicitly racist and anti-Semitic" by the *New York Times* and has been labeled as the "bible of the racist right" by the Southern Poverty Law Center.[74]

Because of its influence on contemporary patriot/militia movements, the plot summary of *The Turner Diaries* is provided here:

> The narrative starts with a foreword set in 2099, one hundred years after the events depicted in the book. The bulk of the book then quotes a recently discovered diary of a man named Earl Turner, an active member of the white Aryan revolutionary movement that caused these events. The book details a violent overthrow of the United States federal government by Turner and his militant comrades and a brutal contemporaneous race war that takes place first in North America, and then the rest of the world.
>
> The story starts soon after the federal government has confiscated all civilian firearms in the country under the fictional Cohen Act, and the organization to which Turner and his cohorts belong goes underground and engages in a guerrilla war against the

"System," which is depicted as the totality of the government, media, and economy that is under left-wing Jewish control. The "Organization" starts with acts such as the bombing of FBI headquarters and continues to execute an ongoing, low level campaign of terrorism, assassination and economic sabotage throughout the United States. Turner's exploits lead to his initiation into the "Order," a quasi-religious inner cadre that directs the Organization and whose existence remains a secret to both the System and ordinary Organization members.

Eventually, the Organization seizes physical control of Southern California, including the nuclear weapons at Vandenberg Air Force Base; ethnically cleanses the area of all blacks and summarily executes all Jews and other "race traitors." The Organization's response to a white woman who had a black man as a lover is summary execution. The Organization has little use for most white "mainstream" Americans. Those on the left are seen as dupes or willing agents of the Jews, while conservatives and libertarians are regarded as misguided fools, for, the Organization states, the Jews "took over according to the Constitution, fair and square." Turner and his comrades save their special contempt for the ordinary people, who are seen to care about nothing beyond being kept comfortable and entertained.

The Organization then uses both their Southern Californian base of operations and their nuclear weapons to open a wider war in which they launch nuclear strikes against New York City and Israel, initiate a nuclear exchange between the United States and the Soviet Union, and plant nuclear weapons and new terrorist cells throughout North America. Many major U.S. cities are destroyed, including Baltimore and Detroit. The diary section ends with the protagonist flying an airplane equipped with an atomic bomb on a suicide mission to destroy The Pentagon, in order to eliminate the leadership of the remaining military government before it orders an assault to retake California. The novel ends with an epilogue summarizing how the Organization continued on to conquer the rest of the world and how people of other races were eliminated (China and the entire eastern half of Asia were destroyed by prolonged bombardments with various weapons of mass destruction and made into an enormous desert; blacks were exterminated in Africa as well as America; Puerto Ricans, described as "a repulsive mongrel race," were exterminated and the island re-settled by whites).[75]

In the reprinting of *The Turner Diaries* in September 1990, the narrative is moved forward in several parts to coincide with the dozen years that have passed from the first printing in 1978. In both printings of the book, there is an epilogue that extols the "birth of the Great One [whose] dream of a White world finally became a certainty." This is a direct reference to Adolf Hitler, who was greatly admired by William Pierce and thus became an inspiration for his book.

Bob Mathews's fealty to *The Turner Diaries* would become evident in his choice for a new name for his group that he hoped would foment the global revolution envisioned by the book. In September 1983, Mathews gathered with eight associates on his property in Washington and founded the group known as the Order, after the group in *The Turner Diaries*. Mathews made each man assembled swear an oath of allegiance to their cause, which was the maintenance and protection of the White race, and a vow to fight against all elements that stood in the way of their goals being accomplished: the U.S. government and all minority and other groups that fought against the white race.[76] Mathews had the members swear their oath while the one-month-old daughter of one of those assembled lay in the middle of the circle they had created. This white child, Mathews reportedly told those assembled, was the future of the white race and the reason they would initiate violence and rebellion: in order to protect her and all others like her.[77]

Mathews would come to view the Order as a silent brotherhood, wherein each man was bound by an oath of silence to protect the others in the group, no matter what violence they had committed. Those assembled with Mathews on that day included members of Aryan Nations and members from the National Alliance. With what he believed to be a loyal cadre of supporters about him, Mathews began a series of violent acts to support the cause of white separatism. Many of the activities undertaken by the group mimicked those taken by the Order in *The Turner Diaries*. The group began by robbing an adult book store, but, considering this too dangerous, moved on to counterfeiting and robbing banks. Mathews acted alone in robbing a bank just north of Seattle, while other burglaries of various kinds netted monies for the cause. Yet altogether, the money that the Order had secured was less than $100,000.[78] This changed in March 1984 when members of the Order set a bomb in a Seattle theater to mislead police while other members of the group robbed an armored car of nearly $500,000.[79] This haul was greatly surpassed just a few weeks later when the group held up an armored car near Ukiah, California, that netted more than $3.6 million in cash.[80] At the time, this was the largest armored car heist in American history. Much of the money that the group had stolen would end up in the coffers of like-minded white supremacist groups, such as Pierce's National Alliance and the White Patriot Party.[81] The group also purchased parcels of land in Idaho and Missouri to be used as paramilitary training camps. With their penchant for violent actions, the Order very quickly rose to rank among the most wanted on the Federal Bureau of Investigation's (FBI's) Most Wanted List.

In the midst of the robberies, Mathews and other members of the group orchestrated the assassination of Denver talk show host Alan Berg. Berg, a controversial Jewish talk-radio personality, had made his career goading right-wing and white-supremacist extremists on his call-in radio program.[82] On June 18, 1984, Order member Bruce Pierce killed Alan Berg as he stepped out of his car at his home. Berg had been shot at least a dozen times.[83] The killing was meant to send a message to all opponents of the group but particularly to its number-one nemesis—Southern Poverty Law Center founder Morris Dees. After the killing of Berg, the FBI had managed to exert pressure on one member of the group—Tom Martinez—who had been arrested on counterfeiting charges. With many of the Order members dead, in jail, or awaiting trials that promised long prison sentences, the group was rapidly disappearing from view. As the FBI was led to Mathews's hiding place, he escaped and began a one-man crusade against the FBI and the federal government. Prior to his death, Mathews composed a long letter that effectively stated his attention to declare war on the United States government. In this letter, he describes threats made against his family by the FBI as well as a number of attempts on his life at the behest of government-led agencies. Stating he "quit being hunted and [would instead] become the hunter," Mathews determined to go down fighting. He wrote:

> I am not going into hiding, rather I will press the FBI and let them know what it is like to become the hunted. Doing so it is only logical to assume that my days on this planet are rapidly drawing to a close. Even so, I have no fear. For the reality of my life is death, and the worst the enemy can do to me is shorten my tour of duty in this world. I will leave knowing that I have made the ultimate sacrifice to ensure the future of my children.
>
> We all knew it would be like this, that it would be our own brothers who would first try to destroy our efforts to save our race and our terminally ill nation. Why are so many white men so eager

to destroy their own kind for the benefit of the Jews and the mongrels?

I see three FBI agents hiding behind some trees to the north of the house. I could have easily killed them, I had their faces in my sights. They look like good racial stock yet all their talents are given to a government which is openly trying to mongrelize the very race these agents are a part of. Why can't they see?

White men killing white men, Saxon killing Dane; When will it end, the Aryan's bane?

I knew last night that today would be my last day in this life. When I went to bed I saw all my loved ones so clearly, as if they were there with me. All my memories flashed through my mind. I knew then that my tour of duty was up.

I have been a good soldier, a fearless warrior. I will die with honor and join my brothers in Valhalla.

For blood, soil, and honor. For faith and for race. For the future of my children. For the green graves of my sires.[84]

On December 8, 1984, Mathews was surrounded by federal agents in a home on Whitley Island near Foreland, Washington. Though called upon to surrender, Mathews refused, whereupon smoke grenades were shot into the house in an attempt to force Mathews out. Unbeknownst to the FBI, Mathews was in possession of a gas mask that allowed him to keep firing at the agents. Several flares were then shot into the house that ignited a box of hand grenades and stockpiles of ammunition near Mathews. As the house burned, Mathews continued to fire at the agents, but the shots suddenly stopped as the fire reached the second floor where Mathews had barricaded himself. When his body was found, his pistol was still in his hand.

After Mathews's death, most of the Order members were convicted on a variety of charges, including racketeering, conspiracy, counterfeiting, transporting stolen money, armored car robbery, and violation of civil rights. Some were tried for but acquitted of sedition. For many in the white nationalist and white supremacist movements, Bob Mathews is considered a martyr who was mercilessly hunted by a government intent on stripping him of his rights to protect his home and family from the undesirable elements of modern society.

The end of the 1980s saw the formation of new groups that, though not as violent as the Order, were nevertheless committed to antigovernment and other illegal activities. These groups would grow in number and ferocity with the election of a "liberal" president in 1992.

THE ELECTION OF WILLIAM JEFFERSON CLINTON

The election of 1992 pitted George H. W. Bush, the protector of the Reagan legacy, against a relatively unknown candidate in the person of William Jefferson "Bill" Clinton. Bush was fresh off a resounding victory in the Gulf War in which U.S. and coalition forces had driven Saddam Hussein and his Iraqi forces out of Kuwait after Iraq had invaded the small country only a few months earlier. With an air war of six weeks and a ground campaign that took only 100 hours the United States military stood preeminent in the world. Bush, who had already been riding the wave of popular opinion because of the fall of the Berlin Wall in 1989, was now bolstered by his resounding military victory and almost assured of reelection. After all, the Cold War was all but over, and before the year was out, the Cold War adversary of the United States—the Union of Soviet Socialist Republics—would cease to exist, being known first as the Commonwealth of Independent States (CIS) and then as the constituent republics of the former Soviet Union, including the Russian Federation.

Standing in the way of George H. W. Bush's reelection was Bill Clinton. A two-term governor of Arkansas, Bill Clinton was exactly what conservatives (and the patriot/militia groups to which this study addresses itself) hated. Clinton was young—only 46 on inauguration day—making him the youngest president to serve since John F. Kennedy. Though considered a "Southern Democrat," Clinton nevertheless had built his populist coalition with environmentalists, tax-and-spend liberals, minority groups (particularly African Americans), and war protestors. Clinton himself was the epitome of what many in post–World War II America feared the most: a child of the 1960s who had, by some accounts, dodged the draft to protest the Vietnam War instead of serving in it. Clinton was a Democrat, and the previous Democratic president—Jimmy Carter—had led the country into the worst recession since the Great Depression and had promoted policies that weakened the United States vis-a-vis the Soviet Union as well as alienated allies that had since become powers unfriendly to the United States and its foreign policies. In this atmosphere, conservative and extremist groups flourished.

As Ronald Reagan left the presidency in 1989, there were conservative elements in the United States that feared for the future of the place of religion in public life that had been reinvigorated during Reagan's presidency. Indeed, religious leaders such as Billy Graham and others had been regular visitors to the White House during Reagan's presidency. Though George H. W. Bush was a Republican, he certainly was not Ronald Reagan, and his conservative credentials were not as well documented or understood. In 1989, after his failed attempt to secure the Republican presidential nomination, Pat Robertson used the remainder of his campaign resources to create the Christian Coalition. This organization was composed mostly of evangelical Protestant Republicans and was created to preserve what like-minded individuals perceived as traditional American culture. At its height, the group lobbied in support of traditional religious values, market capitalism, school choice, and school prayer while opposing abortion, gun control, and secular influence in the United States.[85] At its height, the group had more than two million members, but these numbers waned after 1999. Nevertheless, the Christian Coalition was the quintessential "American values" organization of the 1990s and epitomized the mood of many in the United States who feared what the "New World Order" would bring.

THE NEW WORLD ORDER

On September 11, 1990, President George H. W. Bush delivered a speech before a joint session of Congress titled "Toward a New World Order." The speech was intended to chart a course for the United States in the post–Cold War era. The speech included several points related to U.S.–Soviet cooperation (the Soviet Union would not disintegrate until the end of 1991) and postulated a bipolar new order of U.S. power and United Nations moral authority, "the first as global policeman, the second as global judge and jury. The order would be collectivist, in which decisions and responsibility would be shared."[86]

The idea of a "New World Order, of course, was nothing new. British author H. G. Wells had published a book in 1940 titled *The New World Order* in which he envisioned a world without war and governed by law and order emanating from a world governing body. However, this idea to some is malicious and insidious inasmuch as the New World Order is envisioned as an environment dominated by a powerful and secretive elite class determined to promulgate a globalist agenda through a dominant and preeminent authoritarian world government. To conspiracy theorists such as these, the New World Order will replace the age of the sovereign nation-state and will idealize the era of peace and coexistence that is created as the highest achievement of humankind.

During the McCarthy era of the 1950s in the United States, the New World Order became closely associated with the menace of communism, as that ideology articulated welfare-state policies that would gradually evolve to collectivism that would inevitably lead to nation-states being replaced with a communist one-world government.[87] Right-wing groups in the United States, such as the John Birch Society, would seize upon the idea of the New World Order and campaign for U.S. withdrawal from the United Nations. Others would claim that the creation of the U.S. Federal Reserve System in 1913 was a plot by "international bankers" to seize control of the U.S. government. This plot included the formation of the Council on Foreign Relations in 1921 that effectively served as a "shadow government." As noted by author Chip Berlet, "'international bankers' would have been interpreted by many readers as a reference to a postulated 'international Jewish banking conspiracy' masterminded by the Rothschilds."[88]

Those who see conspiracy in the New World Order believe that it will be implemented gradually and not at one specific point in time. Adherents point to the proliferation of international and regional organizations that have formed over the years (e.g., the League of Nations, the United Nations, the World Health Organization, the European Union, the African Union, the Union of South American Nations, etc.), as well as national and international monetary institutions (e.g., the U.S. Federal Reserve System, the International Monetary Fund, the World Bank, the World Trade Organization, etc.) as proof of the "gradualism" by which the New World Order is taking hold in the world.[89]

Prior to the dissolution of the Soviet Union in 1991, right-wing conspiracy theorists in the United States believed the United States was being ruled by a conspiratorial elite with secret desires to bring the United States under control of a world government, most likely dominated by communism. With the end of the Soviet Union, however, the new protagonist that would foster the arrival of the New World Order was the United Nations. This shift in emphasis from the evils of the Soviet Union to the evils of the United Nations occurred very easily, as New World Order conspiracists viewed the agenda of the United Nations—population control, women's empowerment, global equity, and so forth—as antithetical to the natural "anarchical" state of nation-states and human relations.

Televangelist Pat Robertson, founder of the Christian Coalition discussed earlier, wrote a book in 1991 titled *The New World Order* in which he popularized the notion of the conspiratorial New World Order by noting the coincidental nature of the Order with changes and/or additions to American politics and policy. Robertson believed that these changes were nudging the United States "constantly and covertly" in the direction of a global government that would be in service of the Antichrist.[90]

The idea of an end times as espoused by apocalyptic millennial Christians conveniently coincides with the notion of a New World Order. Adherents of this point of view believe those who populate the "shadowy" governments now agitating for world government have made a "deal with the devil" to gain wealth and power in pursuit of some utopian ideal. Some believe that the Antichrist may turn out to be the president of the European Union or the Secretary-General of the United Nations.[91]

Observers have noted that the galvanization of right-wing conspiracy theories, such as that of the New World Order, have resulted in militancy that has contributed to the rise of the militia movement.[92] Because of the militancy of militia groups, an antigovernment ideology has been propagated through the venues these groups populate—rallies and meetings, gun shows, radio talk shows, Internet websites, and so forth. The "viral" nature of the latter has probably done more than anything else to spread the fallacy that is churned over time and time again at each subsequent gathering.[93]

What did more to galvanize patriot/militia groups in the 1990s, however, was not necessarily conspiracy theories about the United States but the actions of the United States government. The ideas that have hitherto been the focus of this study—allegiance to a notion of liberty in an idealized past that is now being contravened by a system and government that have become precisely what the Founding Fathers feared, abusive and unresponsive—can nowhere be more clearly illustrated than in the cases of the incidents at Ruby Ridge, Idaho, and Waco, Texas. These two events taken together probably did more to solidify the modern patriot/militia movements as we know them today than any other pair of events in the history of the republic to this point.

NOTES

1. "U.S. Government Spending History from 1900." 2014. *Usgovern mentspending.com.* http://www.usgovernmentspending.com/past_spend-ing. (Accessed 3/20/2014).

2. Ibid.

3. Sarup, Madan. 1993. *An Introductory Guide to Post-Structuralism and Postmodernism.* University of Georgia Press, p. 6.

4. Salberg, Daniel, Robert Steward, Karla Wesley, and Shannon Weiss. 2009. "Postmodernism and Its Critics." *Anthropological Series*. University of Alabama, Department of Anthropology. http://anthropology .ua.edu/cultures/cultures.php?culture=Postmodernism%20and%20 Its%20Critics. (Accessed March 3, 2014).

5. Boyne, Roy, and Ali Rattansi. 1990. "The Theory and Politics of Postmodernism: By Way of an Introduction." In Boyne, Roy, and Rattansi, Ali, eds., *Postmodernism and Society*. MacMillan Education LTD, pp. 1–45.

6. "Islam, Modernity, and Terrorism." 2006. *Pew Research Global Attitudes Project*. http://www.pewglobal.org/2006/06/22/iii-islam-modernity-and-terrorism/. (Accessed February 15, 2014).

7. Zafirovski, Milan, and Daniel G. Rodeheaver. 2013. *Modernity and Terrorism: From Anti-Modernity to Modern Global Terror*. Brill Publishing. See also http://www.brill.com/modernity-and-terrorism.

8. Excerpt from Sayyid Qutb's article "Amrika allati Ra'aytu" ("The America That I Have Seen"). *Milestones*, p. 139. See also Calvert, John. 2000. "'The World is an Undutiful Boy!': Sayyid Qutb's American Experience." *Islam and Christian-Muslim Relations*, II (1): 87–103.

9. Von Drehle, David. 2006. "A Lesson in Hate: How an Egyptian Student Came to Study 1950s America and Left Determined to Wage A Holy War." *Smithsonian Magazine*. (February). Found at http://www. smithsonianmag.com/history/a-lesson-in-hate-109822568/.

10. Excerpts from the "Anti-Government Movement Guidebook." 1999. *The National Center for State Courts*. See also http://www.tulanelink. com/pdf/anti-gov_movement_guidebook.pdf. (Accessed November 10, 2013).

11. Ibid.

12. Ibid.

13. Ibid.

14. "Paranoia as Patriotism: Far Right Influences on the Militia Movement." 1991. *The Nizkor Project*. See also http://www.nizkor.org/ hweb/orgs/american/adl/paranoia-as-patriotism/posse-comitatus.html. (Accessed November 3, 2014).

15. Smith, Brent L. 1995. *Terrorism in America: Pipe Bombs and Pipe Dreams*. SUNY Press, pp. 57–58. See also Pitcavage, Mark. n.d. "Common Law and Uncommon Courts: An Overview of the Common Law Court Movement," *Militia Watchdog Archives*. Anti-Defamation League. Found at http://archive.adl.org/mwd/common.html.

16.   http://www.nola.com/crime/index.ssf/2012/08/picture_of_5_ suspects_in_st_jo.html; see also http://www.reuters.com/article/2012/08

/18/us-usa-louisiana-shooting-idUSBRE87G0ZN20120818. (Accessed December 1, 2013).

17. "Anti-Government Movement Guidebook," pp. 3–5.

18. Ibid.

19. Ibid.

20. Ibid.

21. The Nizkor Project. "Paranoia as Patriotism: Far Right Influences on the Militia Movement." Found at http://www.nizkor.org/hweb/orgs/american/adl/paranoia-as-patriotism/the-order.html.

22. "Anti-Government Movement Guidebook," pp. 3–5.

23. Ibid.

24. Ibid.

25. Ibid.

26. Ibid.

27. "What Is a Sovereign Citizen?, Message to Students." n.d. *Militia Watchdog Archives*. Anti-Defamation League. Found at http://archive.adl.org/learn/ext_us/scm.html?xpicked=4.

28. "New Multi-Million Dollar Scam Takes Off in Antigovernment Circles." 2002. *Southern Poverty Law Center Intelligence Report*. (Winter). See at http://www.splcenter.org/get-informed/intelligence-report/browse -all-issues/2002/winter/beyond-redemption. (Accessed December 10, 2013).

29. §2A6.1. Threatening or Harassing Communications; Hoaxes; False Liens.

30. Chamberlain, Robert, and Donald P. Haider-Markel. 2005. "'Lien on Me': State Policy Innovation in Response to Paper Terrorism," *Political Research Quarterly* 58 (3): 449–460. See also Pitcavage, Mark. 1998. "Paper Terrorism's Forgotten Victims: The Use of Bogus Liens against Private Individuals and Businesses." Anti-Defamation League. (June 29). Found at http://archive.adl.org/mwd/privlien.html.

31. Marks, Kathy and Adolph Caso. 1996. *Faces of Right Wing Extremism*. Branden Books, p. 146.

32. "Christian Posse Comitatus Newsletter," n.d. In Kenneth S. Stern, *A Force Upon the Plain: The American Militia Movement and the Politics of Hate.* 1996. Simon & Schuster, p. 50.

33. "What Is a 'Sovereign Citizen'?" Found at http://www.splcenter. org/get-informed/intelligence-files/ideology/sovereign-citizens -movement.

34. "Low Trust in Federal Government Rivals Watergate Era Levels." http://www.gallup.com/poll/28795/low-trust-federal-government -rivals-watergate-era-levels.aspx. (Accessed May 6, 2014).

35. Currie, Elliott. 1998. *Crime and Punishment in America.* Metropolitan Books. http://www.nytimes.com/books/first/c/currie-crime.html. (Accessed March 5, 2014).

36. "A Time of Malaise." n.d. *ushistory.org*. http://www.ushistory.org/us/58.asp. (Accessed March 10, 2014).

37. Gamble, Richard. 2009. "How Right Was Reagan?" *The American Conservative*. (May 4). http://www.theamericanconservative.com/articles/how-right-was-reagan/. (Accessed May 1, 2014).

38. Ibid.

39. Manning, Jason. n.d. "The Midwest Farm Crisis of the 1980s." *The Eighties Club*. See at http://eightiesclub.tripod.com/id395.htm. (Accessed March 21, 2014).

40. Ball, Heather, and Leland Beatty. 1984. "Blowing Away the Family Farmer: The Debt Tornado." *The Nation* 239 (November 3): 442–444.

41. Eason, Henry. 1984. "Agriculture at the Crossroads." *Nation's Business* 72 (August): 34–36.

42. Ball and Beatty, p. 443. As Ball and Beatty point out, "Farms with gross annual sales of $40,000 to $250,000 (24 percent of U.S. farms) produced 41 percent of total commodities; farms with gross annual sales of $250,000 to $500,000 (3 percent of U.S. farms) produced 17 percent; farms with gross annual sales above $500,000 (1 percent of U.S. farms) produced 32 percent. Noncommercial farms—under $40,000 in gross annual sales—produced only 10 percent of all farm commodities and lost money every year from 1980 to 1985; nonfarm income offset these losses somewhat. These figures show that the middle-level farm operators—those most affected by the debt crisis, produced nearly 60 percent of total commodities. Dept. of Agriculture, The U.S. Farm Sector, iv–v.). But the farm largesse of the 1970s had swelled the number of mid-level farmers to more than 675,000 by 1985, an astonishing increase of more than 250 percent from the 1970s."

43. Huntley, Steve. 1986. "Winter of Despair Hits the Farm Belt." *U.S. News & World Report* 100 (January 20): 21–23. See also Hammer, Joshua. 1983. "Double Slaying in Rural Minnesota Spotlights the Distress of America's Debt-Ridden Farmers." *People Magazine*, 20 (18). October 31, 1983. Also found at http://www.people.com/people/archive/article/0,,20086276,00.html.

44. Ball and Beatty, p. 442. The federal government claimed that by 1986, total farmland debt had fallen to $92 billion, having peaked at $113 billion in 1983. (Dept. of Agriculture, Economic Research Service, "Issues in Agricultural Policy: New Approaches to Financing Long-Term Farm Debt." AIB-511, March 1987, 3).

45. "The Flight of the Farmer." 1985. *America* (March 23): 227.

46. DeMarco, Susan. "A Fresh Crop of Ideas: State Sows the Seeds of a New Agriculture," *The Progressive*, 53 (January 1989), p. 26.

47. Quoted in Eason, p. 38.

48. McLaughlin, John. 1985. "Farm Blues," *National Review*, 37 (March 22): 24. According to the Department of Agriculture, 8 percent of farms with $100,000 or more in sales were insolvent by 1986, but less than 2 percent with sales under $40,000 were insolvent. (Dept. of Agriculture, "Challenges in Designing U.S. Farm Policy," p. 6.).

49. Manning, http://eightiesclub.tripod.com/id395.htm.

50. Ibid.

51. Aucoin, James. 1986. "Missouri Farmers on the Front Lines." *The Progressive* (July 1986): 33.

52. Downs, Peter. 1986. "Seeds of Discontent: Farmers Plow New Political Ground." *The Progressive* 50 (July): 30–33.

53. McBride, Bob. 1986. "Broken Heartland: Farm Crisis in the Midwest." *The Nation* 242. (February 8): 132.

54. Downs, p. 32.

55. Walljasper, Jay. 1986. "Farmers and the Left: Little Cells on the Prairie." *The Nation* 243 (October 25): 402.

56. Manning, http://eightiesclub.tripod.com/id395.htm.

57. Ibid.

58. Barkun, Michael. 1996. *Religion and the Racist Right: The Origins of the Christian Identity Movement*. University of North Carolina Press, Preface, xii, xiii.

59. Quarles, Chester L. 2004. *Christian Identity: The Aryan American Bloodline Religion*. McFarland & Company, p. 68. See also Mason, Carol. 2002. *Killing for Life: The Apocalyptic Narrative of Pro-Life Politics*. Cornell University Press, p. 30.

60. "Christian Identity." n.d. *Extremism in America*. Anti-Defamation League. http://archive.adl.org/learn/ext_us/christian_identity.html?xpicked=4&item=Christian_ID. (Accessed January 23, 2014).

61. Roberts, Charles H. 2003. *Race over Grace: The Racialist Religion of the Christian Identity Movement*. iUniverse Press, pp. 40–60.

62. Carroll, Charles. 1900. *The Negro a Beast . . . or . . . In the Image of God*. American Book and Bible House. See at http://www.cimmay.com/pdf/carroll.pdf. (Accessed February 2, 2014).

63. Ibid.

64. Ago, James Alfred. 1995. *The Politics of Righteousness: Idaho Christian Patriotism*. University of Washington Press, p. 86.

65. Kaplan, Jeffrey. 2002. *Millennial Violence: Past, Present, and Future*. Routledge, p. 38.

66. Ago, p. 86.

67. Ibid.

68. "William Potter Gale." n.d. Church of Jesus Christ Christian— Aryan Nations. See at http://www.aryan-nation.org/gale.index.html. (Accessed May 22, 2014).

69. http://www.splcenter.org/get-informed/intelligence-files/groups /aryan-nations. (Accessed March 5, 2014).

70. "The Order." 2005. *ABC News Special Report*. (October).

71. "The Federal Liquidation of Bob Mathews." n.d. *American USSR*. See at http://www.americanussr.com/american-ussr-mathews- matthews-bob-robert-jay.htm. (Accessed May 22, 2014). Also see "Tribute to Robert Jay Mathews" at http://vnnforum.com/showthread. php?t=4096.

72. "A Call to Arms, Part One of Two." n.d. *WNTube.net*.

73. "*The Turner Diaries*." 2005. *Extremism in America*. Anti-Defamation League. See at http://archive.adl.org/learn/ext_us/turner_diaries.html. (Accessed March 5, 2014).

74. See also Harkavy, Ward. 2000. "The Nazi on the Bestseller List." *The Village Voice* (November 15). Found at http://www.village- voice.com/2000-11-14/news/the-nazi-on-the-bestseller-list/.

75. Anti-Defamation League. 2005. "*The Turner Diaries*." *Extremism in America*. See at http://archive.adl.org/learn/ext_us/turner_diaries. html?LEARN_Cat=Extremism&LEARN_SubCat=Extremism_in_ America&xpicked=5&item=22. (Accessed May 25, 2014).

76. "The Order."

77. Ibid.

78. Martinez, Thomas, and John Guinther. 1999. *Brotherhood of Murder*. iUniverse.

79. "Paranoia as Patriotism: Far Right Influences on the Militia Movement." 1991. *The Nizkor Project*. See also http://www.nizkor.org/ hweb/orgs/american/adl/paranoia-as-patriotism/posse-comitatus.html. (Accessed November 3, 2014).

80. Cashman, John R. 1999. *Emergency Response to Chemical and Biological Agents*. CRC Press, p. 5.

81. Martin, Gus, ed. 2011. *The SAGE Encyclopedia of Terrorism*. 2nd ed. Sage, p. 450.

82. "Paranoia as Patriotism: Far Right Influences on the Militia Movement."

83. "The Order."

84. "Robert Jay Mathews' Last Letter." 1984. *The Savitri Devi Archives*. http://www.mourningtheancient.com/mathews1.htm. (Accessed March 1, 2014).

85. "Christian Coalition." n.d. *Infoplease*. See at http://www .infoplease.com/encyclopedia/us/christian-coalition.html. (Accessed March 6, 2014).

86. Bush, George. 1991. "Address Before a Joint Session of the Congress on the State of the Union." The American Presidency Project. (January 29). See also at http://www.presidency.ucsb.edu/ws/?pid= 19253. (Accessed May 25, 2014).

87. Berlet, Chip. 1998. "Dances with Devils: How Apocalyptic and Millennialist Themes Influence Right Wing Scapegoating and Conspiracism." (Fall 1998, Revised 4/15/99). Found at http://www .publiceye.org/apocalyptic/Dances_with_Devils_1.html.

88. Ibid.

89. Barkun, Michael. 2003. *A Culture of Conspiracy: Apocalyptic Visions in Contemporary America*. University of California Press.

90. Ibid.

91. Ibid. See also Hughes, Richard T. 2011. "Revelation, Revolutions, and the Tyrannical New World Order." *Huffington Post*. (February 24). See at http://www.huffingtonpost.com/richard-t-hughes/revolutions-in-the-middle_b_827201.html. (Accessed March 10, 2014).

92. Berlet, http://www.publiceye.org/apocalyptic/Dances_with_ Devils_1.html.

93. Ibid.

CHAPTER 5

Striking the Match

RUBY RIDGE

In the 1980s, Randy Weaver moved to northern Idaho with his wife and family to escape what he and his wife considered a "corrupted world."[1] Weaver's wife Vicki chose to home-school her children, believing that the apocalypse was imminent and that in the rough and remote mountainous terrain, they could survive. In 1984, Randy Weaver had a legal dispute with a neighbor. Eventually, the neighbor—Terry Kinnison—was ordered to pay Randy Weaver the amount of the original dispute ($3,000) plus $2,100 in court costs and damages.[2] In retaliation, Kinnison wrote letters to the FBI, the U.S. Secret Service, and the local county sheriff that alleged that Weaver had threatened to kill prominent public officials, including the president of the United States. In January 1985, the FBI and the Secret Service started an investigation. Randy and Vicki Weaver were both interviewed by federal officers, but no charges were filed. Although the FBI had been informed that Weaver was a member of Aryan Nations and maintained a large weapons stockpile at this home, there was no firm evidence to support these accusations.[3]

The federal investigators did note that Weaver associated with Frank Kumnick, who was believed to be a member of Aryan Nations, though Weaver claimed that Kumnick was "associated with the Covenant, Sword, and Arm of the Lord."[4] On February 28, 1985, Randy and Vicki Weaver filed an affidavit at the Boundary County (Idaho) courthouse

alleging that their enemies were attempting to provoke the FBI into at-
tacking and killing the Weaver family.[5] In May 1985, the Weavers sent a
letter to President Ronald Reagan claiming that their enemies had sent
a threatening letter to the president under a forged signature. Though
no evidence of a threatening letter was ever found, the alleged 1985 letter was cited by federal prosecutors in 1992 as proof of a Weaver family
conspiracy against the federal government.

In July 1986, Randy Weaver attended his first meeting of Aryan
Nations. He attended the meeting with Frank Kumnick, who had
been the original target of a federal investigation. At the meeting,
Weaver was introduced to an individual who, unbeknownst to him,
was an informant of the Bureau of Alcohol, Tobacco, and Firearms
(ATF). Over the next three years, the ATF informant and Weaver
would meet several times.[6] (In October 1989, the ATF claimed that
Weaver sold their informant two sawed-off shotguns, with the overall
length less than the legally allowed limit set by federal law. When the
ATF informant's cover was blown, his handler attempted to enlist
Weaver to become an ATF informant on the activities of the Aryan
Nations. Weaver, claiming that the sawed-off shotgun charge was false,
as the ATF informant had himself sawed the guns off, refused to
be a "snitch" for the ATF, whereupon the ATF filed gun charges
against Weaver, claiming that he was also a bank robber with criminal
convictions (both false charges, as Weaver had no criminal record at
the time).[7]

In early 1991, Randy and Vicki Weaver were arrested when they
pulled over to assist what appeared to be stranded motorists. The motorists were, in actuality, members of the ATF lying in wait to arrest the
Weavers. After several miscommunications among Weaver, his lawyer,
and his probation officer, Randy Weaver's trial was scheduled to begin
on February 20, 1991. However, the letter sent to Weaver by U.S.
Probations Officer Richins indicated that his trial would start March 20,
1991.[8] When Weaver failed to appear for the February 20 trial date, the
judge issued a warrant for his arrest. However, upon finding a copy of
the letter that clearly indicated the erroneous date, the chief probation
officer contacted the judge's clerk, the U.S. Marshals Service (USMS),
and Weaver's lawyer. Upon learning of the mix-up in dates, the judge
refused to withdraw the bench warrant. Nevertheless, the USMS determined that it would not serve the warrant until after March 20 to
determine if Weaver would show up on the appointed date. Before this
could happen, the U.S. Attorney's Office (USAO) empaneled a grand
jury that issued an indictment for failure to appear, even though evi-

dence of the erroneous date on the summons letter was not made available to the grand jury.[9]

With the failure-to-appear indictment, Weaver's case passed from the ATF to the USMS, the law enforcement arm of the federal court. Weaver had not fled the jurisdiction, however. He was simply holed up in a house on his land at Ruby Ridge, threatening to resist any attempt to take him by force.[10] As noted, Weaver distrusted the government and most, if not all, federal officials. This mistrust was not allayed by the inconsistent messages regarding his trial date or the failure of his lawyer to provide clarification. Weaver was convinced of a conspiracy against him and his family and had become convinced that he could not receive a fair trial in the courts of the federal government. As noted by author Jess Walter, "his distrust grew when he was erroneously told by his magistrate that if he lost the trial he would lose the land that would essentially leave Vicki homeless and the government would take away his children."[11]

The USMS made several attempts to have Weaver peacefully surrender, but he refused to leave his cabin or his property. As a result, the USMS ordered an operation code-named Northern Exposure that was meant to place surveillance teams around the Weaver property to record activity and monitor the movements of Weaver and his family.[12] U.S. Marshals observed that the Weaver family responded to the approach of vehicles and other visitors "by taking up armed positions around the cabin until the visitors were recognized."[13]

Other instances fueled Randy Weaver's suspicions of the government's intentions. When a deputy U.S. Marshal asked Bill Grider, an acquaintance of the Weavers, about Randy Weaver's intentions, Grider said: "Let me put it to you this way. If I was sitting on my property and somebody with a gun comes to do me harm, then I'll probably shoot him."[14] When this was reported to government officials, Grider's words were attributed to Weaver and viewed as a threat.[15]

Another misinterpretation of events took place surrounding an incident on April 18, 1992. In a helicopter flyover conducted for Geraldo Rivera's *Now It Can Be Told* television program, the USMS received reports that Weaver had fired shots at the helicopter as it flew overhead.[16] U.S. Marshals who were near the Weaver property that day setting up surveillance cameras reported seeing the helicopter but not hearing any shots fired.[17] Weaver later granted an interview to a newspaper reporter denying that he, any member of his family, or any of his friends fired on the helicopter.[18] The pilot of the helicopter, Richard Weiss, also denied that the helicopter had been fired upon.[19]

Notwithstanding the denial by Weaver and others that they had not fired upon the Rivera helicopter, the unsubstantiated reports that shots had been fired at the Rivera helicopter from Weaver's property prompted the FBI to draw up rules of engagement in the case of Randy Weaver and his family. These rules would dictate in what manner federal officials could engage with Weaver.

On August 21, 1992, six United States Marshals were sent to Ruby Ridge to scout the area to determine a suitable place removed from Weaver's cabin where he could be apprehended and arrested.[20] The marshals were dressed in camouflage and were equipped with M-16 assault rifles and night-vision goggles.[21] At one point, one of the marshals, Art Roderick, threw rocks at the Weaver cabin to determine the reaction of the dogs the Weavers maintained to alert them to intruders.[22] As the dogs reacted, Weaver's friend, Kevin Harris, and Weaver's 14-year-old son Samuel ("Sammy") emerged from the cabin to investigate. As Harris and Samuel Weaver began to advance into the woods, the marshals retreated to a "Y" juncture in the paths leading to the cabin, about 500 yards away. Randy Weaver took a trail separate from Harris and Samuel, while the rest of Weaver's family remained in the cabin.

Randy Weaver came upon the marshals first. Reportedly, Marshal Roderick identified himself and those with him as U.S. Marshals and ordered Weaver to stop and/or surrender. Weaver reportedly responded by cursing and retreating back up the path toward the cabin. About a minute later, Harris and Sammy Weaver came upon the Marshals' position, whereupon a firefight erupted.[23] The accounts of all involved differ at this point, and there was controversy about who fired first—the marshals or Harris and Sammy Weaver. At this point, Deputy U.S. Marshal (DUSM) Art Roderick shot and killed Weaver's dog that was accompanying Harris and Sammy, after which Sammy returned fire at Roderick. As all of the marshals began to fire, Samuel Weaver retreated back toward the cabin and was shot dead. DUSM Bill Degan was subsequently shot and killed by Kevin Harris.[24]

In the version of the firefight related by DUSMs Art Roderick and Larry Cooper, the Weavers' dog, followed by Harris and Sammy, came out of the woods upon the marshals' position. When DUSM Degan challenged Harris, Harris shot him dead without Degan firing a single shot. Roderick then shot the dog and Sammy fired at Roderick twice. Cooper fired two three-shot bursts at Harris and believed that he had killed Harris, while Sammy ran from the scene.[25] In Harris's version of events, Roderick shot the Weaver dog in front of Sammy, who cursed Roderick and shot at him. Degan emerged from the woods at this point firing his M-16 and hit Sammy in the arm. Harris then fired at Degan, hitting him in the chest and knocking him down. Cooper then fired on Harris who had ducked for cover and fired on Sammy as he was retreating, hitting him in the back. Upon checking Sammy's body, Harris discovered that he was dead and retreated to the cabin.[26]

In testimony offered after the firefight in 1993, Larry Cooper admitted that things happened quickly, and a narrative that may have taken a minute only occurred within a matter of a few seconds. Ballistics experts Martin Fackler and Lucien "Luke" Haag testified in June 1993 that the physical evidence did not contradict either the prosecution or defense theories on the firefight. Fackler testified that DUSM Roderick shot and killed the Weavers' dog, DUSM Degan shot Sammy through the right elbow, Kevin Harris shot and killed DUSM Degan, and Cooper "probably" shot and killed Sammy. The 1993 trial jury accepted the defense theory of the firefight and acquitted Kevin Harris on grounds of self-defense. In 1997, Boundary County Sheriff Greg Sprungl conducted an independent search of the "Y," and Lucien Haag confirmed that a bullet found in that search matched Cooper's gun and contained fibers that matched Sammy Weaver's shirt.[27]

After the firefight, the USMS was alerted by the FBI that a federal marshal had been killed. The FBI then mobilized the Hostage Rescue Team (HRT) from Quantico, Virginia, to Idaho. Additional agents from the ATF, Marshals Service, FBI, and U.S. Border Patrol were mobilized, as well as the majority of the Boundary County Sheriff's Office. Idaho Governor Cecil Andrus declared a state of emergency existed in Boundary County that allowed the FBI to call up units of the Idaho National Guard that deployed armored personnel carriers to the scene.[28]

The day after the confrontation at the "Y," sniper/observer teams were deployed to the cabin, while an armored personnel carrier approached the cabin to make a surrender callout. Prior to these actions, HRT Commander Richard Rogers briefed the sniper teams on the rules of engagement (ROE) that had been approved for use at Ruby Ridge. Some snipers would later say that the ROE gave them the "green light" to "shoot on sight."[29] The ROE were drawn up on reports from the USMS and the FBI and were fueled by unconfirmed media reports that were accepted by the federal officers on the scene. The reports, most agree, exaggerated the threat posed by the Weavers.

The military-style ROE varied from the FBI's standard practice on the use of deadly force, which was, "Agents are not to use deadly force against any person except as necessary in self-defense or the defense of another, when they have reason to believe they or another are in danger of death or grievous bodily harm. Whenever feasible, verbal warning should be given before deadly force is applied."[30] The ROE in the case of Ruby Ridge were as follows:

1. If any adult male is observed with a weapon prior to the announcement, deadly force can and should be employed, if the shot can be taken without endangering any children.

2. If any adult in the compound is observed with a weapon after the surrender announcement is made, and is not attempting to surrender, deadly force can and should be employed to neutralize the individual.

3. If compromised by any animal, particularly the dogs, that animal should be eliminated.

4. Any subjects other than Randall Weaver, Vicki Weaver, Kevin Harris, presenting threats of death or grievous bodily harm, the FBI rules of deadly force are in effect. Deadly force can be utilized to prevent the death or grievous bodily injury to oneself or that of another.[31]

As per these rules:

Under the Ruby Ridge Rules of engagement 3 and 4, the Weaver dogs, the Weaver children, and third parties were subject to the standard deadly force policy and could only be shot in self-defense if they presented a danger of death or grievous bodily harm. However, under the Ruby Ridge ROE 1 and 2, deadly force against the Weaver adults should be used without the justification of defense and without any verbal warning.[32]

The Denver FBI SWAT team assigned to Ruby Ridge reportedly believed the Ruby Ridge ROE to be crazy and agreed among themselves to use the standard FBI deadly force policy noted earlier. However, most of the FBI and HRT snipers believed that they had the "green light" to shoot any armed males on the Weaver property "on sight." The FBI negotiator at Ruby Ridge is said to have been "shocked and surprised" at the ROE, as he saw them as inconsistent with standard FBI policy and the most severe rules he had ever encountered in his more than 300 hostage negotiations.[33]

Guided by the ROE, on August 22, 1992—the day after the death of Sammy Weaver and USMS Bill Degan—an FBI sniper, Lon Horiuchi, shot and wounded Randy Weaver from a position of more than 200 yards as Weaver lifted the latch on a shed to visit the body of his dead son.[34] The shot hit Weaver in the back and exited his right armpit. As a wounded Weaver, his 16-year-old daughter Sara, and Kevin Harris retreated back toward the cabin, agent Horiuchi fired a second shot that struck and killed Vicki Weaver, who was standing in the door through which those fleeing the shooting were attempting to enter the house. At the time of the shooting, Vicki Weaver was holding her 10-month-old baby Elisheba in her arms.[35] A Department of Justice (DOJ) report (Office of Professional Responsibility [OPR] Ruby Ridge Task Force Report) would state in 1994 that the second shot fired by Horiuchi that killed Vicki Weaver did not "satisfy constitutional standards for legal use of deadly force."[36] The DOJ report would also find that the lack of a request for surrender in the case of the shooting on August 22 was "inexcusable" given that Harris and the Weavers were running for cover at the time of the second shot and that they did not pose an imminent threat, as they were not returning fire. FBI sniper Horiuchi was blamed for firing at the retreating individuals through a door, not knowing whether someone was on the other side of the door. The DOJ report also condemned the Ruby Ridge ROE for allowing shots to be fired without a request for surrender.[37] On August 24, 1992, the fourth day of the siege at Ruby Ridge, the deputy assistant director of the FBI wrote a memo in which he intimated that Weaver was in a strong legal position given the events then transpiring on the Weaver property.[38] On August 26, 1992, the Ruby Ridge rules of engagement were revoked.

The siege at Ruby Ridge was ultimately resolved when negotiators, including Bo Gritz, were told by federal authorities that if Weaver did not surrender, the situation would be resolved through tactical assault.[39] Gritz, a decorated United States Army Special Forces officer, was sympathetic to Weaver. In 1988, Gritz had run as the vice presidential candidate on the presidential ticket of David Duke, former Grand Wizard of the Ku Klux Klan. Gritz was a vocal proponent of racial segregation and advocated that states should have the right to reinstitute segregationist policies if they saw fit. In 1992, Gritz ran for political office on the U.S. Taxpayer's Party platform under the slogan "God, Guns and Gritz" and published a manifesto extolling the virtues of isolationism and survivalism. In the manifesto—"The Bill of Gritz"—Gritz called for a complete closing of the border with Mexico and the dismantling of the Federal Reserve.[40] Gritz opposed the New World Order and taught military and survivalist skills because he believed that the United States was headed toward total sociopolitical and economic collapse. For a time, Gritz associated with the Christic Institute, a group that pursued lawsuits against the U.S. government over charges that the government helped foster drug trafficking in both Southeast Asia and Central America.[41] Gritz had also been associated with the Christian Patriot movement and the Christian Identity movement.[42] Four years after Ruby Ridge, Gritz would attempt to mediate a settlement in a standoff between the patriot/militia group Montana Freemen and law enforcement officials of the federal government.

With Gritz's intervention, Randy Weaver and his daughters surrendered on August 31, 1992. Both Kevin Harris and Weaver were arrested and his daughters were released to the custody of family members, though there was some thought at the time of charging Weaver's oldest daughter—16-year-old Sara—as an adult.[43]

At his trial, Weaver's defense attorney, Gerry Spence, would not call a single witness on behalf of the defense. Instead, he used as his defense strategy the cross-examination and discrediting of government witnesses and the evidence that the government had presented. Ultimately, Weaver was acquitted of all charges except the failure-to-appear charge and the violation-of-probation charge. He was sentenced to 18 months and fined $10,000. Credited with time served, Randy Weaver served an additional four months in jail. The defense of both Randy Weaver and Kevin Harris was that federal agents had themselves been guilty of serious wrongdoing in the siege they perpetrated upon Weaver, his family, and friends on Ruby Ridge. On June 10, 1994, the DOJ finished a "Ruby Ridge Task Force," which delivered a 542-page report to the DOJ Office of Professional Responsibility. Though the report was never officially released, a redacted version was later circulated.[44]

In the aftermath of the siege at Ruby Ridge, a 1995 Senate subcommittee reported that the rules of engagement utilized at Ruby Ridge were unconstitutional.[45] The surviving members of the Weaver family filed a $200 million wrongful death lawsuit against the federal government. In an out-of-court settlement in 1995, the U.S. government awarded Randy Weaver $100,000 and his three daughters $1 million each, while never admitting any wrongdoing in the deaths of Weaver's son and wife.[46] On the condition of anonymity, a DOJ official admitted in a *Washington Post* article that he believed that the Weavers would have been awarded the full amount of the lawsuit had it gone to trial.[47] FBI Director Louis Freeh would admit before a U.S. Senate hearing investigation that the siege was "synonymous with the exaggerated application of federal law enforcement" and stated "law enforcement overreacted at Ruby Ridge."[48]

FBI HRT sniper Lon Horiuchi was indicted for manslaughter in 1997, but the trial was moved from the jurisdiction of Boundary County, Idaho, to a federal court, where the charges were dismissed. Kevin Harris was charged with first-degree murder in the death of DUSM Bill Degan, but the charge was dismissed on the grounds of double jeopardy inasmuch as Harris had been acquitted of the same charge in the federal trial that had taken place in 1993. Harris's attorney filed a civil suit against the U.S. government for damages. The government, however, vowed that it would never pay someone who had killed a U.S. Marshal. Yet in September 2000, after several appeals, Harris was awarded a settlement of $380,000 from the government.[49]

Randy Weaver and his daughters would eventually relocate to Montana. He and his daughter Sara would write a book titled *The Federal Siege at Ruby Ridge: In Our Own Words*.

AFTERMATH

The siege at Ruby Ridge was, for patriot and militia devotees, the epitome of "government gone wild." From the patriot/militia point of view, Randy Weaver and his family were falsely accused, harassed, and eventually targeted for death by a federal government that had no higher authority to which it was accountable. Miscommunications on the part of the court system had caused Randy Weaver to be labeled a criminal when he had, in fact, committed no criminal act for which he was convicted. The actual siege on Weaver's private property was yet another example of a government that disregarded constitutional guarantees of freedom, liberty, and due process. The manner in which the siege was conducted (e.g., the Ruby Ridge rules of engagement) was testimony to a government apparatus that had degenerated into a lawless collection of agencies that answered to no authority and certainly not to the people. Although three individuals died in the case of Ruby Ridge, not one person spent one day in jail as a result. The assault on liberties that Ruby Ridge represented to patriot/militia adherents was just one of the "last straws" that broke the proverbial camel's back, reinvigorating existing groups and creating new ones throughout the United States.

THE BRANCH DAVIDIANS AND THE SIEGE AT WACO

Together with the siege at Ruby Ridge, Idaho, the siege on the Branch Davidian compound near Waco, Texas, from February to April 1993 did more to galvanize and mobilize extremist groups in the United States than any other event in history. Occurring only a few short months after the events of Ruby Ridge, the siege upon the Branch Davidians once again provided for extremists undeniable proof that the federal government had run amok. Indeed, taken together, Ruby Ridge and Waco would become synonymous with a government that had completely lost touch with the people and one that, at best, was simply oblivious to the tyrannical nature of its actions and that, at worst, was a blatant attempt to destroy the freedoms and liberties of the American people regardless of the consequences.

The siege at Waco began with a hail of gunfire on February 28, 1993, and ended on April 19, 1993, in a cataclysmic inferno. Federal law enforcement officers, together with Texas law enforcement units and elements of the U.S. military, laid siege to the Branch Davidian compound at Mount Carmel, Texas, for 51 days. In the end, the conflagration that consumed the Branch Davidian compound ignited the extremist elements of the patriot/militia movement that inspired many of the groups that exist today.

The Branch Davidians were a religious group that was formed in 1955 from a schism that occurred in the Seventh Day Adventist Church of the Shepherd's Rod (Davidians) following the death of the Shepherd's Rod founder, Victor Houteff. Houteff founded the Davidians on the belief that the biblically prophesied apocalypse was imminent and that God's people should gather to await the Second Coming of Jesus Christ.[50] The "gathering" took place on a hilltop nine miles east of Waco, Texas, that the Davidians named Mount Carmel, after a mountain in Israel that is mentioned in the Old Testament in Joshua 19:26.[51] After Houteff's death, his widow, Florence Houteff, predicted that Armageddon was imminent, whereupon many Davidians built houses, sold their possessions, and squatted in tents, trucks, and buses.[52]

When the predicted apocalypse and Second Coming of Christ failed to materialize, control of Mount Carmel fell to the organizer of the group known as the Branch Davidian Seventh-Day Adventist Association (Branch Davidians), Benjamin Roden. Upon his death, control fell to his wife, Lois, who considered her son, George Roden, unfit to assume the mantle of prophet that had been bestowed upon the rightful leader of the Branch Davidians. In the place of her son, Lois

Roden anointed Vernon Howell (later known as David Koresh) as her successor. Upon her death, a struggle for control of the Branch Davidians ensued between George Roden and Vernon Howell. Roden gained the upper hand and drove Howell and his followers off of Mount Carmel.[53] After an armed incursion in which Howell and several of his followers attempted to seize control of Mount Carmel from George Roden, a trial acquitted Howell and his followers for the attempted murder of George Roden. During the firefight with Howell, Roden had been wounded and was himself under indictment. After being jailed on contempt charges in the case, it came to light that Roden had killed a Davidian named Wayman Dale Adair in 1989 when Adair came to visit Roden to discuss his (Adair's) vision of god choosing him to be the chosen messiah. Roden had killed Adair with an axe. Claiming insanity, Roden was committed to a mental hospital, whereupon Howell was able to finally wrest control of Mount Carmel from those of Roden's followers who remained.[54]

On August 5, 1989, Howell released an audiotape titled "New Light" in which he stated that God had ordered him to procreate with the women of the Branch Davidians in order to establish a "House of David." Howell explained that married couples would be separated and that husbands would be expected to become celibate while he had sexual relations with the wives.[55] Howell also claimed in the audiotape that God had commanded him to build an "Army for God" to prepare for the end of days and ensure the salvation of his followers.[56] On May 15, 1990, Howell petitioned the Supreme Court of California to legally change his name "for publicity and business purposes" to David Koresh. His petition was granted on August 28, 1990.[57]

In May 1992, Chief Deputy Daniel Weyenberg of the McClennan County Sheriff's Department called the ATF to notify them of suspicions that the Branch Davidians were stockpiling weapons. The sheriff's department had been tipped off by a UPS driver, who reported that a package delivered to the Branch Davidian compound had broken open during delivery, revealing firearms, grenade casings, and black powder. In June, a formal investigation into the case was opened and classified as "sensitive."[58]

Reports of automatic gunfire at Mount Carmel prompted the ATF to begin surveillance of the property in the fall of 1992. This investigation of the Branch Davidians was augmented by the assignment of an undercover agent, Robert Rodriguez, who was to infiltrate the compound and gather information. The ATF undercover operation was clumsily handled, as a house had been established across the road from the compound with ATF agents posing as "college students." However, these "students" were in their thirties, owned new cars, and were discovered as not being registered in any schools proximate to the location. Moreover, the "students" did not keep a schedule that would suggest that they were attending classes or otherwise gainfully employed.[59]

At least one Branch Davidian who had left the Mount Carmel compound claimed that the group was stockpiling parts to convert AR-15s to machine guns, violating the Hughes Amendment to the Firearm Owners Protection Act of 1986, which outlawed civilian ownership of any machine gun manufactured after the date of the promulgation of the Act.[60] An ATF investigator presented an affidavit to a U.S. Magistrate on February 25, 1993, in which he stated that the Branch Davidians had purchased many legal guns and gun parts from various legal vendors. Though these purchases were not in and of themselves illegal, the ATF investigator, David Aguilera, stated that in his experience and training, past purchases of the gun parts being bought by the Branch Davidians indicated a strong possibility that the parts would be modified into automatic weapons. The affidavit Aguilera presented claimed that there were more than 150 weapons at the compound. The paperwork that Aguilera had traced back to the Branch Davidians' purchases of AR-15 components demonstrated that these purchases were, in fact, legal. Nevertheless, Aguilera told the judge: "I have been involved in many cases where defendants, following a relatively simple process, convert AR-15 semi-automatic rifles to fully automatic rifles of the nature of the M-16."[61]

Though reports of automatic gunfire at the Mount Carmel compound had been reported, Aguilera failed to report to the judge that these reports had been investigated by the Waco sheriff, who had determined that the guns owned by the Branch Davidians were legal.[62] Moreover, the Branch Davidians were well-known participants in local and regional gun shows and partly supported themselves by trading at gun shows, taking care to ensure that they always had the relevant paperwork to prove that their transactions were legal.[63] Branch Davidian Paul Fatta was a licensed federal firearm dealer, and the group operated a retail gun business known as the Mag Bag.

Using the affidavit filed by Aguilera, the ATF obtained search and arrest warrants for David Koresh and others based on the allegations that the Branch Davidians were in violation of federal law by converting semi-automatic to automatic weapons. The ATF also claimed that Koresh was operating a methamphetamine lab in order to obtain funds to purchase military assets under federal legislation that allowed for such actions under the War on Drugs. The evidence to support this claim, however, was not based on any factual evidence but on claims from disgruntled Branch Davidians who had left the compound six years earlier. Koresh had dismantled the lab when he took over Mount Carmel and given all of the components to the Waco sheriff for destruction.[64]

The search warrant requested by the ATF was authorized, and a search of the Mount Carmel compound was scheduled to occur on or before February 28, 1993, between 6:00 a.m. and 10:00 p.m. The day before the February 28 deadline, the *Waco Tribune-Herald* began publishing "The Sinful Messiah," a series of articles that alleged that Koresh had physically abused children in the compound and committed statutory rape on several underage girls by taking them as wives. The opening passage of the series began:

If you are a Branch Davidian, Christ lives on a threadbare piece of land 10 miles east of here called Mount Carmel. He has dimples, claims a ninth-grade education, married his legal wife when she was 14, enjoys a beer now and then, plays a mean guitar, reportedly packs a 9mm Glock and keeps an arsenal of military assault rifles, and willingly admits that he is a sinner without equal.[65]

According to the paper, Koresh was husband to more than 140 wives and was entitled to any female in the group he desired. He was also reportedly the father of a least a dozen children, some of these with mothers who had become Koresh's brides as early as age 12 or 13.[66]

Although it is believed that the *Waco Tribune-Herald* had held the Koresh story for days or perhaps even weeks, the ATF later claimed that the publication of "The Sinful Messiah" caused its preparations to be moved up, though these claims would have contradicted the original warrant that mandated a deadline of 10:00 p.m. on February 28.

Though the ATF would have preferred to arrest David Koresh outside of Mount Carmel, this proved difficult, as Koresh rarely left the safety of the compound. Thus, the ATF attempted to execute the search and arrest warrant on Sunday morning, February 28, 1993. Any element of surprise that the ATF might have hoped for was dashed when a reporter for a local TV station, who had been tipped off about the raid, asked for directions to Mount Carmel from a U.S. Postal Service mail carrier who happened to be Koresh's brother-in-law.[67] Despite being informed that the Branch Davidians knew they were coming, the ATF commander ordered that the raid on the compound proceed, though success depended on the Branch Davidians not being armed and not engaging the agents as they served the warrant. While not typical procedure in instances of federal agents serving warrants, ATF agents nevertheless had their blood type written on their arms or necks for quicker blood type identification in the event of injury.[68] The ATF approached the compound with agents hidden in cattle trailers pulled by pickups.

As the agents disembarked, shooting began in the compound. ATF "dog teams" had been sent to kill dogs in the kennels on the compound, but it is not clear if this began the gunfire or if an accidental discharge on either side precipitated the shootings.[69] Three National Guard helicopters flying over the compound and being used as distractions were fired upon by Branch Davidians, though the occupants of the helicopters reportedly did not return fire.[70] During the first few moments of shooting, David Koresh was wounded in the wrist. Within a minute, Branch Davidians were calling emergency services pleading for the shooting to stop.

As the exchange of gunfire continued, ATF agents put two ladders up against the side of one of the buildings where the arms cache was believed to be located. As the agents crouched by an open window waiting to enter what was believed to be Koresh's room, one agent was struck and killed, while another was wounded. Another agent was killed after shooting a shotgun at several Branch Davidians firing at him. Inside the arms room, ATF agents killed a Branch Davidian gunman and discovered a large cache of weapons. However, coming under heavy fire, two ATF agents were wounded and had to retreat. An agent providing covering fire for the retreating agents was shot by a Branch Davidian and killed instantly. Another agent was killed by gunfire as agents attempted to neutralize a Branch Davidian sniper who was firing at the ATF teams from on top of a water tower. The exchange of gunfire lasted about 45 minutes until the ATF began to run low on ammunition. One ATF agent later wrote, "About 45 minutes into the shootout, the volume of gunfire finally started to slacken. We were running out of ammunition. The Davidians, however, had plenty."[71] The shooting continued sporadically for two hours, after which the McLennan County Sheriff's Department was able to negotiate a ceasefire.[72] During the ceasefire, the Branch Davidians allowed the ATF to secure their dead and evacuate their wounded.

As a result of the exchange between the ATF and the Branch Davidians, four ATF agents were killed and another 16 were wounded. Five Branch Davidians were killed and several were wounded, including Koresh. The local sheriff claimed that he had not been apprised of the raid beforehand. A government report would later state that the Branch Davidians did not ambush the ATF, as they "apparently did not maximize the kill of ATF agents." Rather, as the report explained, they were "desperate religious fanatics expecting an apocalyptic ending, in which they were destined to die defending their sacred ground and destined to achieve salvation."[73] A 1999 FBI report on the ATF raid on Mount Carmel later noted:

> The violent tendencies of dangerous cults can be classified into two general categories—defensive violence and offensive violence. Defensive violence is utilized by cults to defend a compound or enclave that was created specifically to eliminate most contact with the dominant culture. The 1993 clash in Waco, Texas at the Branch Davidian complex is an illustration of such defensive violence. History has shown that groups that seek to withdraw from the dominant culture seldom act on their beliefs that the endtime has come unless provoked.[74]

After the death of four federal agents, the FBI took overall command at the Mount Carmel site. FBI agent Jeff Jamar, head of the FBI's San Antonio field office, took overall command as site commander, while the FBI HRT was also deployed. Ironically, the leader of the HRT was Richard Rogers, who only six months before had been instrumental in the disastrous events at Ruby Ridge, Idaho. As he did at Ruby Ridge, Rogers often overrode the site commander (Jamar). Moreover, the lack of HRT reserves to maintain a lengthy siege created pressure to resolve the situation quickly in a tactical fashion.

Immediately after the raid, the Branch Davidians had telephone contact with local news media and Koresh gave several phone interviews. However, after the FBI cut all telephone lines into the compound, the Branch Davidians did not communicate again for the next 51 days. In the first few days of the siege, FBI negotiators believed that they had secured a resolution to the crisis when Koresh was allowed to broadcast a message via national radio. In return, Koresh had stated that the Branch Davidians would leave the compound peacefully. After the broadcast, Koresh told negotiators that God hold told him to remain at Mount Carmel and "wait."[75] However, negotiators were able to secure the release of 19 children, ages five months to 12 years. Ninety-six people remained on the compound.

Allegations of child abuse within the compound could not be corroborated even though some of the 19 children that had been released were interviewed for hours by FBI agents and Texas Rangers. Nevertheless, the FBI would put forth claims of child abuse as justification for launching tear gas attacks to force the Branch Davidians out of the compound.[76]

During the siege, the FBI sent a video camera in to the Branch Davidians. Koresh used the video camera to introduce his children and his wives to the FBI, including several minors who claimed to have fathered children by Koresh. A week into the siege, the Branch Davidians sent out a videotape in which everyone in the compound seemed to be staying of their own free will. The FBI was concerned that the release of these tapes to the media might produce sympathy for the Branch Davidians.[77] The videos confirmed that 23 children remained in the compound. As the siege continued, Koresh negotiated for more time, as he stated that he needed to complete several religious documents before he could surrender. Koresh's stalling tactics alienated the federal negotiators, who began to increasingly believe that the situation was deteriorating into a hostage crisis.

As the siege developed, two factions began to develop within the FBI. The first believed that continued negotiations were the best method to resolve the crisis, while the second believed in forcing the Branch Davidians out through sleep deprivation and cutting off supplies of water and electricity to the compound. On the perimeter of the compound property, nine Bradley Fighting Vehicles and other U.S. Army vehicles began patrols. The armored vehicles destroyed fencing and outbuildings and crushed cars belonging to Branch Davidians.[78] One armored vehicle reportedly drove over the grave of a Branch Davidian. Criticism was later leveled at the tactics of using sleep deprivation and peace-disrupting tactics against the Branch Davidians: "The point was this—they were trying to have sleep disturbance and they were trying to take someone that they viewed as unstable to start with, and they were trying to drive him crazy. And then they got mad 'cos [sic] he does something that they think is irrational!"[79]

Despite the aggressive tactics employed by the FBI, Koresh and most of his followers refused to give up. Koresh did order 11 people to leave the compound, though all of the children who remained stayed with the rest of the Branch Davidians. FBI negotiators were not prepared for the religious zeal of Koresh and his followers. A number of experts on apocalypticism in religious groups attempted to persuade the FBI that its siege tactics only reinforced the belief of those inside that the Branch Davidians "were part of a Biblical end of times confrontation that had cosmic significance."[80] The experts pointed out that while the Branch

Davidians' beliefs may have seemed extreme, their behavior was consistent with their beliefs inasmuch as those inside the compound were likely to sacrifice themselves rather than submit.[81] The FBI voiced concern over this assessment, believing that Koresh might order the collective suicide of those in the compound, similar to the cult suicide committed by Jim Jones and the 900 people of the People's Temple in Jonestown, Guyana, in 1978. Koresh himself professed that he embodied the Second Coming of Jesus Christ and that he had been commanded by his father in heaven to remain in the compound.[82]

Believing that child abuse and the possibility of mass suicide were real, U.S. Attorney General (AG) Janet Reno consulted with President Bill Clinton on the deteriorating conditions at the Branch Davidian compound. Clinton stated that he told AG Reno to proceed if she thought an assault on the compound would prevent further loss of life.[83] Reno had also voiced concerns that Linda Thompson and the Unorganized Militia of the United States were on their way to Waco in order to aid or attack Koresh.[84]

Because it was known that the Branch Davidians were heavily armed, the FBI's plan was to pump tear gas into the compound's buildings until the occupants were forced out. The assault consisted of armored vehicles equipped with booms so that holes could be punched in the buildings by which the canisters of tear gas could be delivered. Loudspeakers were used to inform the Branch Davidians in the buildings that no armed assault was taking place but that they needed to surrender. As the armored vehicles approached the buildings, they were fired upon, whereon the FBI ordered more tear gas to be pumped into the buildings. After more than six hours, no Branch Davidians had left any buildings, instead sheltering in a cinder-block room and using gas masks.[85] The FBI claimed that the armored vehicles had been punching holes in the buildings to allow the occupants to escape the tear gas.

On April 19, 1993, at approximately 12:07 p.m., three fires broke out almost simultaneously in the buildings that composed the Mount Carmel compound. Fanned by high winds, the fire spread quickly through the wooden structures, and within 45 minutes, every building was burned to the ground. Only 9 people of the 85 who had been in the compound survived the fire. Among the 76 Branch Davidians who died were 20 children who were under 18 years old.[86]

After the fire, the government maintained that they had not taken any action that would have caused the fire. Government officials made the claim that the Branch Davidians had set the fires deliberately.[87] Some of the Branch Davidian survivors maintained that the fires were accidentally or deliberately set by the actions of the FBI and the assault perpetrated upon the compound by the federal government.[88] The children and adults who died in the fire were either buried alive by rubble, burned to death, suffocated by the effects of the fire, or shot. Though there was some evidence that some of the fatalities had died from cyanide poisoning, consistent with burning tear gas, the government maintained that the last canister of tear gas had been delivered at least an hour before the flames erupted. At least 20 Branch Davidians died from gunshot wounds and not from the effects of the fire. Among these were five children under the age of 14. A three-year-old was stabbed in the chest. An expert retained by the U.S. Office of the Special Counsel concluded that many of the gunshot wounds were mercy killings by the Branch Davidians, who performed them when there was no chance of escape from the fire.[89] According to an FBI official, Koresh's top aide shot and killed Koresh and then committed suicide with the same gun. Television footage of the FBI assault and the fire that consumed the compound at Mount Carmel was broadcast live on local and national television.

Soon after the events of April 19, a federal grand jury indicted 12 surviving Branch Davidian members on charges of conspiring to cause and aiding and abetting in causing the murder of federal agents. After a jury trial of two months, four of the Branch Davidians were acquitted on all charges. The remaining eight were acquitted of all of the murder-related charges. However, five of the eight Branch Davidians were convicted on lesser charges, including aiding and abetting the voluntary manslaughter of federal agents, while all eight were convicted on firearms charges.[90]

After a plethora of appeals in which the convicted Branch Davidians appealed their sentences—challenging, among other things, the constitutionality of the prohibition on possession of machine guns—the U.S. Supreme Court made recommendations that cut 25 years off the sentences of five Branch Davidians and 5 years off of the sentence of another. As of July 2007, every Branch Davidian who served prison time as a result of the siege at Waco had been released from prison.[91] Civil suits against the federal government brought by surviving Branch Davidians were all dismissed.

Though surviving Branch Davidian members claimed that the activities of the government had started the fire that led to the deaths of Branch Davidians, U.S. Attorney General Janet Reno had specified that no pyrotechnic devices were to be used in the assault.[92] Between 1993 and 1999, FBI spokespeople continually denied that any pyrotechnic devices had been used at Mount Carmel. Nevertheless, three pyrotechnic grenades were found in the rubble of the fire that the FBI later admitted had been used to penetrate an outlying structure that was away from the main buildings.[93] However, these grenades were fired three hours before the fire erupted and could not have caused the blaze that engulfed the buildings on the compound. But when FBI documents were turned over to Congress for an investigation in 1994, the page listing the possible use of any pyrotechnic devices was missing.[94] Because of inconsistencies in FBI statements and reports, Attorney General Reno directed that an investigation be initiated.[95] The investigation was complicated by the fact that Texas authorities had bulldozed the compound site less than a month after the fire (May 19). Nevertheless, it was finally revealed that as many as 100 FBI agents had known that pyrotechnics had been present at Mount Carmel, but none of them came forward until six years after the fire (1999).[96]

By the time of the revelations in 1999, public opinion had begun to believe that there had been serious misconduct by the federal government at Waco. A *Time* magazine poll conducted on August 26, 1999, found that 61 percent of the public believed that law enforcement officials had started the fire on the Branch Davidian compound.[97] Because of the lingering questions, Attorney General Janet Reno appointed former U.S. Senator John Danforth to investigate the matter. A year-long investigation, in which the Office of the Special Counsel interviewed more than 1,000 witnesses and sifted through 2.3 million pages of documents, yielded no conclusive physical evidence that the fire that consumed the Branch Davidian compound had been started by the actions of the government. The Danforth Report, issued on November 8, 2000, thus concluded that all allegations that the government had started the fire at Mount Carmel were meritless. David Koresh's attorney called the Danforth Report a "whitewash," whereas former U.S. Attorney General Ramsey Clark, who had represented several Branch Davidians in their lawsuits against the government, said that the report "failed to address the obvious." Clark stated, "History will clearly record, I believe, that these assaults on the Mt. Carmel church center remain the greatest domestic law enforcement tragedy in the history of the United States."[98]

Aftermath

Though the government had been held blameless by the Danforth Report, the reaction within extremist elements of the public was swift. As reported by the Anti-Defamation League (ADL),

More than any other issue, though, the deadly standoffs at Ruby Ridge, Idaho, in 1992 and Waco, Texas, in 1993 ignited widespread passion. To most Americans, these events were tragedies, but to the extreme right, they were examples of a government willing to stop at nothing to stamp out people who refused to conform. Right-wing folk singers like Carl Klang memorialized the children who died at Waco with songs like "Seventeen Little Children." These events provided new life to a number of extremist movements, from Christian Identity activists to sovereign citizens, but they also propelled the creation of an entirely new movement consisting of armed militia groups formed to prevent another Ruby Ridge or Waco.[99]

The fact that Ruby Ridge and Waco both involved government action in response to what were deemed "illegal firearms" added fuel to the fire that prompted the formation of the militia groups we know today. Most patriot and militia leaders of this time were radical gun-rights advocates who believed that the 2nd Amendment meant that there was no such thing as illegal firearms. Ruby Ridge and Waco intensified the fear and suspicion among these groups that confiscation of all guns by the government was just around the corner. In 1992, Larry Pratt, leader of a radical gun-rights group and an advocate for the formation of militias to protect the American public from government action, issued a statement in the wake of the Rodney King riots in Los Angeles that urged the L.A. Police Department to "take advantage of what the Founding Fathers called the unorganized militia" in order to prevent further unrest.[100] The ranks of militia groups swelled during this time, as many in the public felt that such groups were needed to protect their inherent rights to keep and bear arms. Even today, the zealous advocacy of a citizen's gun rights is at the core of most militia ideology.

As noted by ADL,

The combination of anger at the government, fear of gun confiscation and susceptibility to elaborate conspiracy theories is what formed the core of the militia movement's ideology. Although there were white supremacists in the movement, and although groups and individuals within the movement often made common cause with or at least tolerated hate groups, the orientation of the militia movement remained primarily anti-government and conspiratorial. The militia movement appealed to many radical libertarians just as it appealed to traditional proponents of extreme right-wing causes.[101]

THE FORMATION OF THE MILITIA OF MONTANA

The siege at Ruby Ridge, Idaho, convinced many in patriot/militia circles that the federal government was exercising undue power and usurping the rights of American citizens. This sentiment, fueled by Ruby Ridge, exploded after the events of Waco.

In January 1994, the Militia of Montana (MOM) was formed by brothers John and David Trochmann, as well as David's son, Randy. The organization evolved out of the remnants of an earlier organization known as United Citizens for Justice.

In the aftermath of both Ruby Ridge and Waco, MOM was a response to what was seen as the growing threat posed by the federal government. MOM began a push to "return our government to a position of service to the people and to defender of individual rights as our forefathers intended."[102] Though it portrayed itself ostensibly as a human rights group, most of its members and supporters were white supremacists, many associated with Aryan Nations.[103]

In its infancy, the Trochmann brothers and other adherents of MOM portrayed themselves as "sovereign citizens" owing no allegiance to either a state or national government with which they had not entered into a social contract.[104] Like many who had come before and others who would come after, MOM members believed that it was federal overreach to require citizens to obtain a driver's license or to be required to have a Social Security number assigned to them. The Trochmann brothers were followers of the common law movement (see discussion in Chapter Four) and believed that property taxes were invalid. MOM believed that the only powers granted to the federal government were those enumerated in the Constitution. Thus, like many others, they were Constitutional literalists.

Though MOM portrayed itself as the protector of citizen rights, its white supremacist bent exposed it as a radical organization. Since MOM believed that laws promulgated after the Founding were essentially illegitimate, only white males were sovereign citizens. All nonwhites and non-Christians were "second-class" citizens.[105]

In June 1994, more than 800 people gathered in Kalispell, Montana, to hear an address by MOM's cofounder, John Trochmann, a retired maker of snowmobile parts.[106] In a 1995 interview, Trochmann stated that "Gun control is people control," intimating that the government's attempt to control certain weapons in the aftermath of Waco was a blatant attempt to subvert liberties and bring the United States under the domination of a global government.[107] At its height, MOM had perhaps

12,000 members "trained in guerilla warfare, survivalist techniques, and other unconventional tactics in preparation for withstanding the federal government onslaught presaged by the Waco siege.[108]

Adherents to the Militia of Montana fit the bill of the typical militia member of the time. They engaged in endless speculation about government conspiracies, including one in which a convicted felon maintained that his execution for the killing of an Arkansas state trooper was related to a series of scandals related to President Bill Clinton.[109] The felon, Richard John ("Wayne") Snell, alleged that 25 individuals had met "strange" deaths because of their knowledge of then-Governor Clinton's activities. Snell was being executed, according to MOM, because he "was and still is heavily involved in exposing Clinton for his trail of blood to the White House."[110]

MOM also proved to be a very vocal opponent of the Brady Handgun Violence Prevention Act ("Brady Bill") and the Federal Assault Weapons Ban, both of which had been proposed in the aftermath of horrendous events.[111] MOM, and many other groups of the time, saw these gun control attempts as direct threats to the liberties provided by the 2nd Amendment and believed that such attempts were "orchestrated by financial and corporate elites in a global conspiracy."[112] MOM held that these unseen powers "were using the United Nations to overturn the Constitution and invoke martial law as they absorbed the United States into an international totalitarian state."[113] Resisting the New World Order became a central theme to MOM adherents, as well as serving as a core ideological and rhetorical theme of the patriot/militia movement.[114] One MOM member even compiled a "Blue Book" that purported to contain a map that denoted occupation zones that would exist in the United States after the United Nations takeover of the country.[115]

The Militia of Montana never directly confronted the government as would one of its offshoot organizations, the Montana Freemen. Instead, MOM orchestrated public appearances and took to the television and radio airwaves to espouse its views. Along with these appearances, MOM members pushed literature and paraphernalia that helped support the organization. These tactics brought derision to the group, as other, more militant patriot/militia groups were demanding more aggressive action against the activities of the federal government.

As noted by one source, however:

MOM flourished despite criticism. Along with its proficient salesmanship, two other reasons stand out. First, John Trochmann proved a formidable leader. With the thick gray beard and intense stare of an avenging prophet, his belligerency toward the government was in fact leavened by a relatively soft manner and speaking style—qualities that made him especially attractive to mainstream media. His influence undoubtedly contributed to the second reason for MOM's success, namely its ability to cultivate and promote a paranoid-style world view without descending into racism or anti-Semitism.

Although bigots were associated with the group from its start, Trochmann went to great lengths to emphasize that the militia's concern was with the threat posed by conspiratorial powers against the rights of all Americans. In his way, he pioneered a militia "don't ask, don't tell policy" toward the racists in his group, while downplaying (at least publicly) aspects of MOM's views that bolstered intolerance.[116]

As stated on its website, the Militia of Montana's current statement of purpose can be distilled into three essential points:

1. Now, more than ever before, the information highway is reaching into millions of homes all across America. Everywhere a person goes (Anytown, USA) you can find a conversation taking place about the direction our nation is heading—keeping it's sovereign status, or becoming a state under the governance of the United Nations.

2. We, at the Militia of Montana, are dedicated to ensuring that all Americans are educated to make an informed decision as to which direction America should go. Along with being physically prepared to withstand the onslaught which will erupt no matter where we end up, we must at all costs, keep reaching those who have not had the opportunity to decide for themselves.

3. The Militia of Montana has been, and continues to be, a national focal point for assisting Americans in forming their own grass roots organization dedicated to American's sovereignty and status as an independent nation among the nations of the world.[117]

The website currently maintained by MOM hosts several links pertaining to survivalism and survival supplies, news items, a list of appearance by MOM members, e-mail alerts, and the like. In an attempt to convince skeptics, the last section of the website is titled "What is the Militia?" The following are brief excerpts from this document:

The Federal government has made claims over and over that the militia is the National Guard, portraying, and in many cases literally calling the militia groups of Citizens Terrorists, White Supremacists, Extremists, Radicals, and many other slanderous, defaming names.

First of all, no where in the Constitution does it say that the militia is the National Guard. This is proven when taking into consideration that the Constitution was written in the 1700s, and the National Guard was not created until January 21, 1903, under the name of its founder, "The Dick Act."

On January 3, 1916, president Wilson usurped (Usurped: to make claim to something you have no lawful right to) the powers of the People as a "Militia" under U.S. Code, Title 32. Under Title 32, the National Guard is Federally funded through the U.S. Treasury, and the commanding officer of the National Guard is the president. Not as a president, but as the senior officer, in accordance with Title 32 USC 104(c)(d)(e)(f). Such a position makes the National Guard the president's own private army! U.S. Code, Title 32, completely alters the definition of the militia, its services, who controls it and what it is. Title 32 violates every article and section of the Constitution, including the Second Amendment!...

. . . Our forefathers knew that countries with a militia excelled, and nations without a militia usually failed. They knew that without certain safeguards inserted in our constitution, this nation would also fail. One safeguard is the Second Amendment. The Second Amendment is an absolute right, reserved respectively to the people. . . .

. . . If the militia is to protect the Citizens against tyranny in government, and if the National Guard was the Militia, the president, being the commander/senior officer of the National Guard, surely wouldn't order the overthrow of tyranny in the government in which he is a part of, no matter how much the people proclaimed tyranny. The National Guard is not the Militia. NOTHING, in the Constitution states that the Militia is the National Guard. The Militia has always been the "Sovereign Citizens." Anything else would be in contrast with the Constitution. It wouldn't make any sense to create safeguards against tyranny in government, and then put that same government in control of such safeguards. . . .

. . . We, the Sovereign Citizens of the United States of America are the true Militia under the Constitution, and when the Citizens see (as stated in the Declaration of Independence) "a long train of abuses and usurpations, pursuing invariably the same Object evinces a design to reduce them under absolute Despotism, it is their right, it is their duty, to throw off such Government, and to provide new Guards for their future security."

The only power the government has over The People is their ignorance. When tyrants act in the name of government, violating ethics, they break the trust of the Citizens. The natural result should be to pull back power.

Learn about our Constitution before its to [sic] late. Unchecked power in government is the foundation of tyranny. It is our duty as Citizens to use our power to control the government in order to stem the tide of oppression and tyranny. . . .[118]

MONTANA FREEMEN

Perhaps one reason the Militia of Montana remains today and the reason it did not disappear as other patriot/militia groups of this time did is its decision not to directly confront the United States government. Like members of the Militia of Montana, the Montana Freemen espoused individual sovereignty and rejected the authority of the United States government over any citizen of the United States. They began their own system of government in "Justus Township" (the term members used to refer to their land holdings) near Jordan, Montana, and believed in common-law courts and devised their own systems of banking and credit.[119] In late 1994, foreclosure proceedings were begun on the land that comprised Justus Township. The Freemen, however, refused to be evicted from the land. They had previously openly demonstrated their contempt for all state and federal government jurisdiction when they conducted their own mock trials of public officials and issued a writ of execution for the federal judge—U.S. District Judge Jack Shanstrom of Billings, Montana—who had begun the foreclosure proceedings against Justus Township.[120] The Freemen briefly took over the Garfield County, Montana, courthouse in January 1994 in an attempt to establish the "Supreme Court of Garfield County-comitatus."[121] The Freemen had also issued bounties of $1 million for anyone thought to be involved in the foreclosure proceedings, including Judge Shanstrom, and issued wanted posters for Shanstrom and county officials who were to be brought in "dead or alive."[122]

On March 3, 1995, two Freemen were arrested after being stopped for driving without license plates in Musselshell County, Montana. Law enforcement officials found several guns, ammunition, and other suspicious material in the car, including a map with the judge's home circled.[123] When several Freemen appeared at the jail where the two were being held, they were carrying guns and demanding the release of their compatriots. Though charges against the individuals were eventually dropped, law enforcement officials were "astonished" at the brazenness of the Freemen's actions.[124] Such contempt would only portend what was to come.

In early 1996, the one-time leader of the Freemen and a "dean in the antigovernment 'Patriot' movement," LeRoy M. Schweitzer, was arrested on charges of conspiracy, bank and wire fraud, failure to file federal income tax returns, fugitive possession of a firearm, and threatening a federal judge.[125] Schweitzer was eventually convicted on 25 charges related to these charges and was sentenced to 22 years in a federal prison. Yet Schweitzer's convictions were just a few of those handed down to more than a dozen Freemen over the next few years. The Freemen had printed their own checks and had written fraudulent checks in amounts totaling more than $18 billion, of which $1.8 million was cashed. The Freemen also "put millions of dollars worth of liens on property owned by anyone who opposed them. They presented workshops showing others how to use their methods."[126] When presented at trial, their defense attorneys contended that the Freemen, because of their beliefs in no governmental authority higher than the local level, had acted in good faith.[127]

What propelled the Montana Freemen onto the national and international stage was a standoff with the federal government that began on March 25, 1996. On that day, undercover FBI agents lured Schweitzer and two other Freemen from the Justus Township compound and arrested them. More than 100 agents surrounded the area where about 20 Freemen remained. But the federal government had learned from the lessons of Ruby Ridge, Idaho, and Waco, Texas, where rash and inadvisable actions had led to the deaths of those who had expressed antigovernment sentiments. In the case of the Montana Freemen, the FBI deployed more than 40 third-party negotiators, attempting to talk the Freemen out of their compound. No offensive action was taken, and after 81 days, the remaining Freemen at Justus Township surrendered to federal authorities.[128] The surrender came after one of the remaining Freemen had been allowed to consult with Schweitzer, who was being held in jail on a variety of charges.

LeRoy Schweitzer, who would eventually die in the maximum-security portion of the Federal Correctional Complex in Florence, Colorado, in September 2011, was typical of those who found their way to the patriot/militia movement. As noted by one author,

Schweitzer's introduction to the radical right came after he had a run-in with the Internal Revenue Service. . . .

. . . Schweitzer balked when the federal government said he owed $700 more in taxes in 1977. He relied on advice from his accountant and attorney, and didn't believe he owed another dime, his former associates told *The Spokesman-Review* in 1996.

When the IRS then froze $6,000 in his business account, Schweitzer's partner paid the delinquent taxes. "He couldn't believe his bank would let anybody touch his money," a friend told the Spokane newspaper in 1996.

I can remember LeRoy saying, "The IRS can steal my money, but nobody else can," the friend said. "That's where his trust in banks went down the drain, and his hatred of the government began."

In 1978, Schweitzer was audited again by the IRS. He eventually stopped paying federal income taxes and became a "full-blown tax protester."[129]

Though it was ultimately declared that Schweitzer died in his jail cell of natural causes at age 73, his supporters suspected foul play. Just over two weeks after his death in September 2011, one Freemen sympathizer wrote a piece titled "The Untold Story of the Montana Freemen."[130] Author Pat Shannan asked the question, "Why was he (Schweitzer) still under lockdown 24 hours a day, seven days a week, next to such notorious killers as mob hit men and alleged 'Unabomber' Ted Kaczynski?"[131] Among other accusations, Shannan contends that the federal government had targeted Schweitzer and the Freemen because they had exposed the illegal and corrupt practices of the federal government. For instance, Schweitzer and fellow Freeman Dan Petersen had for years conducted "in-depth legal research" to educate citizens on the chicanery of the government. "Their legal instruction included the fraud committed against American citizens by the Federal Reserve system, and more importantly, how to counter it."[132]

But the Freemen, Shannan contends, went beyond the mere pointing out of the government's evil. Instead, they actually engaged in the same activities themselves in order to draw the attention of the American people to the crimes of the Federal Reserve and, perhaps, bring it down. They did this by "suing federal judges and others while securing what they believed to be 'perfected liens' that they converted into certified bank drafts, which were then used to pay off government debt, mainly farm foreclosures and IRS liens."[133]

But "feeling the heat" that its scams had been exposed, the federal government falsely lured Schweitzer and Petersen out of Justus Township and "stungunned and beat them into submission."[134] Author Shannan contends that on at least one occasion, on a visit to Justus Township he was shown

> 38 instances where Schweitzer had signed drafts, drawn from funds created from unchallenged summary judgments, and not only paid off liens but received in many cases five-figure government refunds for overpayment. The bank drafts were obviously "money," at least as legitimate as the thin air creations by the Fed.
>
> That's why the federal government considered these men dangerous—not because they might have owned guns and not because they were a physical threat to anyone. It was the Freemen's knowledge—and their passing it on to others—that created the Fed's fear of exposure of its fraudulent system.[135]

Thus, for Shannan, the Freemen's exposure of the fraudulent practices of the federal government "may have arrived on the scene just a bit too early."[136]

MICHIGAN MILITIA

One of the most prominent groups formed in the aftermath of Ruby Ridge and Waco was the Michigan Militia. The militia was formed in 1994 by Norman Olson, a former U.S. Air Force noncommissioned officer. Members of the Michigan Militia believe that Ruby Ridge and Waco marked a new era of demonstrations of force by the federal government against citizens who had not been convicted of any federal crimes. Rather, such actions were gross overreactions to individuals and groups believed to have views that were contrary to the government. Because of antigun legislation passed during the Clinton administration, the Michigan Militia was among those groups that emerged that were fearful of government attacks on the 2nd Amendment rights of Americans.

The militia was initially organized with four divisions (later nine), each consisting of several brigades, organized by country. Each brigade has a commander who holds the rank of lieutenant colonel and is elected by members of her or his brigade.[137] The commanding officer of the Militia holds the rank of brigadier general and is elected at large by all Michigan Militia Corps members on an annual basis, with each brigade getting one vote. At its peak, the Michigan Militia claimed membership of more than 10,000. Today, however, the Militia numbers in the hundreds.[138] The group's main focus is paramilitary exercises and emergency response.

In the aftermath of the Oklahoma City bombing, founder Norman Olson, together with militia leaders from other states, testified before the United States Subcommittee on Terrorism. Olson's opening statement spoke directly to the long-standing positions of militias in the American system of government:

Not only does the Constitution specifically allow the formation of a Federal Army, it also recognizes the inherent right of the people to form militia. Further, it recognizes that the citizen and his personal armaments are the foundation of the militia. The arming of the militia is not left to the state but to the citizen. However, should the state choose to arm its citizen militia, it is free to do so (bearing in mind the Constitution is not a document limiting the citizen, but rather limiting the power of government). But should the state fail to arm its citizen militia, the right of the people to keep and bear arms becomes the source of the guarantee that the state will not be found defenseless in the presence of a threat to its security. It makes no sense whatsoever to look to the Constitution of the United States or that of any state for permission to form a citizen militia since logically, the power to permit is also the power to deny. If brought to its logical conclusion in this case, government may deny the citizen the right to form a militia. If this were to happen, the state would assert itself as the principle of the contract making the people the agents. Liberty then would depend on the state's grant of liberty. Such a concept is foreign to American thought.

While the Second Amendment to the U.S. Constitution acknowledges the existence of state militia and recognizes their necessity for the security of a free state; and, while it also recognizes that the right of the people to keep and bear arms shall not be infringed, the Second Amendment is not the source of the right to form a militia

nor to keep and bear arms. Those rights existed in the states prior
to the formation of the federal union. In fact, the right to form militia and to keep and bear arms existed from antiquity. The enu-
meration of those rights in the Constitution only underscores their
natural occurrence and importance.

According to the Tenth Amendment, ultimate power over the
militia is not delegated to the Federal government by the Constitution nor to the states, but resides with the people. Consequently,
the power of the militia remains in the hands of the people. Again,
the fundamental function of the militia in society remains with the
people. Therefore, the Second Amendment recognizes that the militia's existence and the security of the state rests ultimately in the
people who volunteer their persons to constitute the militia and
their arms to supply its firepower. The primary defense of the state
rests with the citizen militia bearing its own arms. Fundamentally,
it is not the state that defends the people, but the people who defend the state.[139]

In his closing remarks before Congress, Olson noted the long-held
belief in the limitations of the government as outlined in the
Constitution—a consistent belief among most patriot/militia groups.
He stated:

> One other important point needs to be made. Since The
> Constitution is the limiting document upon the government, the
> government cannot become greater than the granting power. That
> is, the servant cannot become greater than its master. Therefore,
> should the chief executive or the other branch of government or all
> branches together act to suspend The Constitution under a rule of
> martial law, all power granted to government would be cancelled
> and deferred back to the granting power. That is the people.[140]

Though its numbers diminished toward the end of the 1990s, the
Militia made a slight comeback with Y2K fears and, in 2009, coinciden-
tally just after the election of the first African-American president (and
a liberal Democrat) to the presidency in 2008. Its numbers are increasing again, with at least 17 counties in Michigan claiming to have elements of the Militia that are active.

In 2014, the Michigan Militia celebrated 20 years of existence.
Members conduct several paramilitary exercises per year.[141] Like most
patriot/militia groups, the Michigan Militia takes great exception to

anything that its members deem to be government overreach, and they challenge the government on the constitutionality of many of the laws that it has passed in recent years.

An example of such a law is the National Defense Authorization Act of 2012 (NDAA) (H.R. 1540). This act, termed the Belligerent Act by Michigan Militia members, states that any person who has committed a "belligerent act" (defined as hostilities against the U.S. government) is subject to "detention under the law without trial until the end of hostilities. . . ."[142] As noted by the Michigan Militia, "Prior to this Act, such a distinction would have to be decided in a court of law by a jury of a citizen's peers. With the signing of the NDAA, the government is claiming the right to decide this unilaterally, without any judicial proceedings and no legal representation afforded to the accused."[143] Members of this group, as well as others, ask whether the U.S. government can declare as a "belligerent act" any protest that is legally conducted against the government. As they point out, the act of protest is constitutionally protected, yet they are sure that the U.S. government is going to deny these rights, particularly as they pertain to groups that may have antigovernment sentiments. As the Militia notes, the Bill of Rights specifically protects American citizens from an intrusive central government:

These are the most basic, most essential protections of human liberty upon which the United States was founded. It would be no exaggeration to claim that the primary purpose of those who founded the United States was the creation of a nation where exactly these protections were guaranteed to all citizens. And with the signing of the NDAA, the present government of the United States has claimed the legal right to kill these constitutional protections.[144]

The Militia intoned that the "Rule of Law" is the most fundamental premise of the American system of governance:

Under the Rule of Law and under the Constitution, citizens of the United States are presumed innocent until deemed guilty of a crime by a jury of their peers. Under the Rule of Law and under the Constitution, no citizen of the United States can be incarcerated without recourse to legal counsel and the justice system in a timely manner. These principles are what separate the Rule of Law from dictatorship. These principles are what separate the Rule of Law from totalitarianism. These principles are what separate the

Rule of Law from every political regime that the U.S. has rhetorically scorned over the history of its existence as a nation.[145]

The Militia's opposition to the NDAA even caused it to agree with what would, under normal circumstances, be a fair-weather ally, the American Civil Liberties Union (ACLU).[146] As pointed out, on the day of the signing of the NDAA, Anthony D. Romero, executive director of the ACLU, stated:

President Obama's action today is a blight on his legacy because he will forever be known as the president who signed indefinite detention without charge or trial into law. The statute is particularly dangerous because it has no temporal or geographic limitations, and can be used by this and future presidents to militarily detain people captured far from any battlefield.[147]

The closing paragraphs of the protest against this act state:

The point is that this law really makes it possible for a US government, whether this one or a future one, to lock up US citizens who are protesting against, and threatening to replace, that government. Even if this law were never used, it radically changes the relationship between the government and the citizens of the United States. Unless and until it is repealed, this Act gives the government legal grounds to use the military and the threat of indefinite military detention without trial to put down any form of protest that it decides is a threat to itself by simply defining the protest as a "belligerent act."

Think about this: those in Congress and the President have taken a lot of political heat for passing this law and a host of other recent legislation that curtails the Constitutional rights of U.S. citizens. Why would they take the political risk of offending their constituents if they were not anticipating a day when they would need to protect themselves against those constituents?

The authors of this site [http://belligerentact.org/] perceive the National Defense Authorization Act of 2012 itself as a belligerent act committed against the people of the United States by the self-same government officials who have sworn a solemn oath to serve the citizens and uphold the Constitution.

We protest and demand the repeal of Subtitle D, SEC. 1021 of the National Defense Authorization Act of 2012, along with any other legislation that abrogates the protections of human liberty guaranteed under the Constitution.[148]

The Michigan Militia, like most patriot/militia groups in today's political environment, prepare themselves for an eventual showdown with the United States government. This group and others like it insist that the United States government has been in inexorable decline for decades and that the government continues to trample on the rights of the people, all the while neglecting the spirit and the letter of the Constitution. To the Michigan Militia and similar groups, the government is intent on its survival regardless of the wishes and aspirations of those it supposedly serves—the people. As many patriot/militia groups are wont to do, they look to the past—particularly to the words of the Founding Fathers—for their guidance and inspiration. Thomas Jefferson is among their favorites. And it was Jefferson who intoned that:

> The commotions which have taken place in America, so far as they are yet known to me, offer nothing threatening. They are a proof that the people have liberty enough, and I would not wish them less than they have. If the happiness of the mass of the people can be secured at the expense of a little tempest now & then, or even of a little blood, it will be a precious purchase. Malo libertatum periculosum quam quietam servitutem. ("I prefer dangerous liberty to a quiet servitude.") To Ezra Stiles, Paris, December 24, 1786.[149]

Even more famous than this quote is Jefferson's reference to the "blood of patriots," which is often used in defense of violent acts. As Jefferson once said: "The tree of liberty must be refreshed from time to time with the blood of patriots & tyrants. It is natural manure."[150]

That quote would become particularly significant in the most destructive case of domestic terror ever perpetrated in the United States— the bombing of the Alfred P. Murrah Federal Building in Oklahoma City, Oklahoma, on April 19, 1995.

THE MAKING OF A PATRIOT: TIMOTHY MCVEIGH AND THE OKLAHOMA CITY BOMBING

Timothy McVeigh had grown up in a middle-class home in upstate New York, where his father had been employed in the local factory for decades. When McVeigh's father lost his job, the young boy's world was turned upside down. This disruption was compounded when McVeigh's mother left the family when McVeigh was only 10 years old. McVeigh and his two sisters were left to be raised by their father. Frequently a target of bullying, McVeigh retreated into a fantasy world, where he dreamed of retaliating and getting even with those who had bullied him.[151] Near the end of his life, McVeigh would state that the United States government was the ultimate bully.[152]

McVeigh showed promise in high school as a computer programmer and even bragged once that he had hacked into government computers. However, his grades never warranted any indication that he would attend college. McVeigh became intensely interested in firearms and stated that he wished to own a gun shop in the future. McVeigh would sometimes bring guns to school to impress his classmates. McVeigh began to speak forcefully in favor of gun rights and contended that the 2nd Amendment to the Constitution needed to be protected. McVeigh was known to read magazines such as *Solider of Fortune*.

McVeigh turned to the military to satisfy his increasingly violent desires. In May 1988 at the age of 20, he graduated from U.S. Army Infantry School at Fort Benning, Georgia.[153] While in the military, McVeigh would spend much of his spare time reading about firearms, sniper tactics, and explosives. He was once reprimanded for purchasing a "White Power" t-shirt at a Ku Klux Klan protest in retaliation for what he perceived to be "Black Power" t-shirts worn by black servicemen around the base.[154]

McVeigh was deployed to Fort Riley, Kansas, where he met Terry Nichols, who would become his coconspirator in the Oklahoma City bombing. In Nichols, McVeigh found a kindred spirit who had drifted from job to job and place to place before enlisting in the military. It was Nichols who began to fuel McVeigh's antigovernment rage when he introduced him to the fantasy novel *The Turner Diaries*.[155] When McVeigh was deployed to Operation Desert Storm in 1991, he claimed that he was ordered to execute surrendering Iraqi prisoners. In interviews after his capture, McVeigh claims that his hatred of the U.S. government intensified while he was in Iraq.

McVeigh aspired to become part of the U.S. Army Special Forces. He had been decorated several times as a result of his service during the Gulf War, including the Bronze Star and the National Defense Medal.[156] Yet after returning from the Gulf War and entering the Special Forces selection program, McVeigh quit after being deemed "unsuitable" for the Special Forces based on his psychological profile.[157]

After leaving the Army, McVeigh increasingly began to voice his dissatisfaction with the U.S. government and its policies. On February 11, 1992, McVeigh's hometown newspaper, the *Union-Sun & Journal*, published a letter he wrote to the editor of that newspaper:

Crime is so out of control. Criminals have no fear of punishment. Prisons are overcrowded so they know they will not be imprisoned long. This breeds more crime, in an escalating cyclic pattern.

Taxes are a joke. Regardless of what a political candidate "promises," they will increase. More taxes are always the answer to government mismanagement. They mess up. We suffer. Taxes are reaching cataclysmic levels, with no slowdown in sight.

The "American Dream" of the middle class has all but disappeared, substituted with people struggling just to buy next week's groceries. Heaven forbid the car breaks down!

Politicians are further eroding the "American Dream" by passing laws which are supposed to be a "quick fix," when all they are really designed for is to get the official re-elected. These laws tend to "dilute" a problem for a while, until the problem comes roaring back in a worsened form (much like a strain of bacteria will alter itself to defeat a known medication).

Politicians are out of control. Their yearly salaries are more than an average person will see in a lifetime. They have been entrusted with the power to regulate their own salaries, and have grossly violated that trust to live in their own luxury.

Racism on the rise? You had better believe it! Is this America's frustrations venting themselves? Is it a valid frustration? Who is to blame for the mess? At a point when the world has seen communism falter as an imperfect system to manage people; democracy seems to be headed down the same road. No one is seeing the "big" picture.

Maybe we have to contribute ideologies to achieve the perfect utopian government. Remember, government-sponsored health care was a communist idea. Should only the rich be allowed to live long? Does that say that because a person is poor, he is a lesser human being; and doesn't deserve to live as long, because he doesn't wear a tie to work?

What is it going to take to open the eyes of our elected officials? America is in serious decline!

We have no proverbial tea to dump, should we instead sink a ship full of Japanese imports? Is a civil war Imminent? Do we have

to shed blood to reform the current system? I hope it doesn't come
to that. But it might.[158]

McVeigh later wrote another letter to a U.S. Congressman in which
he complained about the arrest of a woman who had been carrying
Mace. He wrote that "Firearms restrictions are bad enough, but now a
woman can't even carry Mace in her purse?" McVeigh became increasingly paranoid about the reach of the U.S. government, even claiming at
one point that the Army had implanted a microchip in him to keep track
of his movements.[159]

McVeigh became increasingly frustrated at his inability to hold a job
and turned to gambling, where he racked up thousands of dollars in
debt. When he was informed by the government that he had been over-
paid $1,058 while in the Army and would have to pay the money back,
McVeigh responded with an angry letter in which he stated:

Go ahead, take everything I own; take my dignity. Feel good as you
grow fat and rich at my expense; sucking my tax dollars and
property.[160]

At this point, McVeigh began to increasingly read antigovernment
literature, much of which he shared with his sister. When his father
showed little interest in his rants, McVeigh moved out of his childhood
home and took an apartment with no phone. He also quit the National
Rifle Association (NRA), viewing their stance on the protection of gun
rights as too weak to adequately prevent the government from eventually seizing the guns of private citizens.[161]

In early 1993 as the standoff between federal agents and the Branch
Davidians dragged on in Waco, Texas, McVeigh drove to Waco to show
his support for the besieged at Mount Carmel. At the scene, McVeigh
distributed pro–gun rights literature and bumper stickers supporting
gun rights. He told a student reporter at the scene:

The government is afraid of the guns people have because they
have to have control of the people at all times. Once you take away
the guns, you can do anything to the people. You give them an inch
and they take a mile. I believe we are slowly turning into a socialist
government. The government is continually growing bigger and
more powerful and the people need to prepare to defend themselves against government control.[162]

McVeigh was outraged at the deaths of the Branch Davidians and held the U.S. government personally responsible for their deaths.[163] For the next several months, McVeigh traveled to gun shows around the United States. Reportedly, he traveled to 40 states and visited more than 80 gun shows.[164] While working at the gun shows, McVeigh handed out free cards that had Lon Horiuchi's name and address on them. Horiuchi was the FBI sniper accused of killing Randy Weaver's wife at Ruby Ridge, Idaho, while she held their baby daughter in her arms. McVeigh reportedly made death threats to Horiuchi and for a time considered killing Horiuchi rather than bombing a federal building.[165] In his travels, McVeigh found that the farther west he traveled, the more antigovernment sentiment he encountered. It was on a trip such as this that McVeigh first reportedly encountered what he called "the People's Socialist Republic of California."[166]

Besides handing out literature at the gun shows he attended, McVeigh handed out copies of Andrew Macdonald's (pen name for William Pierce) fantasy novel *The Turner Diaries*. This novel, which by this time had become standard fare at gun shows around the country, opined about a group known as "the Order," which plotted the overthrow of the United States government and all of the elements that supported it. In the novel, the Order perpetrates an attack on a federal building using a truck bomb. The bomb detonates near 9:00 a.m. McVeigh's fascination with this novel would become chillingly clear within less than two years. But McVeigh was not alone, for he found those sympathetic to his views at the gun shows. Indeed, there were many in attendance who were as angry as he was. As one author said:

> In the gun show culture, McVeigh found a home. Though he remained skeptical of some of the most extreme ideas being bandied around, he liked talking to people there about the United Nations, the federal government and possible threats to American liberty.[167]

McVeigh would end up in Michigan at the farm of an ex-army buddy who shared his antigovernment views—Terry Nichols. At the Nichols farm, Terry Nichols and his brother began to instruct McVeigh in the making of explosives out of readily available materials. The destruction of Waco had so enraged McVeigh that he determined that it was time to take action. He became increasingly convinced of a government cover-up as the events surrounding Waco came to light. For instance, McVeigh himself had been exposed to the effects of 0-chlorobenzalmalononitrile

(CS) gas (as the Branch Davidians allegedly had been) as part of his military training and knew its effects. McVeigh also believed that the disappearance of evidence in the case, such as the bullet-riddled steel-reinforced door of the Mount Carmel complex, suggested that the government was engaging in a massive cover-up to hide its true motivation, the methodical dismantling of the freedoms of law-abiding Americans everywhere.[168]

At this time, McVeigh's antigovernment rhetoric became even more extreme than it had been in the past. He began to imagine ATF hats riddled with bullet holes and flare guns that he claimed could shoot down ATF helicopters.[169] He produced videos detailing the U.S. government's misdeeds at Waco and Ruby Ridge and handed out pamphlets that openly stated that the government was engaged in "open warfare" against Americans.[170] McVeigh was also angry at new firearms restrictions that had been put in place in 1994 as a consequence of the activities at Ruby Ridge and Waco.

In what appeared to be a final break with his past, McVeigh sent a 23-page farewell letter to his boyhood friend Steve Hodge. In the letter, McVeigh proclaimed his everlasting devotion to the United States Declaration of Independence, explaining to Hodge in detail what every sentence meant to him (McVeigh). In his rantings, McVeigh declared that:

> Those who betray or subvert the Constitution are guilty of sedition and/or treason, are domestic enemies and should and will be punished accordingly.
>
> It also stands to reason that anyone who sympathizes with the enemy or gives aid or comfort to said enemy is likewise guilty. I have sworn to uphold and defend the Constitution against all enemies, foreign and domestic and I will. And I will because not only did I swear to, but I believe in what it stands for in every bit of my heart, soul and being. I know in my heart that I am right in my struggle, Steve. I have come to peace with myself, my God and my cause. Blood will flow in the streets, Steve. Good vs. Evil. Free Men vs. Socialist Wannabe Slaves. Pray it is not your blood, my friend.[171]

About the time of this letter, McVeigh and Nichols began to stockpile ammonium nitrate and agricultural fertilizer, ostensibly to resell to survivalists but also to make large explosive devices for actions that were being contemplated.[172] Moreover, rumors were circulating that the government would soon ban large purchases of the materials, making any large-scale device impossible to construct.

McVeigh confided in another war buddy, Michael Fortier, that he intended to blow up a federal building, just as the patriots had done in *The Turner Diaries*. Fortier and his wife declined to participate in McVeigh's plot. Prior to the planned action, McVeigh composed two letters to the ATF, the first titled "Constitutional Defenders" and the second "ATF Read." In the letters, he denounced government officials as "fascist tyrants" and "storm troopers" and warned:

ATF, all you tyrannical people will swing in the wind one day for your treasonous actions against the Constitution of the United States. Remember the Nuremberg War Trials.[173]

McVeigh also tried to enlist the support of one of his survivalist "customers" who had demonstrated an interest in what McVeigh was saying:

A man with nothing left to lose is a very dangerous man and his energy/anger can be focused toward a common/righteous goal. What I'm asking you to do, then, is sit back and be honest with yourself. Do you have kids/wife? Would you back out at the last minute to care for the family? Are you interested in keeping your firearms for their current/future monetary value, or would you drag that '06 through rock, swamp and cactus . . . to get off the needed shot? In short, I'm not looking for talkers, I'm looking for fighters. . . And if you are a fed, think twice. Think twice about the Constitution you are supposedly enforcing (isn't "enforcing freedom" an oxymoron?) and think twice about catching us with our guard down—you will lose just like Degan did—and your family will lose.[174]

McVeigh had considered a plan of assassination against government officials but believed that the bombing of a federal building would be much more of a political statement.[175] After the event, McVeigh said he sometimes wished that he had carried out the assassinations instead of the bombing.[176]

On April 19, 1995, a bomb transported by a Ryder rental truck and containing 5,000 pounds of ammonium nitrate and nitromethane (agricultural fertilizer) exploded in front of the Alfred P. Murrah Federal Building at 9:02 a.m., just as offices were opening for the day. The blast killed 168 people, including 19 children in a day care center that was operated on the second floor of the building. More than 680 other people were injured in the explosion.[177] In addition to blowing away half of the Murrah Building, the blast destroyed or damaged 324 nearby buildings, destroyed or burned 86 cars, and shattered glass in another 258 buildings. In all, the bombing caused an estimated $652 million in damage.[178] Though McVeigh claimed that he may have been given pause on the target had he known that there was a day care in the building, Terry Nichols contended that McVeigh knew about the day care and simply didn't care.[179]

This callous attitude would seem to be confirmed in McVeigh's later statements, in which he proclaimed:

> To these people in Oklahoma who have lost a loved one, I'm sorry but it happens every day. You're not the first mother to lose a kid, or the first grandparent to lose a grandson or a granddaughter. It happens every day, somewhere in the world. I'm not going to go into that courtroom, curl into a fetal ball and cry just because the victims want me to do that.[180]

Shortly after the bombing, McVeigh was arrested for driving with no license plate on his car and carrying a concealed weapon. Upon his arrest, McVeigh was wearing a t-shirt with a picture of Abraham Lincoln and the motto *sic semper tyrannis* ("thus always to tyrants") printed on the front. On the back of the shirt was a picture of a tree with three droplets of blood dripping from it and a quote by Thomas Jefferson: "The tree of liberty must be refreshed from time to time with the blood of patriots and tyrants."[181] Within 72 hours, McVeigh was identified as the subject of the nationwide manhunt that was then taking place for the perpetrator of the Murrah Building bombing.

On August 10, 1995, McVeigh was indicted on 11 federal counts, including conspiracy to use a weapon of mass destruction, use of a weapon of mass destruction by explosive device, and eight counts of first-degree murder.[182] At his trial, McVeigh instructed his lawyers to use a necessity defense—to claim that the bombing took place in defense of an imminent danger that McVeigh perceived emanated from the U.S. government. Though the lawyers balked at such a defense, McVeigh made the point that "imminent danger" did not have to equate with "immediate danger." In other words, the "illegitimate" actions of the U.S. government, while not posing an "immediate" threat to McVeigh, nevertheless posed an "imminent" threat inasmuch as the continuation of policies being conducted by the government would certainly bring about the "imminent" destruction of freedom and liberty in the United States. McVeigh's lawyers claimed that the bombing of the Murrah Federal Building was a justifiable response to what McVeigh believed were the crimes committed by the U.S. government at both Ruby Ridge, Idaho, and Waco, Texas.[183]

On June 2, 1997, McVeigh was found guilty on all 11 counts of the federal indictment:

> Although 168 people, including 19 children, were killed in the April 19, 1995, bombing, murder charges were brought against McVeigh for only the eight federal agents who were on duty when the bomb destroyed much of the Murrah Building.
>
> Along with the eight counts of murder, McVeigh was charged with conspiracy to use a weapon of mass destruction, using a weapon of mass destruction and destroying a federal building.
>
> Oklahoma City District Attorney Bob Macy said he would file state charges in the other 160 murders after McVeigh's co-defendant, Terry Nichols, was tried.[184]

On June 13, 1997, Timothy McVeigh was sentenced to death for his crimes. He continued to claim that the bombing was revenge exacted for "what the U.S. government did at Waco and Ruby Ridge."[185] McVeigh frequently quoted from and alluded to *The Turner Diaries*, which justified attacks upon the federal government because the unchecked power of the government had set about to destroy the liberties of the people. In a 1,200-word essay dated March 1998, McVeigh claimed that the bombing of the Murrah Building was the "moral equivalent" to U.S. military actions against Iraq and other foreign lands:

> The administration has said that Iraq has no right to stockpile chemical or biological weapons ("weapons of mass destruction")— mainly because they have used them in the past.
>
> Well, if that's the standard by which these matters are decided, then the U.S. is the nation that set the precedent. The U.S. has stockpiled these same weapons (and more) for over 40 years. The U.S. claims this was done for deterrent purposes during its "Cold War" with the Soviet Union. Why, then, it is invalid for Iraq to claim the same reason (deterrence) with respect to Iraq's (real) war with, and the continued threat of, its neighbor Iran?

The administration claims that Iraq has used these weapons in the past. We've all seen the pictures that show a Kurdish woman and child frozen in death from the use of chemical weapons. But, have you ever seen those pictures juxtaposed next to pictures from Hiroshima or Nagasaki?

I suggest that one study the histories of World War I, World War II and other "regional conflicts" that the U.S. has been involved in to familiarize themselves with the use of "weapons of mass destruction."

Remember Dresden? How about Hanoi? Tripoli? Baghdad? What about the big ones—Hiroshima and Nagasaki? (At these two locations, the U.S. killed at least 150,000 non-combatants—mostly women and children—in the blink of an eye. Thousands more took hours, days, weeks or months to die.)

If Saddam is such a demon, and people are calling for war crimes charges and trials against him and his nation, why do we not hear the same cry for blood directed at those responsible for even greater amounts of "mass destruction"—like those responsible and involved in dropping bombs on the cities mentioned above?

The truth is, the U.S. has set the standard when it comes to the stockpiling and use of weapons of mass destruction.[186]

On May 29, 1998, the Associated Press published the remainder of McVeigh's essay:

Hypocrisy when it comes to the death of children? In Oklahoma City, it was family convenience that explained the presence of a day-care center placed between street level and the law enforcement agencies which occupied the upper floors of the building. Yet, when discussion shifts to Iraq, any day-care center in a government building instantly becomes "a shield." Think about it.

Actually, there is a difference here. The administration has admitted to knowledge of the presence of children in or near Iraqi government buildings, yet they still proceed with their plans to bomb—saying that they cannot be held responsible if children die. There is no such proof, however, that knowledge of the presence of children existed in relation to the Oklahoma City bombing.

When considering morality and "mens rea" [criminal intent], in light of these facts, I ask: Who are the true barbarians? . . .

I find it ironic, to say the least, that one of the aircraft used to drop such a bomb on Iraq is dubbed "The Spirit of Oklahoma."

This leads me to a final, and unspoken, moral hypocrisy regarding the use of weapons of mass destruction.

When a U.S. plane or cruise missile is used to bring destruction to a foreign people, this nation rewards the bombers with applause and praise. What a convenient way to absolve these killers of any responsibility for the destruction they leave in their wake.

Unfortunately, the morality of killing is not so superficial. The truth is, the use of a truck, a plane or a missile for the delivery of a weapon of mass destruction does not alter the nature of the act itself.

These are weapons of mass destruction—and the method of delivery matters little to those on the receiving end of such weapons.

Whether you wish to admit it or not, when you approve, morally, of the bombing of foreign targets by the U.S. military, you are approving of acts morally equivalent to the bombing in Oklahoma City . . . .[187]

Timothy McVeigh was executed by lethal injection on June 11, 2001, at the U.S. Federal Penitentiary in Terre Haute, Indiana. McVeigh's accomplice in the bombing, Terry Nichols, was convicted and sentenced in federal court to life in prison for his part in the conspiracy. Though it was contended by several witnesses that others had been seen with McVeigh and Nichols, no other suspect was ever found or charged.

In the aftermath of the Oklahoma City bombing, the Southern Poverty Law Center (SPLC) reported that another 60 domestic smaller-scale terrorism plots were planned from 1995 to 2005.[188] Mark Potok, SPLC director of the Intelligence Project, estimated that in 1996, there were approximately 858 domestic militias and other antigovernment groups that SPLC tracked. By 2004, the number had dropped to 154.[189] However, as will be demonstrated, since the election of Barack Obama to the U.S. presidency, these numbers have once again surged.

Those who expressed sympathy for McVeigh's actions saw the bombing as a legitimate act of war against an illegitimate power. Noted author Gore Vidal, in his essay "The Meaning of Timothy McVeigh," compared McVeigh to Paul Revere, a hero of American independence. According to Vidal's comments,

the FBI not only knew about the plot, it was involved in it. Having infiltrated the right-wing militia group that planned it, it did nothing because it wanted to pressure President Clinton into pushing through draconian anti-terrorist legislation he was refusing to sign. "Within a week of the bombing, Clinton signed it for 'the protection of the state and of persons,' using the exact language that Adolf Hitler used after the Reichstag fire of 1933."[190]

Vidal contended that the United States was in a "revolutionary situation" in that wealth had become concentrated into the hands of only 1 percent of the population. "The truth is that 80 percent are not doing well, and many of those are farmers out in the mid-west who have been driven off their land by big business. They are the backbone of the militia movement. Many of them are as crazed as you can find. But they number over 4 million, 300,000 of which are active."[191]

As in most cases of disasters that are so large that they cannot easily be explained, several conspiracy theories popped up after the Oklahoma City bombing. Among these was the contention that the government, including President Bill Clinton, knew of the bombing but did nothing to prevent it.[192] Additional theories claimed that the bombing was orchestrated by the government in order to frame the militia movement that by then was increasingly gaining followers in the United States, particularly in the aftermath of Ruby Ridge and Waco.[193] These theories emphasize that McVeigh was framed as a scapegoat for the bombing and that the real reason behind the bombing involved a desire on the part of the government to provide an impetus for new antiterrorism legislation.

This latter point did, in fact, come into being, as the U.S. government, in the aftermath of the Oklahoma City bombing, instituted the Antiterrorism and Effective Death Penalty Act of 1996.[194] This bill was intended to tighten habeas corpus laws in the United States, limiting the power of federal judges to grant relief to those in the postconviction phase. The law survived challenges to it brought before the Supreme Court in 1997 and 2005.[195] Other laws aimed themselves at limiting the amount of agricultural fertilizer that could be purchased at any one time and requiring chemical taggants to be incorporated into dynamite and other explosive devices so that a bomb could be traced to the manufacturer and the place where it had been sold.[196]

Though many who agreed with McVeigh's views believed that the bombing of the Alfred P. Murrah Federal Building was counterproductive to the cause of stemming the tide of government activism, McVeigh himself nevertheless believed that the bombing had a positive effect on government policy. For instance, McVeigh believed that the government was much more measured in its approach to its standoff with the

Montana Freemen than it had been at either Ruby Ridge or Waco. Moreover, the government's decision to reach a $3.1 million settlement with Randy Weaver and his children, together with statements by President Bill Clinton in April 2000 that he regretted the decision to storm the Branch Davidian compound, were indications to McVeigh that his act of civil and political violence had had an effect in that government was moderating its positions. As McVeigh stated, "Once you bloody the bully's nose, and he knows he's going to be punched again, he's not coming back around."[197]

THE 1990S–THE DECADE OF THE PATRIOT

The 1990s proved to be one of the most seminal decades in terms of the effects it had on the patriot/militia movement across the United States. Very early in the decade, the election of Bill Clinton signaled to many of a more conservative political bent a shift in the political winds that had dominated the country since the election 12 years earlier of Ronald Reagan. Clinton's election and his new "liberal" view of the world, coming as it did at the supposed end of the Cold War, created a "perfect storm." This storm was precipitated and fostered by several factors.

First, with the collapse of the Soviet Union at the end of 1991, the United States no longer had an identifiable enemy of the world. Indeed, as the decade dawned the winds of change—which had begun with the fall of the Berlin Wall a year before—began to signal a significant change in geopolitics. As the Soviet Union withdrew from Afghanistan and several former Soviet Bloc countries declared their independence from the Soviet Union and began full-blown independence movements, the world increasingly became unipolar, with the United States as the sole remaining superpower. The official end of the Soviet Union on December 31, 1991, solidified this perception. It also reinvigorated a movement birthed several years before—neoconservatism. Quite simply, neoconservatism held that the United States should use its vast economic and military power to reshape the world into one vast democratic society. This effort had become very clear in the United States's efforts in Iran from 1990 to 1991. In that Gulf War, the United States deployed its vast military power to the Persian Gulf region to roll back the invasion of Kuwait by Iraqi forces led by Saddam Hussein. The United States did not act alone, however. It was joined by a vast coalition of some 50 countries that acted to repel what was seen as an act of aggression no less egregious than

Adolph Hitler's dismemberment of Czechoslovakia some 50 years before.

Second, the "collective action" that took place against Iraq was not merely at the behest or direction of the United States. In fact, for only the second time in its history, countries came together under the auspices and authority of the United Nations. This fact caused even President Bush to declare early in 1991 that a "new world order" had been established, an order that would see the United States working much more in concert with the United Nations and its stated goal of world peace and prosperity. To those who had nurtured a distrust and hatred of government, an appeal to what many supposed to be a "global government" was antithetical to the American way of life and unilateralism that had come to epitomize most of the history of American foreign policy. With Bill Clinton's election in late 1992 and the signing into law soon thereafter of the North American Free Trade Agreement (NAFTA), anger at government began to grow.

Third, the anger that was simmering against the U.S. government because of its growth in scope and power was punctuated by events such as Ruby Ridge and Waco. The actions of the government during these events caused many—even supporters of government—to wonder whether the greatest fears of the Founders were coming true—that there comes a time in the life of every government when it degenerates so far from its original intentions that there is nothing left to do but to begin again. The "over-the-top" actions of the government in relation to its citizens seemed to confirm to many skeptics that the federal system of governance was no longer operating as it had been intended to.

Fourth, the bombing of the Murrah Federal Building in Oklahoma City in April 1995 clearly demonstrated that there were those whose anger at the government was so palpable that they were willing to go to extreme lengths to push forward the need for change. The aftermath of the Oklahoma City bombing, taken in concert with the sieges of Ruby Ridge and Waco, saw increased efforts on the part of the federal government to increase regulatory practices, particularly as they related to firearms and other material that could be used in defending oneself against government excess or striking back at government if the need arose.

Taken together, these events galvanized the patriot/militia movement and laid the groundwork for the groups that still exist today. As noted, the actions of the government during the first half of the 1990s were "examples of a government willing to stop at nothing to stamp out people who refused to conform."[198] Many people during the 1990s joined the fledgling militia groups then forming "as a way to protect more aggressively their right to bear arms; even today, gun-related issues dominate many of the newsletters published by militia groups."[199] Coupled with the suspicions of a heavy-handed and unresponsive government, militia members developed a fascination with conspiracies. As noted by the Anti-Defamation League (ADL), however, they were not content to stick with accepted conspiracy theories. Rather,

> they described a shadowy movement intent on creating a one-world socialist government no matter what the cost. This "New World Order," using the United Nations as its primary tool, had already taken over most of the planet. The United States was still a bastion of freedom, but its own government was collaborating with New World Order forces to strip Americans slowly of their freedoms in preparation for the final takeover. The government was erecting large numbers of concentration camps in which to place American dissenters; meanwhile, the number of United Nations troops secretly encamped in national parks grew by the month. Stickers on the backs of street signs would guide the New World Order to strategic points, while the authorities enlisted urban street gangs to help enforce gun confiscation.[200]

Christian Identity member George Eaton in 1993 wrote that the U.S. government and the media were "fighting a war against independent thinking Christian patriots. . . . The reason they have targeted patriots is simple, they will not conform or submit to the New World Order."[201]

At the same time as the patriot/militia movement was ramping up its physical presence, its message was getting out via the emerging media outlets that were echoing its ideas (e.g., Patriot Voices Radio). Among the more prominent of these sites was the Patriot Post, founded as the Federalist in 1996.[202] The Patriot Post, in its vision statement, articulates many of the same positions and arguments often held by patriots and militia groups, namely, a belief in limited government, a balance of power between the federal government and state governments, and a reverence for the wording and the intentions of the Constitution. In addition to these ideas, the Patriot Post affirms its belief and "reliance upon and commitment to the God of Christendom, the Father, Son, and Holy Spirit."[203]

The Patriot Post makes no apologies that it is an organization on the right side of the political spectrum that espouses conservative values and will cover topics from this perspective. A brief examination of topics on one particular day noted articles that talked of taking from the rich to give to the poor, the travesty of Obamacare, the "Employee Protection Agency" instead of the Environmental Protection Agency, and the "plot to muzzle free speech."[204] Through sites like the Patriot Post, the patriot movement is well versed in the programs and policies of the federal government that lie at odds with their view of the world.

Y2K AND THE PATRIOT MOVEMENT

As the decade of the 1990s drew to a close, membership in many patriot/militia groups declined. At least part of this decline stemmed from government efforts to rein in more violent groups and the pursuit, arrest, and prosecution of some of the more violent members of the militia movement. As the decade closed, federal officials arrested a Florida militia leader and others that were accused of plotting to destroy a nuclear power plant.[205] Another plot discovered in Sacramento, California, accused militia members of plotting to blow up a propane storage facility.[206] These two incidents, along with others, demonstrated the lengths to which some individuals and groups were willing to go in order to disrupt the government. Like the events of Oklahoma City, civilian deaths were of secondary concern. Indeed, had these attacks been carried out, it is quite possible that hundreds and perhaps even thousands of Americans could have been killed. As had been the case all along, the goal of disrupting the federal government for the purpose of change or revolution justified in the minds of many in the patriot and militia movement the need for more and more violent means of political protest.

The approach of the millennium was a boon to many patriot/militia groups, as they saw the anarchy associated with Y2K scenarios as a "clarion call for their followers."[207] As one pundit noted:

> Serving as a touchstone among the movement's conspiracy theories and symbolizing its worst fears of government repression and nationwide anarchy, the Y2K computer "bug" represents [sic] for many of these far-right extremists a problem far beyond the capacity of the Federal Government to control. . . . Relying on computer and fax networks, shortwave radio, AM talk radio, and video and audio tape distribution, the fundamental message was always the same: the U.S. Government is run by a secret network of elites, who are engaged in a vast conspiracy to deny Americans their

constitutional rights and create a New World Order via a globalist
U.N. police state.[208]

The leaders of several patriot/militia organizations chimed in on the
Y2K threat prior to the turn of the millennium. Militia of Montana
(MOM) leader John Trochmann stated that the federal government was
in possession of "secret" reports that assessed the social, economic, and
political fallout that would result from Y2K disruptions in various
American cities. He also claimed that branches of the U.S. military
were involved in a coordinated effort to ensure the unpreparedness of
the American public in the event of Y2K breakdowns. As he stated:

Folks, the deception has just been blown away. Branches of the
U.S. Government have known, apparently for quite some time,
that Y2K was likely to result in major infrastructure failures in
highly populated cities. They deliberately withheld this information from the American people. . . .
. . . We need to expose corruption in America. . . . I believe when
Y2K hits there will be Federal troops on every street corner. I've
got documents to prove it.[209]

One of the founders of the Michigan Militia, Norm Olson, also
chimed in on the Y2K threat. His call for action was somewhat more
ominous than Trochmann's. He stated,

It appears that the devastation of Y2K is only now being truthfully
considered. That alone ought to give us pause, but still greater in
scope and scale is what may follow; for, unless there is a miraculous
spiritual and moral change in the attitude of this nation, armed
revolution is inevitable. Nothing can stop it. And so we prepare.
That, my friends, is what the militia is all about.[210]

Leading up to Y2K, many patriot/militia groups attempted to "cash
in" on the fears being perpetrated in the popular media as well as those
being circulated among the groups themselves. Leading up to the turn
of the millennium, "preparedness expos" at which patriot and militia
members could browse through survival products and discuss conspiracy theories in roundtable settings peppered the calendar. The topics
often included "the virtues of various types of firearms, how to build
underground shelters, purify water and survive underground for a
lengthy period of time."[211]

Fears of the chaos caused by Y2K exacerbated calls against the New World Order—a popular target of the patriot/militia movement. At one preparedness expo, it was intimated that the Y2K crisis was being precipitated by the "leftist revolution" in the United States. Organizations that preyed upon the fears of financial collapse also began to spring up. One such organization—the National Organization for the Repeal of the Federal Reserve Act and the Internal Revenue Code [NORFED]—promoted "liberty currency." This currency claimed to be

> America's only silver-backed Currency—[which] provides you with a legal Warehouse Receipt which is your title of ownership to pure .999 fine silver. Redeemable in pure silver at over 100 Redemption Centers throughout the nation, this currency will not be devalued in any coming financial collapse, such as may follow the year 2000 "Y2K" computer crash.[212]

Perhaps the most brazen of the patriot/militia profiteers was Bo Gritz—former Green Beret, presidential candidate, and negotiator at Ruby Ridge, Idaho—who purportedly trained hundreds of antigovernment individuals in techniques designed to thwart the New World Order. In 1999, he told a crowd of hundreds in Kansas City, Missouri, that "Y2K could bring chaos to the nation and the world. . . . For the general good, regulations could be imposed that turn you into less than an American."[213] Gritz also established SPIKE—Specially Prepared Individuals for Key Events—where he taught participants all manner of survival skills and techniques. Gritz also attempted to sell plots of land in a common law community called Almost Heaven, offering buyers an escape from cities, where the effects of Y2K would no doubt be the worst. Gritz also sold dozens of different survival products ranging in price from a few dollars to several hundred dollars.[214]

Though Y2K failed to materialize, the problems presented by the patriot/militia community became more acute to government officials and emergency planners. As noted by the Anti-Defamation League,

> The onset of the millennium and its Y2K problem confront our society with an important and potentially dangerous challenge: how to deal with the prospect of hundreds, perhaps thousands, of extremists in possession of a large supply of firearms and survival gear, suspicious of government and of major social institutions and preparing for the worst, being urged by conspiratorial propaganda toward some "emergency" action against perceived "enemies."[215]

As the millennium dawned and massive disruptions failed to materialize, the patriot/militia movement stalled for a brief period of time. The election of a conservative candidate, George W. Bush of Texas, in the November 2000 U.S. presidential election quieted groups for a brief period of time. The hiatus was brief, however, as the attacks of September 11, 2001, brought patriot/militia groups back to the forefront, particularly as these groups tended to perpetuate the conspiratorial ideas that the U.S. government itself had orchestrated 9/11 and that all Jews who worked in the World Trade Center and the Pentagon had been warned to stay away from work on the morning of September 11.[216] As noted by the SPLC, the number of hate groups in the United States rose 56 percent from 2000 to 2013. The SPLC speculates that the surge was fueled by a poor economy, the influx of illegal immigrants into the United States, and a diminishing white majority.[217]

The sentiment about the dangers of illegal immigration was famously echoed in a book by noted author Samuel P. Huntington, who wrote *Who Are We: The Challenges to America's National Identity* in 2005.[218] Huntington, a tenured professor of government at Harvard University, was widely seen as a conservative voice in an otherwise liberal field of study (i.e., political science). Yet his works had always been largely characterized by large doses of realism, as illustrated in his texts *The Soldier and the State: The Theory and Politics of Civil-Military Relations* (1957) and *The Clash of Civilizations and the Remaking of World Order* (1996). In a review of *Who Are We?* in the journal *Foreign Affairs*, commentator Alan Wolfe noted that Huntington "eschews realistic treatment of American history in favor of romantic nostalgia for Anglo-Protestant culture."[219] Wolfe continues that the book is inherently "fatalistic," with Huntington often reminding the readers that he is a "patriot . . . deeply concerned about the unity and strength of my country based on liberty, equality, law and individual rights."[220] Wolfe notes that Huntington points out that average Americans tend to be more "patriotic and nationalistic" than liberal elites.

Huntington, who espouses what some have called the American Creed, wrote that the United States had always been characterized as an Anglo-Protestant country where immigrants had assimilated and accepted the general concept of the creed. Yet illegal immigration, particularly from Hispanic-Catholic lands, is changing the demographic characteristics of the United States, so much so that Huntington was left to pose the question "Who are we?" Wolfe concludes his review by noting that Huntington points out that it is "perfectly reasonable to ask people without Anglo-Protestant roots to adapt their culture to the one that existed here from the beginning."[221] Huntington does not go so far as to bemoan the end of the white race in America, but he does resort to "nativism." According to Wolfe, Huntington does not believe that nativism should be defined by "extremist militias and the Ku Klux Klan but rather should be embraced by those who fear that an internal minority is on its way to becoming a majority."[222]

Huntington's query to "average America," which he believes is much more in tune with patriotism and nationalism than the political and liberal elites who govern, is indicative of the types of sentiments expressed by patriot/militia groups. However, within these communities, these sentiments quickly turn to frustration and rage as patriots and militia members confront the new realities of the modern world. As they have in the past, these frustrations suggest that there exists a real possibility that violence (i.e., domestic terrorism) may ensue in the future as groups that formerly considered themselves empowered (i.e., white males) find themselves marginalized by the changing dynamism of a culture that is becoming less white and a culture in which women are increasingly flexing more of their political muscles. Much like the phenomenon in the international realm in which we see Islamic extremists "striking back" because of the perception that they have been ignored, disenfranchised, marginalized, and the like, and that the culture in which they were raised is no longer their own, American patriot/militia groups are beginning to articulate some of these same sentiments. In the immediate aftermath of President Barack Obama's reelection in 2012, an article in the journal *Foreign Policy* noted that white nationalist groups were thrilled by the reelection of Barack Obama, as they believed that it would reenergize "traditional America" and "the white establishment" to come to the realization that they are now politically "impotent," giving rise to the possibility of widespread violence and rebellion. This possibility is becoming reality.

In April 2014, a feud between a Nevada cattle rancher, Cliven Bundy, and the United States Bureau of Land Management (BLM) escalated into a standoff between Bundy and his supporters and the federal government. The feud between Bundy and the BLM had been simmering for 20 years but came to head in March 2014 when the BLM decided to close nearly 145,000 acres of federal land where cattle had grazed for years. The BLM decided to close the range and "capture, impound, and remove trespass cattle."[223] As BLM officials began a cattle roundup on April 5, 2014, a group of protestors, some of whom were armed, blocked their way. The BLM ended the cattle roundup in order to prevent an escalation of the conflict.

In the ensuing weeks, the views of Cliven Bundy and many of his neighbors in the area surrounding the BLM land became known. Bundy can rightly be described as an adherent of the ideas and philosophies of Posse Comitatus. Thus, he believes that the county sheriff is the highest legal authority, with authority greater than that of any federal law enforcement officer, elected official, or local law enforcement.[224] Bundy has stated categorically that he does not recognize nor will he submit to federal police power, believing instead that federally owned land belongs to the "sovereign state of Nevada."[225] Bundy has said, "I abide by all Nevada state laws. But I don't recognize the United States government as even existing."[226] Bundy denies the power of federal courts over Nevada land, telling his supporters, "We definitely don't recognize [the BLM director's] jurisdiction or authority, his arresting power or policing power in any way."[227] Bundy has frequently used language consistent with that of the sovereign citizen movement, which believes that the U.S. government is illegitimate, and has gained the support of such groups as the Oath Keepers, White Mountain Militia, and the Praetorian Guard militias.[228]

The sovereign citizen movement is characterized by the FBI as one of the top domestic terrorist threats in the United States.[229] Cliven Bundy's views have been characterized by the SPLC as being consistent with "the self-described 'patriot' groups [who are] focused on secession, nullification, state sovereignty, and the principle that 'powers not delegated to the United States by the Constitution, nor prohibited by it to the States, are reserved to the States respectively, or to the people,' and their views overlap with other groups organized around hate."[230]

As Bundy's feud with the federal government continues at this writing, a Nevada congressman has said that Bundy's supporters need to vacate the area. Self-described "citizen soldiers," many brandishing semi-automatic weapons, have been standing outside of Cliven Bundy's ranch for weeks. These self-proclaimed militia members are "serving their purpose," according to Bundy's wife.[231] And while many conservative lawmakers initially sided with Bundy and his fight with the federal government, noting it was an example of "federal overreach," they have since recanted much of this support when Bundy made very pointed and disparaging remarks about African Americans.[232]

Cliven Bundy's supporters are not confined to Nevada, however. Protestors in Utah have also disregarded directives of the Bureau of Land Management. In direct violation of a BLM directive that closed an area of southwestern Utah known as Recapture Canyon, protestors intended to ride all-terrain vehicles (ATVs) into the closed area, claiming that the federal government has no right to close the land to the public. Many of the militia who had been standing watch outside of Bundy's ranch in Nevada traveled to Utah to participate in the ATV protest ride. When Carol Bundy, Cliven Bundy's wife, was asked whether the militia members were armed, she responded, "They're militia. Of course they're carrying weapons."[233]

Cliven Bundy's story is only one of dozens now taking place in areas around the United States. Patriot groups and self-styled militias are growing increasingly frustrated over their perceptions of an unresponsive and overreaching federal government that takes little note of citizen concerns. As noted by Samuel P. Huntington earlier, these individuals view the "Washington elite" as disconnected from the average, real American, who is much more patriotic and conservative than they are. Hearkening back to President Richard Nixon's claim that there was a vast "silent majority" that supported the U.S. cause in Vietnam, patriot/militia groups today believe that more and more Americans are waking up to the excesses of the liberal elite, who have pushed an agenda that includes, among other things, gender and marriage equality, environmentalism (including appeals to global warming), increased taxation, more social programs, decreased military spending, and more stringent gun control laws—just to name a few. The "patriots" of today embrace a philosophy of limited government, the sanctity of the U.S. Constitution, the inviolate nature of the 2nd and 10th Amendments, and a desire to return the United States culture to a simpler, more easy time. In their pursuit of these goals, they often come face to face with the reality of a modern, globalized world that does not share, nor does it easily tolerate, views that attempt to bring about cultural devolution. This, then, is the tension that the American patriot of today faces.

NOTES

1. Suprynowicz, Vin. 1999. "The Courtesan Press, Eager Lapdogs to Tyranny." *Send in the Waco Killers—Essays on the Freedom Movement, 1993–1998*. Mountain Media, p. 288. See also *Randy Weaver interview at Ruby Ridge*. 2000. Reality Productions Group for TLC (The Learning Channel).

2. Weaver, Randy, and Sara Weaver. 1998. *The Federal Siege at Ruby Ridge: In Our Own Words*. Ruby Ridge, Inc.

3. Ibid.

4. Department of Justice Office of Professional Responsibility. 1994. Ruby Ridge Task Force Report, June 10.

5. Walter, Jess. 2002. *Ruby Ridge: The Truth and Tragedy of the Randy Weaver Family*. Harper Perennial, pp. 63–65.

6. DOJ Office of Professional Responsibility Ruby Ridge Task Force Report.

7. Ruby Ridge: Report of the Subcommittee on Terrorism, Technology and Government Information of the Senate Committee on the Judiciary. 1995. A federal grand jury would later indict Weaver for "making and possessing, but not for selling, illegal weapons" (DOJ Office of Professional Responsibility Ruby Ridge Task Force Report).

8. "Department of Justice Report Regarding Internal Investigation of Shootings at Ruby Ridge, Idaho During Arrest of Randy Weaver." n.d. *Byington.org*. See at http://www.byington.org/carl/ruby/ruby1.htm. (Accessed January 10, 2014).

9. Ibid.

10. "Feds Have Fugitive 'Under Our Nose.'" 1992. *Spokane Spokesman Review*. (March 1, A19). See also "Marshals Know He's There But Leave Fugitive Alone." 1992. *New York Times*. (March 13, A14).

11. Walter, p. 140.

12. Ibid.

13. DOJ Office of Professional Responsibility Ruby Ridge Task Force Report.

14. Walter, p. 132.

15. DOJ OPR Ruby Ridge Task Force Report, June 10, 1994, attributes the quote "if a man enters my property with a gun to do me harm, you can bet that I'm going to shoot him to protect myself" to Weaver citing Report of Investigation by Mays, March 6, 1991, at 2, and also notes, "Law enforcement regarded the Griders as "more radical and dangerous than Weaver."

16. DOJ OPR Ruby Ridge Task Force Report, June 10, 1994, Section VI Chronology of Events.

17. DOJ OPR Ruby Ridge Task Force Report, Section IV, Specific Issues Investigated, C. Efforts by the Marshals Service to Effect the Arrest of Weaver, footnote 246.

18. Weland, Mike. 1992. "An Interview with the Randy Weaver Family." *Bonners Ferry Herald*. (May 2). See at http://law2.umkc.edu/faculty/projects/ftrials/weaver/dojrubyIVC.htm. (Accessed January 12, 2014).

19. DOJ OPR Ruby Ridge Task Force Report, June 10, 1994, footnote 1196: "Only one of the four people in the helicopter thought he heard shots; the other three heard nothing but were certain that

the helicopter had not taken fire." A photographer in the helicopter saw someone gesture at the helicopter and thought he heard two shots on a boom microphone. FD-302 Interview of Dave Marlin, September 16, 1992. However, another passenger said that no shots had been fired and that "it would have been 'grossly unfair' to accuse the Weavers of shooting." FD-302 Interview of Richard Weiss, September 11 & 18, 1992, at 1–2; see FD-302 Interview of Brooke Skulski, September 28, 1992. Weaver denied that shots had been fired at the helicopter. See also "Fugitive: No Surrender." 1992. *Coeur D'Alene Press* (May 3, p. 1).

20. DOJ Office of Professional Responsibility Ruby Ridge Task Force Report. "Report of the Ruby Ridge Task Force to the Office of Professional Responsibility of Investigation of Allegations of Improper Governmental Conduct in the Investigation, Apprehension and Prosecution of Randall C. Weaver and Kevin L. Harris." 1994. USDOJ. See at http://www.justice.gov/opr/readingroom/rubyreportcover_39.pdf. (Accessed March 10, 2014).

21. Suprynowicz, p. 288.

22. DOJ Office of Professional Responsibility Ruby Ridge Task Force Report, p. 12.

23. "Ruby Ridge: Report of the Subcommittee on Terrorism, Technology and Government Information." 1992. "Firefight." *United States Marshal Service*. (August 21, Section B), pp. 38–49. See also Walter, pp. 163–180.

24. Suprynowicz, p. 291. See also Lynch, Tim. 2002. "Remember Ruby Ridge." CATO Institute. (August 21). See at http://www.cato.org/publications/commentary/remember-ruby-ridge. (Accessed January 12, 2014).

25. U.S. Department of Justice, Office of Professional Responsibility, Ruby Ridge Task Force Report, June 10, 1994, Section IV. Specific Issues Investigated, D. Marshals Service Activities Between August 17 and August 21, 1992.

26. Weaver and Sara Weaver.

27. Walter, p. 390.

28. DOJ OPR Ruby Ridge Task Force Report, June 10, 1994. "USMS Crisis Center Log August 21, 1992, placed U.S. Border Patrol among respondents at Ruby Ridge." DOJ OPR Ruby Ridge Task Force Report, June 10, 1994, p. 235.

29. DOJ OPR Ruby Ridge Task Force Report, June 10, 1994, Section IV. Specific Issues Investigated, F. "FBI'S Rules of Engagement" and "Operations" on August 21 and August 22, 1992.

30. Walter, Jess. 1995. *Every Knee Shall Bow: The Truth and Tragedy of Ruby Ridge & the Randy Weaver Family*. HarperCollins, p. 190.

31. DOJ OPR Ruby Ridge Task Force Report, June 10, 1994, Section IV. Specific Issues Investigated, F. "FBI'S Rules of Engagement" and "Operations" on August 21 and August 22, 1992.

32. Ibid.

33. Ibid., pp. 156–193, 200–208.

34. Witkin, Gordon. 1995. "The Nightmare of Idaho's Ruby Ridge." *US News & World Report*. (September 11).

35. Hewitt, Bill. 1995. "A Time to Heal." *People Weekly*. (September 25). See also Norganthau, Tom. 1995. "The Echoes of Ruby Ridge." *Newsweek*. (August 28).

36. Concurring, the Ruby Ridge: Report of the Subcommittee on Terrorism, Technology and Government Information of the Senate Committee on the Judiciary, 1995, stated, "Legality of the Second Shot—The Subcommittee believes that the second shot was inconsistent with the FBI's standard deadly force policy and was unconstitutional. It was even inconsistent with the special Rules of Engagement."

37. Witkin, p. 24.

38. Ruby Ridge: Report of the Subcommittee on Terrorism, Technology and Government Information of the Senate Committee on the Judiciary. 1995. See also Coulson, Danny, and Elaine Shannon. 1999. *No Heroes: Inside the FBI's Secret Counter-Terror Force*. Pocket Books.

39. Walter. See also Bock, Alan W., and Dean Koontz. 1995. *Ambush at Ruby Ridge: How Government Agents Set Randy Weaver Up and Took His Family Down*. Dickens Press.

40. Bringhurst, Newell G., and Craig L. Foster. 2008. *The Mormon Quest for the Presidency*. John Whitmer Books, pp. 208–226.

41. Berlet, Chip, and Matthew N. Lyons. 2000. *Right-Wing Populism in America: Too Close for Comfort*. Guilford Press, p. 340.

42. Bringhurst and Foster, pp. 208–226.

43. Neiwert, David A. 1999. *In God's Country: The Patriot Movement in the Pacific Northwest*. Washington State University Press, p. 66.

44. "Department of Justice Report: Internal Investigation of Shootings at Ruby Ridge, Idaho During Arrest of Randall Weaver (1994)." See at http://law2.umkc.edu/faculty/projects/ftrials/weaver/dojruby1.html. (Accessed January 15, 2014).

45. Ruby Ridge: Report of the Subcommittee on Terrorism, Technology and Government Information, 1995. See at http://law2.umkc.edu/faculty/projects/ftrials/weaver/weaversenate.html. (Accessed January 15, 2014).

46. Labaton, Stephen. 1995. "Separatist Family Given $3.1 Million from Government." *New York Times* (August 16). See also Ostrow, Ronald J. 1995. "U.S. to Pay $3.1 Million for '92 Idaho Shootout: Court: Settlement in Weaver case reflects loss of mother, son in Ruby Ridge incident. But wrongdoing is denied." *Los Angeles Times* (August 16).

47. Lynch, http://www.cato.org/publications/commentary/remember-ruby-ridge.

48. Opening Statement of Louis J. Freeh, Director Federal Bureau of Investigation, before the Subcommittee on Terrorism, Technology, and Government Information Committee on the Judiciary—Ruby Ridge Hearing, United States Senate, October 19, 1995. See at http://www.fas.org/irp/congress/1995_hr/s951019f.htm. (Accessed January 17, 2014).

49. Walter, pp. 392–393.

50. "Scholars Tackle 'Cult' Questions 20 Years after Branch Davidian Tragedy." 2013. WacoTrib.com: Religion. *WacoTrib.com*. (April 13). Found at http://www.wacotrib.com/news/religion/scholars-tackle-cult-questions-years-after-branch-davidian-tragedy/article_a3fa463e-d1b4-5eda-b49e-95327bc276d7.html.

51. Ibid.

52. "Stairway to Heaven; Treating Children in the Crosshairs of Trauma." Excerpt from Perry, Bruce, and Maia Szalavitz. 2007. *The Boy Who Was Raised as a Dog: And Other Stories from a Child Psychiatrist's Notebook*. Basic Books.

53. "Adventists Kicked Out Cult Leader." 1993. *Chicago Tribune*. (March).

54. Breault, Mark, and Martin King. 1995. *Inside the Cult: A Member's Chilling, Exclusive Account of Madness and Depravity in David Koresh's Compound*. Signet.

55. Breault and King. See also Fantz, Ashley. 2011. "18 Years After Waco, Davidians Believe Koresh Was God." CNN.com. (April 14). Found at http://www.cnn.com/2011/US/04/14/waco.koresh.believers/.

56. Breault and King, n.p.

57. Linedecker, Clifford L. 1993. *Massacre at Waco: The Shocking True Story of Cult Leader David Koresh and the Branch Davidians*. St. Martin's Paperbacks, p. 94.

58. Higgins, Steve. 1995. "The Waco Dispute—Why the ATF Had to Act." *The Washington Post*. (July 2).

59. "Tripped Up By Lies: A Report Paints a Devastating Portrait of ATF's Waco Planning—or, Rather, the Lack of it." 1993. *Time Magazine*. (October 11).

60. In United States law, a machine gun is defined (in part) by the National Firearms Act of 1934, 26 U.S.C. § 5845(b) as "any weapon which shoots . . . automatically more than one shot, without manual reloading, by a single function of the trigger."

61. Affidavit for search and seizure warrant by Aguillera, Special Agent, U.S. Treasury Department, BATF, Austin, Texas, signed February 25, 2009.

62. "A Believer Says Cult in Texas Is Peaceful, Despite Shootout." 1993. *New York Times*. (March 6).

63. Bates, Albert K. 1993. "Showtime at Waco." *Communities Magazine*. Thefarm.org. (February 23). Found at http://www.thefarm. org/lifestyle/albertbates/akbwaco.html.

64. U.S. House of Representatives Report, "Activities of Federal Law Enforcement Agencies Toward the Branch Davidians," Section 5, 1.3 c. the alleged drug nexus: "ATF did not mention a drug lab or possession of illegal drugs as suspected crimes in its search warrant." See also Lujan, Thomas R. 1997. "Legal Aspects of Domestic Employment of the Army." *Parameters: U.S. Army War College Quarterly* XXVII(3).

65. England, Mark, and Darlene McCormack. 1993. "The Sinful Messiah." *Waco Tribune-Herald* (February 27), p. 1A.

66. Ibid.

67. Rawles, Neil. 2007. *Inside Waco* (television documentary). Channel 4/HBO.

68. "Agents Prepared for Worst Before Waco Raid." 2000. *Associated Press* (July 5). See also "Davidian Criminal Trial Transcripts," Richardson—Cross (Mr. Rentz), pp. 2054–2055.

69. Bovard, James. 1995. "Not So Wacko." *The New Republic* (May 15). Bovard reports that "Rolland Ballestros, one of the first ATF agents out of the cattle trucks, told Texas Rangers and Waco police shortly after the raid that he thought the first shots came from agents aiming at the Davidians' dogs."

70. U.S. House of Representatives Report, "Pre-raid Military Assistance Requested by ATF and Assistance Actually Received." 1996. See at http://www.gpo.gov/fdsys/pkg/CRPT-104hrpt749/html/ CRPT-104hrpt749.htm. (Accessed February 24, 2014).

71. Gazecki, William. 2003. *Waco—The Rules of Engagement* (film documentary). New Yorker Video.

72. Rawles, *Inside Waco*.

73. "Report and Recommendations. Concerning the Handling of Incidents Such as the Branch Davidian Standoff in Waco Texas."

October 10, 1993. See at http://www.pbs.org/wgbh/pages/frontline/waco/stonerpt.html. (Accessed February 25, 2014).

74. FBI. 2000. "Project Megiddo" (January 31), p. 29. See at http://www.fbi.gov/. See also United States Department of Justice, "Operation Megiddo," November 2, 1999.

75. Rawles, *Inside Waco*.

76. Davies, Nick. 1994. "Lost in America." *The Guardian*. (January 14).

77. Dennis, Edward S. G. Jr. 1993, October 8. *PBS Frontline*. Waco Timeline from the USDOJ report. "Evaluation of the Handling of the Branch Davidian Stand-off in Waco, Texas, February 28 to April 19, 1993," p. 11. See at http://www.justice.gov/publications/waco/wacotx.pdf. (Accessed February 28, 2014).

78. http://www.pbs.org/wgbh/pages/frontline/waco/timeline.html.

79. Testimony to the Subcommittee on National Security et al., *Congressional Record*, July, 1995. Referenced at http://www.newworldencyclopedia.org/entry/Waco_%22cult%22_and_fire.

80. Stange, Mary Zeiss. 2001."U.S. Ignores Religion's Fringes." *USA Today*. (October 3). See at http://usatoday30.usatoday.com/news/opinion/2001-10-04-ncguest2.htm. (Accessed May 20, 2014).

81. Ibid.

82. Rawles, *Inside Waco*.

83. Clinton, Bill. 2004. *My Life*. Alfred A. Knopf, pp. 497–499.

84. Rosenbloom, Joe III. 1995. "Waco: More than Simple Blunders?" *Wall Street Journal*. (October 17).

85. Associated Press. 1993. "Tanks, Chemicals Couldn't Break Resolve of Cultists." *Washington Times*. (April 23).

86. http://www.carolmoore.net/waco/TDM-10.html.

87. "Report to the Deputy Attorney General on the Events at Waco, Texas/The Aftermath of the April 19 Fire: 'The Fire Development Analysis' section." See at http://www.justice.gov/publications/waco/wacotocpg.htm. (Accessed March 10, 2014).

88. *Waco: "The Rules of Engagement."* 1997 (film). Directed by William Gazecki. Produced by Michael McNulty. See also Congressional testimony and interviews of Branch Davidian survivors David Thibodeau, Clive Doyle, and Derek Lovelock. See also Thibodeau, David, and Leon Whiteson. 1999. *A Place Called Waco: A Survivor's Story*. HarperCollins.

89. Danforth, John C. Special Counsel. 2000. "Final Report to the Deputy Attorney General Concerning the 1993 Confrontation at the Mt. Carmel Complex, Waco Texas." (Issued November 8). See at http://www.cesnur.org/testi/DanforthRpt.pdf. (Accessed March 25, 2014).

90. Associated Press. "Indictment of Branch Davidians is Expanded." 1993. Deseret News. (August 7).

91. "Six Branch Davidians due for Release 13 Years After Waco Inferno." 2006. *FoxNews* (April 19).

92. Klaidman, Daniel, and Michael Isikoff. 1999. "A Fire That Won't Die." *Newsweek*. (July 19).

93. Ibid.

94. Ibid.

95. Ibid.

96. Ibid.

97. Kopel, David B., and Paul H. Blackman. 1999. "Fanning the Flames of Waco." *CATO Institute*. (September 8). See at http://www.cato.org/publications/commentary/fanning-flames-waco. (Accessed March 26, 2014).

98. "Koresh's Lawyer Critical of Danforth Report." 2000. *UPI*. (July 22). See also Lichtblau, Eric. 2000. "Report Clears Feds in Deaths of Davidians." *Los Angeles Times*. (July 22).

99. Anti-Defamation League. 2005. "The Militia Movement." *Extremism in America*. See at http://archive.adl.org/learn/ext_us/militia_m.html.

100. Ibid.

101. Ibid.

102. Anti-Defamation League, "Militia of Montana."

103. Ibid.

104. Ibid.

105. Ibid. According to the Anti-Defamation League, MOM would largely repudiate these ideas by the end of 1995.

106. Michael, Kelly. 1995. "The Road to Paranoia." *The New Yorker*. (June 19).

107. Hoffman, Bruce. 1998. *Inside Terrorism*. Columbia University Press, p. 104.

108. Ibid.

109. Leap, Dennis. 2000. "America's Militia Threat." *The Trumpet.com*. (March/April). See at http://www.thetrumpet.com/article/255.26165.21.0/world/americas-militia-threat.

110. Ibid.

111. The Brady Bill was proposed in the aftermath of Reagan Press Secretary James Brady's critical wounding during an assassination attempt on President Reagan, and the Assault Weapons Ban had been proposed after 34 children and a teacher were shot in 1989 in Stockton, California, by an individual wielding a semi-automatic replica of an

AK-47 assault rifle. See Adams, Jane Meredith. 1995. "Sparked By School Massacre, Gun Debate Still Rages." *Chicago Tribune*. (May 29). As Adams would write: "Every murder horrifies, but the massacre of five children as they ran screaming that sunny January morning, and the wounding of 30 others, including a teacher, packed such emotional power it ignited the nascent anti–assault weapons movement."

112. Anti-Defamation League, "Militia of Montana."

113. Ibid.

114. Ibid.

115. Ibid.

116. Ibid.

117. Militia of Montana. "Statement of Purpose." See at http://www.militiaofmontana.com/.

118. Maue, Kenneth C. n.d. "What Is the Militia?" Militia of Montana. See at http://www.militiaofmontana.com/whomom.htm. (Accessed March 30, 2014).

119. "1983–1995: Anti-Government Tax Resisters Begin Forming 'Montana Freemen.'" *History Commons*. See at http://www.historycommons.org/timeline.jsp?timeline=us_domestic_terrorism_tmln&haitian_elite_2021_organizations=haitian_elite_2021_freemen.

120. Ibid.

121. Thackeray, Lorna. 2006. "The Freemen Standoff: In 1996, Region Held Its Breath for 81 Days While World Watched." *Billings Gazette* (March 25). See at http://billingsgazette.com/news/state-and-regional/montana/the-freemen-standoff/article_52ea8d8f-c28e-5170-8b65-8c5f71ea4fe9.html. (Accessed March 31, 2014).

122. Ibid.

123. Anti-Defamation League, "Militia of Montana."

124. Ibid.

125. Morlin, Bill. 2011. "Montana Freeman Leader Dies In Prison." 2011. *Hatewatch*. Southern Poverty Law Center. (September 21). See at http://www.splcenter.org/blog/2011/09/21/montana-freeman-leader-dies-in-prison/. (Accessed March 30, 2014).

126. Thackeray,

127. Ibid.

128. Ibid.

129. Morlin,

130. Shannan, Pat. 2011. "Untold Story of the Montana Freemen." *American Free Press Newspaper* (October 7). See at http://americanfree press.net/?p=888. (Accessed March 31, 2014).

131. Ibid.

132. Ibid.

133. Ibid.

134. Ibid.

135. Ibid.

136. Ibid.

137. http://www.michiganmilitia.com/.

138. Potok, Mark. 1996. "Militant Fringe is Setting Off Alarms." *New York Times.* (March 31).

139. Olson, Norman. 1995. Testimony before the Senate Subcommittee on Anti-Terrorism. (June 15). See at http://www.potowmack.org /emerappb.html. (Accessed March 15, 2014).

140. Ibid.

141. http://www.michiganmilitia.com/.

142. NDAA, Sec. 1021.c.1

143. "Belligerent Act." n.d. http://belligerentact.org/.

144. Ibid.

145. Ibid.

146. Militia of Montana. "One Bullet at a Time: That's How You'll Get Our Guns." Found at http://www.militiaofmontana.com/reports. htm.

147. Belligerant Act.

148. Ibid.

149. Kaminski, John P., ed. 2006. *The Quotable Jefferson.* Princeton University Press, p. 390.

150. Ibid., p. 119.

151. "McVeigh author Dan Herbeck Quizzed." *BBC News.* June 11, 2001. See at http://news.bbc.co.uk/2/hi/talking_point/forum/1378651. stm. (Accessed March 3, 2014).

152. Herbeck, Dan. 2001. "Inside McVeigh's Mind." *BBC News.* June 11, 2001.

153. Linder, Douglas O. 2006. "The Oklahoma City Bombing & the Trial of Timothy McVeigh." University of Missouri–Kansas City, Law School Faculty Projects. See at http://law2.umkc.edu/faculty/projects/ ftrials/mcveigh/mcveightrial.html. See also "People in the News: Timothy McVeigh: The Path to Death Row." Transcript of program broadcast on CNN, June 9, 2001, 11:30 p.m. ET.

154. Michel, Lou, and Dan Herbeck. 2001. *American Terrorist: Timothy McVeigh and the Oklahoma City Bombing.* Harper, pp. 61, 87–88.

155. "Road to Oklahoma." 1995. CNN Special.

156. Russakoff, Dale, and Serge F. Kovaleski. 1995. "An Ordinary Boy's Extraordinary Rage." *The Washington Post* (July 2). See at http://

www.washingtonpost.com/wp-srv/national/longterm/oklahoma/bg/
mcveigh.htm. (Accessed May 27, 2014).

157. Couch, Dick. 2008. *Chosen Soldier: The Making of a Special Forces Warrior*. Three Rivers Press.

158. McVeigh, Timothy. 1992. "Letter from Timothy McVeigh to the *Union-Sun & Journal* (of Lockport, NY)." *RepublicanOperative.com*. (February 11). See at http://www.historycommons.org/context.jsp?item =a021192okcmcveighlockport. (Accessed May 15, 2014).

159. Russakoff and Kovaleski.

160. Michel and Herbeck, p. 110.

161. Ibid., p. 111.

162. Morton, Brian. 2009. "The Guns of Spring." *Baltimore City Paper* (April 15). See at http://www2.citypaper.com/eat/story.asp?id =17888.

163. Russakoff and Kovaleski.

164. Ibid.

165. Michel and Herbeck.

166. Ibid., p. 121.

167. Handlin, Sam. 2001. "Profile of a Mass Murderer: Who Is Timothy McVeigh?" *Court TV Online*. See at http://www.crimelibrary. com/serial_killers/notorious/mcveigh/updates.html.

168. Bryce, Robert. 2000. "Prying Open the Case of the Missing Door." *The Austin Chronicle* (August 18). See at http://www.austinchronicle .com/news/2000-08-18/78306/.

169. "Timothy McVeigh: Convicted Oklahoma City Bomber." *CNN*. March 29, 2001.

170. Editors. 2000. "Gun Shows in America." Violence Policy Center.

171. Michel and Herbeck.

172. Ibid., pp. 156–158.

173. Ottley, Ted. n.d. "'Imitating Turner.' Timothy McVeigh & Terry Nichols: Oklahoma Bombing." *Crime Library*. See at http://www. crimelibrary.com/serial_killers/notorious/mcveigh/turner_7.html.

174. Michel and Herbeck, pp. 184–185.

175. Associated Press. "McVeigh Offers Little Remorse in Letters." 2001. *The Topeka Capital-Journal* (June 10). Associated Press. See also Collins, James, Patrick E. Cole, and Elaine Shannon. 1997. "Oklahoma City: The Weight of Evidence." *Time*. (April 28), pp. 1–8. See also Russakoff and Kovaleski.

176. Saulny, Susan. 2001. "McVeigh Says He Considered Killing Reno." *The New York Times*. (April 27).

177. Associated Press. "Victims of the Oklahoma City bombing." 2001. *USA Today*. (June 20). See also Shariat, Sheryll, Sue Mallonee, and Shelli Stephens-Stidham. 1998. "Summary of Reportable Injuries in Oklahoma City." Oklahoma State Department of Health. See at http://www.ok.gov/health2/documents/OKC_Bombing.pdf.

178. Hewitt, Christopher. 2002. *Understanding Terrorism in America: From the Klan to Al-Qaeda (Extremism and Democracy)*. Routledge, p. 106. See also Oklahoma Department of Civil Emergency Management. *Oklahoma City Police Department Alfred P. Murrah Federal Building Bombing After Action Report*. See at http://www.ok.gov/OEM/documents/Bombing%20After%20Action%20Report.pdf.

179. Romano, Lois, and Tom Kenworthy. 1997. "Prosecutor Paints McVeigh as 'Twisted' U.S. Terrorist." *The Washington Post* (April 25, p. A01). See also Vidal, Gore. 2002. *Perpetual War for Perpetual Peace: How We Got To Be So Hated*. Nation Books, pp. 1, 81.

180. "McVeigh Holds No Regrets For Carnage." 2001. *Lubbock Avalanche-Journal*. Lubbockonline.com. (March 29). See at http://lubbockonline.com/stories/032901/nat_032901055.shtml. (Accessed May 25, 2014).

181. *"Turner Diaries* Introduced in McVeigh Trial." 1997. CNN. (April 28). See at http://www.cnn.com/US/9704/28/okc/. (Accessed April 1, 2014).

182. Count 1 was "conspiracy to detonate a weapon of mass destruction" in violation of 18 USC § 2332a, culminating in the deaths of 168 people and destruction of the Alfred P. Murrah Federal Building in Oklahoma City, Oklahoma. Count 2 was "use of a weapon of mass destruction" in violation of 18 USC § 2332a (2)(a) & (b). Count 3 was "destruction by explosives resulting in death," in violation of 18 USC § 844(f)(2)(a) & (b). Counts 4 through 11 were first-degree murder in violation of 18 USC § 1111, 1114, & 2 and 28 CFR § 64.2(h), each count in connection to one of the eight law enforcement officers who were killed during the attack.

183. Linder, Douglas O. 2006. "The Oklahoma City Bombing & the Trial of Timothy McVeigh." University of Missouri–Kansas City, Law School Faculty Projects. See at http://law2.umkc.edu/faculty/projects/ftrials/mcveigh/mcveightrial.html.

184. Eddy, Mark, George Lane, Howard Pankratz, and Steven Wilmsen 1997. "Guilty on Every Count." *Denver Post Online*. (June 3). See at http://extras.denverpost.com/bomb/bombv1.htm.

185. Associated Press. "McVeigh Remorseless About Bombing." 2001. *culteducation.com*. (March 29).

186. McVeigh, Timothy J. 1998. "An Essay on Hypocrisy." *Media Bypass Magazine*. (June). See at http://www.outpost-of-freedom.com/mcveigh/okcaug98.htm.

187. Ibid.

188. House of Representatives, Federal Building Security: Hearing Before the Subcommittee on Public Buildings and Economic Development of the Committee on Transportation and Infrastructure. 104th Congress, April 24, 1996. Interview with Dave Barram, Administrator of GSA, p. 6. See also Talley, Tim. 2006. "Experts Fear Oklahoma City Bombing Lessons Forgotten." *The San Diego Union-Tribune* (April 17).

189. MacQuarrie, Brian. 2005. "Militias' Era All but Over, Analysts Say." *The Boston Globe*. (April 19).

190. Vidal, Gore. 2001. "The Meaning of Timothy McVeigh." *Vanity Fair*. (September). See also Gibbons, Fiachra. 2001. "Vidal Praises Oklahoma Bomber for Heroic Aims." *Guardian*. guardian.co.uk. (August 17).

191. Ibid.

192. Crothers, Lane. 2003. *Rage on the Right: The American Militia Movement from Ruby Ridge to Homeland Security*. Rowman & Littlefield Publishers, pp. 135–136. See also Hamm, Mark S. 1997. *Apocalypse in Oklahoma: Waco and Ruby Ridge Revenged*. Northeastern, p. 219.

193. Ibid. See also Knight, Peter. 2003. *Conspiracy Theories in American History: An Encyclopedia*. ABC-CLIO, pp. 554–555. See also Sturken, Marita. 2007. *Tourists of History: Memory, Kitsch, and Consumerism from Oklahoma City to Ground Zero*, p. 159.

194. Doyle, Charles. 1996. "Antiterrorism and Effective Death Penalty Act of 1996: A Summary." *FAS*. (June 3). See at http://www.webcitation.org/5xGXWAzia.

195. *Felker v. Turpin*, 518 U.S. 651 and *City of Boerne v. Flores* and *Marbury v. Madison*; Denniston, Lyle. 2005. "Is AEDPA unconstitutional?" *SCOTUSblog* (May 5). Found at http://www.scotusblog.com/2005/05/is-aedpa-unconstitutional/.

196. Gray, Jerry. 1995. "Senate Votes to Aid Tracing of Explosives." *The New York Times*. (June 6).

197. Michel and Herbeck, pp. 378–383.

198. Anti-Defamation League, "The Militia Movement."

199. Ibid.

200. Ibid.

201. Ibid.

202. Jackson, Nate. Managing Editor, E-Mail Response to Author. March 25, 2014.

203. https://patriotpost.us/about/more.

204. https://patriotpost.us/. (Accessed May 12, 2014).

205. Anti-Defamation League, "The Militia Movement."

206. Ibid.

207. http://archive.adl.org/y2k/militias.html. (Accessed May 12, 2014).

208. Ibid.

209. Ibid.

210. Ibid.

211. Ibid.

212. Ibid. See also Gillis, Chad. 1999. "As Y2k Looms, Estero Man Offers Silver-back Currency." *The Naples Daily News*. (May 3).

213. http://archive.adl.org/y2k/militias.html.

214. Ibid.

215. Ibid.

216. Friedman, Thomas. 2003. *The Roots of 9/11*. Discovery Channel Documentary.

217. Southern Poverty Law Center. "Hate and Extremism." 2014. See at http://www.splcenter.org/what-we-do/hate-and-extremism.

218. Huntington, Samuel P. 2005. *Who Are We? The Challenges to America's National Identity*. Simon & Schuster.

219. Wolfe, Alan. 2004. "Native Son: Samuel Huntington Defends the Homeland." Foreign Affairs. (May/June). See at http://www.foreign affairs.com/articles/59908/alan-wolfe/native-son-samuel-huntington -defends-the-homeland. (Accessed May 15, 2014).

220. Ibid.

221. Ibid.

222. Ibid.

223. http://www.blm.gov/pgdata/etc/medialib/blm/nv/field_offices/ las_vegas_field_office/cattle_trespass.Par.49759.File.dat/Gold%20Butte %20Cattle%20Trespass%20EA%20DOI-BLM-NVS010-2014-0020-EA %20%282%29.pdf. (Accessed May 1, 2014).

224. MacNab, J. J. 2014. "Context Matters: The Cliven Bundy Standoff—Part 3." *Forbes*. (May 6). See at http://www.forbes.com/sites/ jjmacnab/2014/05/06/context-matters-the-cliven-bundy-standoff-part-3/. (Accessed April 29, 2014).

225. Strasser, Max. 2014. "For Militiamen, the Fight for Cliven Bundy's Ranch Is Far From Over." *Newsweek*. (April 23). See at http:// www.newsweek.com/2014/05/02/militiamen-fight-over-cliven-bundys- ranch-far-over-248354.html. (Accessed April 29, 2014).

226. Ibid. See also Suckling, Kieran. 2014. "A Rancher's Armed Battle Against the US Government Is Standard Libertarian Fare." *The*

Guardian. (April 19). See at http://www.theguardian.com/commentisfree /2014/apr/19/cliven-bundy-nevada-blm-libertarian. (Accessed April 29, 2014).

227. Hernandez, Daniel, and Joseph Langdon. 2014. "Federal Rangers Face Off Against Armed Protesters in Nevada 'Range War.'" *The Guardian*. (April 13). See at http://www.theguardian.com/world /2014/apr/13/nevada-bundy-cattle-ranch-armed-protesters. (Accessed April 30, 2014).

228. Ibid.

229. "Sovereign Citizens: A Growing Domestic Threat to Law Enforcement." 2011. *FBI Law Enforcement Bulletin*. (September). See at http://www.fbi.gov/stats-services/publications/law-enforcement-bulletin /september-2011/sovereign-citizens. (Accessed April 29, 2014). See also "Examining the Sovereign Citizen Movement in the Obama Era." 2014. *Politics & Policy*. (April 28). See at http://politicsandpolicy.org/article /examining-sovereign-citizen-movement-obama-era/. (Accessed April 30, 2014).

230. Milbank, Dana. 2014. "Bundy Saga Reveals the Risk of Cozying up to Extremists." *Washington Post*. (April 25). "The SPLC puts 'patriot' groups in a separate category from white supremacists and others organized around hate. The patriot groups make a constitutional argument to justify antipathy toward the federal government; this can be seen in the noise about secession, nullification, 'state sovereignty' and the primacy of the 10th Amendment."

231. Simon, Richard, and John M. Glionna. 2014. "Cliven Bundy Standoff: Locals Want Armed Militia Out, Lawmaker Says." Los Angeles Times. (May 5). See at http://www.latimes.com/nation/nationnow /la-na-cliven-bundy-congressman-20140507-story.html. (Accessed May 5, 2014).

232. Ibid.

233. Glionna, John M. 2014. "Cliven Bundy II? Utah Protestors Prepare for New Face-Off With Feds." *Los Angeles Times*. (May 9). See at http://www.latimes.com/nation/la-na-utah-blm-militia-bundy-20140509 -story.html#page=1. (Accessed May 9, 2014).

CONCLUSION

Whither the Patriot?

The idea of the "patriot" in the American mythos has changed since the founding of the United States. In the early republic, the patriot was a selfless individual, a possessor of civic virtue, who maintained his vigilance and took up his arms in defense of the American governmental system. This system, however, was in its infancy, and the politics and policies that the patriot defended were largely theoretical—they had not been tested with the passage of time. As the country grew and evolved, so too did the notion of the patriot, not necessarily to the public at large but to those who saw themselves as patriots, or the "true" protectors of government. Thus, over time, the notion of the stalwart patriot, always at the ready with his trusty weapon, changed. The patriot no longer defended the reality of government but the ideal of government. As the roots of American culture embedded themselves in the American psyche and became more and more part of the generational experience, the ideal of American government was threatened, at least from the perspective of the patriot. What emerged from this evolution was a nostalgic longing for the simplicity of the past—not life as it was but life as it should be. As new forces arose to threaten the idyllic view of the past, conservative forces arose to preserve that which was worth saving. This patriot, like his predecessor of two centuries before, could rightly claim allegiance to liberty.

Though the forces that altered the American political landscape had been gathering since the Founding, the middle of the 20th century saw the greatest threats to the American way of life, at least to those who believed that there was a pristine past that epitomized the American experience. Thus, the threat of communism followed by enormous social changes brought on by the new impetus on liberal politics combined to convince the patriot that it was no longer necessary to protect government. Rather, it became incumbent upon the patriot to protect the American ideal—indeed, the very essence of the American way of life—*from* government. As the 1960s and 1970s witnessed, this philosophy sometime took the form of political violence against the government, but this violence came from the left and not the right. Forces that represented this point of view believed that the American experiment had failed and that it should rightly be replaced by one that advocated absolute equality and a classless society. Though such groups may not have called themselves patriots, they were nevertheless acting to preserve what they believed was the essence of the United States: a belief in the equality of individuals—regardless of race, color, sex, or religion—and the firm conviction that government should serve the people. In many respects, these ideals characterize patriots not only from the left side of the political spectrum but from the right side as well.

As the 1980s dawned and conservative forces believed that liberalism had taken a firm hold at all levels of government, a backlash ensued that came to epitomize the current view of the patriot. The election of Ronald Reagan in 1980 seemed to signal to the country and the rest of the world that liberalism had seen its day in the United States. American citizens had elected a president who was fiercely anticommunist, conservative in his political and social views, and willing to spend exorbitant amounts of money to maintain a large and modern military. To the patriots who were cutting their teeth on national politics at this time, it was also important that Ronald Reagan was an avid supporter of the 2nd Amendment as well as an advocate of a smaller federal government, choosing instead to favor state initiatives over federal initiatives. For a brief moment in the 1980s, then, patriots did not fight to rein government in, as they believed they had an advocate in the White House who was doing this for them.

This changed with the election of George H. W. Bush in 1988. Though he had served as Ronald Reagan's vice president for eight years, Bush did not have the conservative credentials of Reagan. A decorated veteran of World War II (which Reagan was not), Bush had served as Ambassador to China, Ambassador to the United Nations, and director of the Central Intelligence Agency. He did preside over the fall of the Berlin Wall and he was president at the time that communism officially crumbled in Eastern Europe. He also had successfully prosecuted the war against Iraq's Saddam Hussein in what was termed a "Hitler-like" attempt to absorb a weaker neighboring country (Kuwait). Nevertheless, these successes were not enough to assuage the trepidations that many conservatives felt about Bush. For instance, though Bush had presided over communism's fall, it was widely believed that it had been Reagan's policies that had precipitated the event. And though Bush had defeated Iraq and Saddam Hussein, he destroyed almost all of his credibility when referring to the New World Order and the manner in which the United Nations would from that time forward play a more substantial role in the arbitration of world affairs. This single event, more than any other, confirmed suspicions among many that Bush was not the conservative he pretended to be. Coupled with the events of Ruby Ridge, Idaho, late in Bush's presidency, there was uneasiness among patriots about the future of the country in the aftermath of the "conservative moment."

The uneasiness that was building under George H. W. Bush grew into full-blown paranoia with the election of Bill Clinton as president in 1992. The liberal agenda dreaded by patriot and militia groups appeared to be geared up to fully change the social landscape in the United States. Almost upon his inauguration, Clinton began to initiate policies that might have been thought impossible only a few years before. The passage of the North American Free Trade Agreement (NAFTA) was seen by patriot/militia groups as the first step in the institution of the New World Order. Almost simultaneously, the formation of the European Union (EU) heralded ominous times for individuals and groups believing that the drive for global governance was just a few years away. But the Clinton policies hated by those of a patriot/militia bent were not limited to things international. Indeed, the domestic policies of the Clinton administration were equally hated. These included a change in the policy of allowing gays to serve in the U.S. military. Clinton's attempt to placate one of his major bases of support resulted in the almost universally detested policy of "don't ask, don't tell." In addition, Bill Clinton undertook an initiative to provide universal health care to Americans, headed by the first lady, Hillary Rodham Clinton. The vitriol that emerged from conservative groups over the issue of a universal health care policy in the United States was only a small foreshadowing of the fight that would take place a generation later under the leadership of another liberal, Democratic president—Barack Obama. In the aftermath of the raid on the Branch Davidian compound at Waco, Texas, and the bombing of the Murrah Federal Building in Oklahoma City in 1995, the Clinton administration put forth proposals for new regulations on the ownership of guns—a clarion call to all patriots, who responded by aligning themselves with conservative groups and politicians to head off the new liberal surge. A vibrant economy during the Clinton years probably prevented the large-scale formation of patriot/militia groups that, although their frustrations with Clinton and what they perceived as the "liberalism of America" ran high, nevertheless were not suffering economically; if they had been, it may have pushed those on the fence into full-scale and open rebellion against the state.

The election of George W. Bush provided a brief respite in the numbers of patriot/militia groups, though Y2K and 9/11 brought brief surges. In fact, whereas active patriot groups had surged during the middle of the 1990s (in response to Clinton administration policies and the Oklahoma City bombing), approaching nearly 1,000 active groups in 1996, by the election of George W. Bush in 2000, there were never more than 200 active groups.[1] Despite a vigorous prosecution of the War on Terror and new governmental authority to conduct surveillance on suspected terrorists both abroad and at home, the number of "patriot" groups saw precipitous declines through the Bush years (approximately 2001–2008). This decline persisted despite the fact that U.S. government spending rose precipitously during this period of time, and the size and scope of government—mostly pertaining to the increased role of intelligence agencies—was larger than ever.[2] Apparently, patriots trusted the goals and policies of a conservative such as George W. Bush. More importantly, they trusted the man himself. As noted by Kathryn Westcott of the BBC:

President Bush clearly loves that cowboy imagery. It's straight from his home state of Texas and he is comfortable with it.

Remember when he branded Saddam Hussein an "outlaw" or declared that he wanted Osama Bin Laden "dead or alive"?

Or his 2002 State of the Union address, when he evoked images of al-Qaeda leaders "running for their lives" from the long arm of American justice?. . .

. . . Cowboy imagery is quite central to Mr Bush's presidential persona. He holds crucial policy talks at his ranch in Crawford.

"The image he is cultivating is that of the mythic cowboy, strong, morally upright, independent and God-fearing—a stalwart figure standing against chaos," says Mr Mitchell.

"The cowboy sees complex issues in simple, morally unambivalent ways. There is the good and the bad and this is how George Bush sees things, much to the consternation of much of the country."

The cowboy represents a popular point of reference in American culture and has been adopted by past politicians.

Teddy Roosevelt was a type of rancher, as was Ronald Reagan, who borrowed heavily from his former film career.[3]

Of President Bush's persona, author David Halberstam would write in *Vanity Fair* at the close of the Bush presidency:

He is infinitely more comfortable with the cowboy persona he has adopted, the Texas transplant who has learned to speak the down-home vernacular. "Country boy," as Johnny Cash once sang, "I wish I was you, and you were me." Bush's accent, not always there in public appearances when he was younger, tends to thicken these days, the final g's consistently dropped so that doing becomes doin', going becomes goin', and making, makin'. In this lexicon al-Qaeda becomes "the folks" who did 9/11. Unfortunately, it is not just the speech that got dumbed down—so also were the ideas at play. The president's world, unlike the one we live in, is dangerously simple, full of traps, not just for him but, sadly, for us as well.[4]

Thus, patriots saw George W. Bush as a kindred spirit. He was often photographed working hard on his ranch, axe, saw, or shovel in hand. Moreover, he hunted—with guns—and enjoyed the outdoors. He was a man's man. During the Bush presidency, there was little need for violence because there was a friend in the White House. And though the liberal agenda was alive and well, it was being tempered by the Bush influence.

This lull came crashing down on November 4, 2008. On this date, Barack Hussein Obama was elected the 44th president of the United States. For those of the patriot and militia ilk, Barack Obama epitomized most everything they distrusted or hated. First, Barack Obama was "black." Though his mother was white, his father—a Kenyan—was black. For those of a racist bent among patriot/militia groups, it was as if Jim Crow was alive and well. It did not matter that Barack Obama was half white. His black half was enough to hate and disregard. For his part, Barack Obama did not shy away from his black heritage, nor did he attempt to portray himself as biracial. In fact, that he was running as the first African American for the highest office in the land was enormously symbolic and cathartic for a population weary of George W. Bush's wars and one longing for change.

Second, Barack Obama's middle name—Hussein—evoked for many Americans the specter of a Muslim in the White House. After all, the United States had spent precious blood and treasure to defeat Saddam

Hussein—a hated dictator and a Muslim besides. The fact that Barack Hussein Obama, Sr., Obama's father, had been raised in Kenya, a country nearly 12 percent Muslim, caused many to suspect that Barack Obama Jr. may have been a Muslim as well. This speculation was fueled by the fact that Obama's mother, Ann Dunham, divorced Obama's father and married a man from Indonesia, the most populous Islamic country in the world. This, coupled with the fact that Barack Obama Jr. spent several years in Indonesia, fueled conspiracy theories that Barack Obama was, in fact, a Muslim and not a Christian as he claimed.

For patriot/militia adherents, Barack Hussein Obama Jr. was both black and Muslim. But a third concern was the question of whether he was eligible to be president, for there were many who believed that he had not been born in the United States and was therefore ineligible to become president. Obama had actually been born in Hawaii, then an American state, and his mother was a natural-born citizen of the United States. Though an original birth certificate showing Obama's birthplace as Honolulu, Hawaii, is now in the public record, there are those who believe that Barack Obama's presidency is illegitimate as he is not a "natural born citizen of the United States," as specified by the U.S. Constitution.[5]

Fourth, as was made evident during the 2008 presidential campaign, Barack Obama had "consorted" with terrorists. During his days as a community organizer in Chicago, Obama had met and spoken with Bill Ayers, who had been part of the Weather Underground in the late 1960s and the early 1970s. For some, the fact that the United States was fighting a war on terror and yet was ready to elect an individual who had been labeled a terrorist was indefensible. Such contradictions did not sit well with patriot militia groups.[6]

Finally, and perhaps most importantly, Barack Obama was a liberal Democrat, cut from the same cloth as Bill Clinton. He ran on a platform of sensible gun control and a national health care system. Many times during the 2008 campaign, he was accused of himself being a terrorist, but worse yet, a socialist or communist.[7] Since the beginning of the Cold War, the patriot/militia movement could not abide anyone with socialist/communist leanings. Thus, in Barack Obama, patriots saw an individual who would most likely take the United States in directions that they did not desire to see it go. Change is always difficult, but change at the hands of someone deemed to not have the best interests of the country at heart was that much more troubling.

A representation of the number of patriot/militia groups active in the United States from 1995 to 2012 is telling:[8]

Year	Patriot Groups	Militia Groups
1995	368	441
1996	488	370
1997	302	221
1998	264	171
1999	49	68
2000	122	72
2001	85	73
2002	89	54
2003	126	45
2004	100	52
2005	97	35
2006	95	52
2007	88	43
2008	107	42
2009	385	127
2010	494	330
2011	940	334
2012	1039	321

Source: Data from http://www.splcenter.org/home/2013/spring/the-year-in-hate-and-extremism.

From 1995 to 2000, the number of patriot/militia groups in the United States dropped from 809 to 194. The large numbers in 1995 were no doubt fueled by the "hangover" from Ruby Ridge, Waco, and Oklahoma City. There is little doubt the hated policies of the Clinton administration—the 1993 Brady Bill and the 1994 ban on assault weapons—contributed to these high numbers. As stated earlier, however, these numbers began to drop as more stringent law enforcement toward patriot/militia groups was undertaken, so much so that by 2000, there was a 75 percent decrease in the number of active patriot/militia groups.

A noticeable lull is apparent during the years of George W. Bush's presidency, though, as noted previously, Bush's presidency saw unprecedented power delegated to the federal government to spy on average American citizens. Yet the conservative credentials of George W. Bush seemed to mute the need on the part of many patriot/militia groups to express their anger against the government during these years.

Enter Barack Obama, a liberal Democrat. The number of patriot/ militia groups rises dramatically beginning in 2009, the first year of Barack Obama's presidency. The number of patriot/militia groups rises from 149 to 1,360, a more than ninefold increase. Yet in the aftermath of shootings in Aurora, Colorado, in July 2012 in which 12 people were killed and 70 others injured and a shooting at the Sandy Hook Elementary School in Newtown, Connecticut, in December 2012 in which 26 people, including 22 children, were killed by deranged individuals wielding multiple weapons, membership in patriot groups remained steady in 2013, with many individuals believing "that the federal government [was] conspiring to take Americans' guns and destroy their liberties as it paves the way for a global 'one-world government.'"[9]

Though President Obama proposed legislation to tighten gun control laws in the aftermath of Aurora and Sandy Hook, even his allies in Congress admitted that such laws would be difficult to pass. Senator Dianne Feinstein, a fierce advocate of gun control, noted that laws that attempt to curb the number and type of guns in the United States will always be blocked by the National Rifle Association (NRA), which she characterized as "venal," noting that many members of Congress owe their support to the NRA and do not wish to cross them.[10] Besides the NRA, however, Feinstein noted the "maze" of gun control laws in the various states; there is a legal avenue to get "military-style assault weapons, gangster-style Tommy guns, World War II–era bazookas, and even sawed-off shotguns."[11]

PATRIOT PLACE: WHAT DOES THE 21ST CENTURY HOLD?

President Obama's efforts went for naught, as not one piece of substantial gun legislation was passed in the aftermath of the Aurora and Sandy Hook tragedies. Yet this did not stop the vitriol that patriot and other groups continued to hurl at the government in general and the Obama administration in particular. Three events that occurred in 2013 were of particular note to the cause of the patriot.

First, in May 2013, the *Washington Post* reported that the Internal Revenue Service (IRS) had engaged in a policy of "targeting" conservative groups that had applied for tax-exempt status.[12] A review of the applications from groups found that nonprofit approvals for groups with "tea party" or "9–11" in their name were not approved. Groups that included "patriot" or "constitution" in their titles were also slowed down. On the other hand, groups that included the word "progressive" in their title saw their applications approved at a much higher rate.[13]

To patriots, this type of action on the part of the federal government was unconscionable. As subsequent investigations showed, the IRS targeted Tea Party members, "patriots," and other conservative groups. United Press International (UPI) reported:

[the] U.S. Internal Revenue Service inquiry of conservative groups included those lobbying to "make America a better place to live," new details emerging about the IRS investigation indicated. That lever goes beyond what the IRS admitted Friday, which was that it targeted groups with "Tea Party" or "patriot" in their names, several media outlets reported Monday, based on draft findings from disclosures to congressional investigators by the Treasury Department's inspector general for tax administration. . . .[14]

The targeting of these groups caused John Avlon of CNN to ask, "How did 'patriot' become a dirty word? . . . Actually," he stated, "it's an interesting story:"

Over the past few years, you might have noticed more than a few political fundraising e-mails addressing you as "Fellow Patriot." They ain't from the ACLU. They tend to be from conservative activist groups, and there is more than a little self-congratulation in their tribal identifier.

The idea, of course, is that their fellow travelers on the right side of the aisle are the "real" patriots—related to Sarah Palin's "Real Americans"—defenders of a political faith and traditional way of life under attack by liberals, Democrats, demographics and above all, President Barack Obama.

The fact that many of these self-styled superpatriots seem to hate their twice-elected president is itself a sign of just how dumb the false dualities that dominate our politics can be. . . .[15]

But Avlon noted that

history teaches us to be wary of people who lord their patriotism over others and use it to divide rather than unite.

The precursors to some of today's more cultish conservative groups emerged during post-war anxiety about the legitimate threat of communism and the McCarthy-ite excesses that flowed out of that era's right wing politics. The us-against-them, "enemy within" rhetoric of the John Birch Society endures today in the polemics of Glenn Beck, Alex Jones and others.

The early growth of self-styled paramilitary groups began in the early 1960s during the presidency of John F. Kennedy—a committed Cold Warrior, but not incidentally a Catholic and a Democrat.

The "Minutemen" were one such group who thrived off survivalist drills and a supposed plan to "confiscate all private firearms by the end of 1965."

We hear similar strains of fearmongering today in the attempts to block the universal gun background check bill. Notably, the Minutemen's founder, Robert Bolivar DePugh, briefly tried to form a political party called—you guessed it—The Patriot Party. They fell into some discredit when DePugh's followers were implicated in a half-baked plot to attack the United Nations.

At the time, former President Dwight Eisenhower, a Republican, felt compelled to weigh in by saying, "I don't think the United States needs Super-Patriots. . . . We need patriotism, honestly practiced by all of us and we don't need these people [who pretend to be] more patriotic than you or anybody else. . . ."[16]

Avlon noted that use of the word "patriot" is a sign of the "culture wars" now being waged in American politics, largely due to the rise of partisan media outlets. He stated, "When the word 'patriot' becomes a pejorative, it is a sign of how much our shared civic faith has been denigrated by the rise of hyperpartisan politics."[17] Though Avlon condemns the activities of the IRS, he does intimate that the term "patriot" has been "hijacked" from its original meaning, in that it no longer denotes one who supports government but, in actuality, is one who hates, distrusts, and fights against government. Such is the pejorative of the term today.

A second facet of the cause of the patriot today is the long-lost notion of nullification. In 2011, the executive director of the Tenth Amendment Center, Michael Boldin, intoned that during the presidency of George W. Bush, stances by the center against Bush policies such as the Patriot Act and RealID "didn't win [the organization] too many conservative friends." However, when taking a "stand for the Constitution—every issue, every time, no exceptions, no excuses—doesn't win us too many friends on the left."[18]

In 2013, nullification burst back onto the political scene with a vengeance. Nullification efforts—or attempts by states to negate federal law—have focused in recent years on three issue areas: gun control, health care, and national standards for drivers' licenses.[19] In at least 37 states in 2013, legislation was introduced that would gut federal gun regulations in some way. Michael Boldin of the Tenth Amendment Center, which favors states' rights, said, "Isn't that what it's supposed to be, 'We, the people'?" he added. "Over the past few years, you've seen this growing. . . . People are getting sick and tired of federal power."[20] As noted by Tai Kopan,

> the state-level anger at the nation's capital has reached such a fever pitch that many of the bills do not even address specific federal laws but rather amount to what is in effect pre-emptive nullification, wiping out, for instance, any federal law that may exist in the future that a state determines violates gun rights.[21]

In Kansas, State Representative John Rubin sponsored legislation, which passed, that stated that federal gun laws do not apply to firearms and accessories made in Kansas. For the Republican lawmaker, his bill was about "states' rights—not gun rights."[22] Rubin continued:

> The federal government doesn't have the authority to do a lot of what it's trying to do these days, from regulating guns within state borders, as my bill deals with, or telling us what kinds of light bulbs to put in our lamps. . . .
>   . . . We have the Obama administration to thank for that. The more federal overreach in Obamacare and elsewhere, the more [the administration] chooses to act in ways we believe are unconstitutional, the more we're going to push back. I would encourage any state to assert to the strongest possible extent against the Obama administration, or any federal administration, rights clearly reserved to the states.[23]

Representative Rubin is echoing the tact of many patriot groups today. Though they still may be armed, believe in conspiracy theories, and have a fear of the federal government and the New World Order, their tactic is not to forcefully confront the government but to obfuscate through legitimate constitutional means. Though their success has been mixed, it nevertheless seems to indicate a somewhat different track than patriot/militia groups have taken in the past.

Finally, like nullification, secession has once again appeared on the American political horizon—spurred on by individuals and groups who are fed up with both overbearing federal *and* state controls. In November 2013, 10 counties on the eastern front range of Colorado voted to secede from the state to form the 51ˢᵗ state of the United States. An 11ᵗʰ county—Moffat County (the birthplace of this author)—voted to secede but instead join Wyoming to become part of that state. Though the secessionist vote failed to win a majority in five counties, the message was clear: people were tired of being ignored and feeling as if their voices were not being heard. Fort Lupton Mayor Tommy Holt intoned that although the secession vote failed, "the publicity would shed light on rural Colorado's grievances. . . . We not only want to be at the table," he said, "but we want a voice at the table as well."[24] Proponents of secession indicate that they have become "alienated" from the more urbanized Front Range and are "unhappy with laws passed during this year's legislative session, including stricter gun laws and new renewable-energy standards." A 51ˢᵗ state advocate, Jeffrey Hare, said, "The heart of the 51st State Initiative is simple: We just want to be left alone to live our lives without heavy-handed restrictions from the state Capitol."[25]

Though not explicitly "patriot" in the use of the term, the Colorado secessionists, as well as the proponents of nullification, echo more than 200 years of resentment expressed by those wishing to hold their government to account. As previously discussed, most who self-identify today as "patriots" would not characterize themselves as "haters" of their government. To the contrary, most would probably express sentiments that are highly favorable of the American system of government, its economic base, and the values that have continued to attract immigrants to the country for more than two centuries. What these patriots want is a government that is limited, transparent, and uncorrupt. Of course, over the course of two centuries, such characteristics have been largely muted by the growth of government and the policies that have allowed the United States to keep pace with other industrialized states. Nevertheless, there is a longing on the part of patriots to once again have a government that hearkens back to the ideals of the Founding.

THEY'RE STILL HERE: WHAT'S OUT THERE TODAY?

The Southern Poverty Law Center (SPLC), the authoritative source on the number, types, and activities of groups characterized as "patriot," "militia," or "hate," indicates that at the end of 2013, there were nearly 1,100 groups that could be categorized as "patriot" groups, whereas 939 groups were categorized as "hate" groups. Both of these figures represent substantial increases since 2000.[26] Though figures for militia groups were not immediately available through SPLC, retired U.S. Army colonel Harry G. Riley has stated there are between 1.2 and 1.8 million militia members in the United States.[27] At times, SPLC has included in the number of "patriot" groups those that are considered to be "militia" groups as well.[28]

Colonel Harry G. Riley in recent days has called upon members of Congress to "come to their senses" and "leave their offices" in a protest to force the resignation of President Barack Obama. Calling for the gathering of militia members and patriotic Americans everywhere, Riley stated that "we are just a bunch of individual patriots who plan on visiting Washington, DC, exercising our constitutional rights, all at the same time."[29] Riley further intoned that the call to assemble in Washington was "a sacrificial effort by patriots who believe our nation is in jeopardy. . . . Our government at the federal level is totally lawless. Our nation is in grave danger right now of internal implosion."[30]

The "patriots" being called upon by Colonel Riley certainly number in the tens of thousands. There are patriot and militia groups found in every state, some groups having a presence in all 50 states. The following is a brief overview of "patriot" groups that can be found in virtually every state.

WE ARE CHANGE

The mission statement of We Are Change seems innocuous. It reads:

> We Are Change is a nonpartisan, independent media organization comprised of individuals and groups working to expose corruption worldwide. We are made up of independent journalists, concerned citizens, activists, and anyone who wants to shape the direction our world is going in. We seek to expose the lies of governments and the corporate elite who constantly trash our humanity. By asking the hard questions the mainstream media refuses to ask, we shine a little more light on truth.
>
> Furthermore, we seek to connect, educate, and motivate those who are interested in alerting the public to the pertinent issues that are affecting our lives each and every day. Our goal is to create a

community of truth-seekers and peacemakers who share a commitment to nonviolent action.

We Are Change is not so much an individual or group, but an idea, an idea that "We the People" are the change we wish to see in this world. Together, as residents of this planet, we can push back against those who wish to dominate our lives and begin to restore liberty to all.[31]

In its 2010 Annual Report, the SPLC listed founding member Luke Rudowski as the "Patriot Journalist," describing him among those who are considered "enablers" of the antigovernment movement.[32] For his part, Rudowski claimed that a quote about how the group known as WeAreChange existed to "lead the way in a peaceful evolution and not revolution" was taken out of context by the SPLC and meant to demonize him.[33] Writing of the SPLC and its tracking of patriot/militia and hate groups, Rudowski opined:

The SPLC describes themselves as "dedicated to fighting hate & bigotry" it seems the majority of the groups and persons they listed on their reports are peaceful and concerned citizens, the exact opposite of hate. The question is, should the SPLC be listed on their own "Hate Reports"? Considering main figures of the "truth movement" hateful and domestic terrorists is outrageous. One is left to wonder, are we all possible domestic terrorists if we question the intentions of our government?. . .[34]

OATH KEEPERS

As of this writing, the Oath Keepers have been very active in supporting the cause of Cliven Bundy in his dispute with the Bureau of Land Management (BLM). On their website, they claim that "99% of the rumors on the internet are either blatantly false or wildly inaccurate."[35] Though there is no explanation of what rumors are being referred to, it is safe to assume that the group was reacting to media reports that portrayed the group as armed militia spoiling for a fight with the federal government. The message on their website was as follows:

We are, however concerned that the domestic enemies of the Constitution that infest the federal government might try to take advantage of folks going home, and attempt to make a move on the Bundy family. We feel certain that they will want to try again at some point, perhaps in a different way, even perhaps by executing a dynamic entry raid to attempt to arrest the Bundys. And we have heard that this is being discussed, though I have not been able to directly confirm it. But it is a real risk.

Therefore, to prevent such a raid, or to at least throw a monkey wrench into any such plans and make it more difficult for them, we're doing the following:. . .[36]

The unidentified blogger on the site calls for Oath Keepers to (1) come to the Bundy ranch to serve as volunteers on an ongoing, rotating watch and, (2) maintain a rotating vigil of friendly state legislators and current serving sheriffs at the Bundy ranch.[37] The blogger then concludes with a call to fellow Oath Keepers members:

There is also some serious perimeter security and Oath Keepers CPTers who volunteer to help with the out-lying security in the desert will find this to be a great training exercise. Bring your gear. Consider this your Minute Man FTX. But however you come, do come. Oath Keepers will not be alone in this. Many other Americans are mobilizing now, millions of Americans are learning about it and are wanting to be helpful. Be part of it. . . .[38]

The website is filled with testimonials from various Oath Keepers, many of them ex-military, praising the Oath Keepers' cause in sustaining Cliven Bundy, his family, and his friends.

TENTH AMENDMENT CENTER

The Tenth Amendment Center was established to protect the idea enshrined in the 10th Amendment to the U.S. Constitution—the right of the several states to reserve to themselves the power not delegated to the federal government in the Constitution. To this end, the Tenth Amendment Center, which calls itself the "Tenther Movement," notes the predicament their unflagging support of the 10th Amendment elicits:

When Republicans are in power, we get lambasted by the right for being "communists" for opposing unconstitutional republican

programs. When Democrats are in power, we get lambasted by the
left for being "racists" for opposing unconstitutional democrat programs. If you're not catching any flak, you're not over the target.
And since our goal is the Constitution, we're always over the target
to the establishment. The Constitution. Every issue, every time.
No exceptions, no excuses.[39]

REPUBLIC FOR THE UNITED STATES OF AMERICA

In what can only be described as a very thorough and detailed website, the Republic for the United States of America contends that the
United States exists in two forms: "The original united [sic] States that
was in operation until 1860; a collection of sovereign Republics in the
union. Under the original Constitution the States controlled the Federal
Government; the Federal government did not control the States and
had limited powers."[40] The site then proclaims that "The Republic for
the United States of America is re-inhabited and is the only lawful civil
authority for the United States of America."[41]

A more detailed description of the beliefs of the Republic for the
United States is as follows:

The lawful government was re-inhabited in 2010 and is in the process of shifting governance from the unlawfully chartered
UNITED STATES municipal corporation to the de jure Republic
for the United States of America. The United States exists today
in two forms: One, is the original de jure United States of America
Republic that was controlled by "We the People" until about 1871.
The government had very little authority since the power was in
the hands of the People. The original Constitution was never removed; it has simply been dormant since about 1871. It is still intact to this day. The other form is the de facto. During the years
around 1871 the original United States of America Republic was
usurped by banking interests and others to create a separate and
different government, a corporation (the UNITED STATES corporation), that poses and acts as our current government. The
UNITED STATES corporation operates under Corporate/
Commercial Law rather than the common law (Constitution)/
Private Law. The rewritten UNITED STATES corporate
Constitution bypasses the original Constitution of the United
States of America, which explains why our Congressmen and

Senators no longer answer to the People and the President can write unlawful Executive Orders. They are following corporate laws that completely strip Americans of their God given unalienable rights. What the Republic for the United States of America (the Republic) is NOT:

The Republic is not part of or associated with sovereign anarchistic groups or movements.

The Republic is not part of or associated with unlawful anarchistic militia groups or movements.

The Republic is not part of or associated with nation state groups or movements.

The Republic is not part of any groups or movements that promote violence of any kind.

The Republic is not part of the unlawfully chartered UNITED STATES municipal corporation, its agents, or any of its sub-corporations, either directly or indirectly. This includes any of its political parties.[42] (Emphasis in original.)

Finally, there is a statement by this group that articulates four points that are what the Republic stands for:

What the Republic for the United States of America is and what it stands for:

1. The Republic is the only lawful government in the United States of America.

2. The Republic has peacefully, honorably, and lawfully re-inhabited the republican form of Governance demanded by the Constitution of the United States of America that was vacated in 1871 by an unconstitutional act of Congress.

3. The lawful Congress of the Republic has been meeting in sessions since 2010 as the provisional interim government. The goal is to bring the United States of America into complete compliance with the Constitution within 10 years.

4. The Republic is a peaceful, honorable, and lawful government which relies on Law as its foundation, not violence or power.[43]

Though the Republic of the United States of America does not promote violence, it does identify the current government of the United States as illegitimate and as having usurped the powers of the people.

Though there are no direct calls for action of any kind, groups like this can inspire what is known as "leaderless resistance" wherein individuals sympathetic to such a cause take it upon themselves to act violently in such a manner as they believe will promote the goals of the organization with which they identify. In such a way, those who write of the injustices and the wrongs of the current government can claim "plausible deniability" of any actions conducted based upon the principles they espouse since there was not a concrete directive to act in such a manner or in the name of the organization. Thus, though groups such as this appear benign, their effects upon the impressionable mind are difficult to ascertain.

NULLIFY NOW!

As the name of this group indicates, its goal is to promote the idea of nullification, which is the process whereby states legislatively sanction the disavowal of federal laws. This group has organized chapters in several states but does not appear to have a centralized structure. A brief review of its website, however, does reveal its intentions.

In a section titled "Institutionalization of State-level Nullification," there are summaries and links to several efforts now being undertaken by states in reference to the nullification of federal law. In the "Proposal for a Federal Action Review Commission (Nullification Commission)," it states that the proposal is a "[d]raft bill proposing amendment to Texas Constitution for establishment of a state grand jury for the review of the constitutionality of the actions of United States government officials and agents, and to authorize state grand juries to investigate public administration. . . ."[44]

In yet another section titled "The Crisis: or, Essays on the Usurpations of the Federal Government," there is reference to the writings of Robert James Trumbull (a.k.a. "Brutus," one of the writers of the *Anti-Federalist Papers*). This essay "discusses the misconstructions of the Constitution by the Supreme Court and Congress from a Jeffersonian standpoint and develops the concept of state-level nullification."[45]

On the Nullify Now! website, there are links to drafts of state laws, flyers they have distributed concerning nullification, YouTube (and other) videos, excerpts from various Founding documents, and any other document that might support the idea of nullification. In an "Attention Visitors" section of the website, there is a disclaimer that reads in part. . . . "For this project to work we also need you to recruit participants that can form a core of dedicated members who don't waste one another's time. This can be the effort that will work, but it takes you to make that happen."[46]

WE THE PEOPLE ORGANIZATION

The We the People Organization identifies itself as being divided into two separate entities. The first is the We the People for Constitutional Education, Inc., a "non-profit educational foundation that cannot engage in partisan political activity. . . ." The second entity is the "We the People Congress," a not-for-profit membership-based entity "focusing on grassroots constitutional activism that can engage in direct political activity. . . ."[47]

Each entity is then outlined in detail:

The We The People Foundation for Constitutional Education has been established to fulfill the need for popular education including education, awareness, and knowledge about the Declaration of Independence and every provision of the federal and state constitutions, about the sovereignty of the people whose will the constitutions are designed to express, and about the government they are meant to control through their constitutions. Its educational program works to inform the public, increase awareness, and encourage appropriate government reform through constitutional processes, including the exercise and enforcement of the First Amendment Right to Petition.

The Foundation is designed to carry out the professional, broad scale educational program required to counteract the public ignorance and apathy we see as hampering the development of citizen vigilance and the acceptance of popular sovereignty essential to the proper governance of our constitutional democratic republics. The Foundation is an organization devoted to the a-political, public interest, teaching of civility "content" and the expression of the Jeffersonian ideal of a way of life rooted in constitutionality and civic action.

Conceptually, the Foundation exercises philosophical leadership in the total program. Eventually, combining a highly professional public education program with the penetrating analytical and legal activity and advocacy of a public-interest law firm, the Foundation is a source of vital information and education, supportive funding and professional legal undertakings on behalf of situations and individuals suffering from non-constitutional governance, all aimed at "the re-invigoration of constitutional constraints on government. . . ."

. . . The We The People Congress has been established for the purpose of developing in the public forum, from the ordinary, non-aligned citizenry, a constituency committed to what Mahatma Gandhi and Martin Luther King Jr. referred to as a "militant, non-violent, mass-movement" with the goal of achieving substantial reforms in the structure and process of government, through political activism.

The Congress is designed as an advocacy organization, to carry the message vocally and politically to the people and to the various legislative and administrative organizations of government, seeking to influence attitudes of the body politic and legislative actions. This is an organization separate from the Foundation, institutionally, but connected by a mutuality of purpose.

The Congress will, by rational, intelligent and professional means make it difficult for those currently wielding political and governmental power to continue in power with a "business as usual" approach and lead the people toward significant improvements in our system of governance. We recognize that the acknowledgment of popular sovereignty as a social and political force is a fundamental need. The Congress is committed to achieving its purposes by all possible means short of violence.

The Foundation and the Congress recognize that the requirements for changes in governmental structure and process will include, but not necessarily be limited to: the clarification of the federal power to tax; the teaching in our schools of the history, meaning, effect and significance of every provision of our founding documents; increased accountability, ethics and efficiency; the clarification and strengthening of public-debt-limiting restrictions; the clarification and strengthening of the prohibitions regarding the gifting of public funds for private purposes; legislative reform including the strengthening of representative democracy and participatory democracy; a reduction in and control over the cost and secrecy of the legislatures; easier access to the ballot for independents and party insurgents; weakening of the power of political parties and of government in general; weakening of the desire of special interests to influence legislative bodies; non-partisan elections; a judiciary that is more independent and accountable; and, laws which do not favor public education over private education.[48]

We the People contends that very few in the United States are aware that a "battle rages," and that "our Republic currently faces its most significant challenge ever—to restore Constitutional Order and reclaim the fundamental Liberties that have been seized by those that would deprive us our Freedom. Despite the sacrifices of over 200 years, our Constitution today hangs only by a thread."[49] The organization further contends that the U.S. government has "systematically" plundered the wealth of the American people while ignoring constitutional checks and balances and destroying the "last vestiges of freedom." The organization charges that the United States is continuing its "dangerous descent into debt, decay, and despotism." The "root cause" of this situation

> is that the People, through ignorance, apathy and institutionalized tyranny, have allowed their servant governments (and those that benefit from its largesse) to "take over the house," i.e., to act without lawful authority in violation of our founding documents, including our federal and state Constitutions.
>
> Our overall purpose is to expose, confront and correct governments operating outside their written, lawful authority and to institutionalize a nationwide program of civic vigilance to prevent future abuses and ensure the continuance of Liberty for our posterity.[50]

While Oath Keepers have not resorted to violent means, it is clear that the rhetoric of the organization lends itself to the patriot cause. Whether such language is inflammatory or "hateful," as the SPLC contends, may be a point of contention. Nevertheless, the language used by the organization certainly sets it on the side of those who see serious problems within the U.S. system of government—problems in need of a serious correction.

THE PATRIOT PARTY

The Patriot Party calls citizens to action as follows: "Patriots of this nation, it's time to unite and put this country back in to the hands of the people!"[51] The "philosophy" of the Patriot Party reads:

> We hold that the United States is a Republic conceived by the Founding Fathers as a Nation whose people were granted

"unalienable rights" by our Creator. Chiefly among these are the rights to "life, liberty and the pursuit of happiness." The Patriot Party stands with our Founding Fathers, as heirs to the Republic, to claim our rights and duties which preserve their legacy and our own. We stand with the Founders, that there exists an inherent benefit to our country when private property and prosperity is secured by Natural Law and the rights of the individual. The intent of the Constitution was to guarantee the rights of the Individual first, to charge the Government with the responsibility of protecting those rights, and to limit the Government by its listed powers and limits.

We believe that social issues are best decided at the state and local levels and they are not and should never be a function of the Federal Government. The Constitution states "Congress shall make no law respecting the establishment of religion, or prohibiting the free exercise thereof." The Constitution does not give the Federal Government the authority to legislate personal responsibility, nor to impose one groups beliefs on the citizens as a whole. Our Founders firmly believed in the personal responsibility and morality of the individual. We believe that responsibility, integrity and ethics is taught and demonstrated, not legislated. We recognize and support the strength of grassroots organizations and promote civic responsibility at local, state, and national levels. We will create partnerships with like minded organizations so our shared principles may succeed. It is the intention of the Patriot Party to unite Americans based upon our core values. Our Party will endorse and / or support representatives who truly respond to the wishes of the people. We support our fellow citizens, and will not allow any special interest group to influence us. The Patriot Party will actively oppose all Government officials, elected or appointed, who disregard our core principles. We expect nothing less than a Government which best serves and protects its citizens liberties and operates under the limitations contained within our Constitution.[52]

ALARM AND MUSTER

Alarm and Muster, sometimes known as the Modern Day Alarm Riders, have chapters in several states, though information on them is somewhat sketchy. As identified in what follows, this group considers itself a militia and is categorized as such by the Southern Poverty Law Center. Though the website of Alarm and Muster does not appear active, it does espouse the values that are associated with this group:

> As a citizen of the United States, you are a member of the Constitutionally guaranteed unorganized militia.
>
> Everything you have heard about militias from the media is likely wrong. Main stream news has primarily reported on the negative stereotypes and criminal activity of groups that have nothing to do with militia. The true militia has exactly the opposite purpose; to uphold the law and the Constitution.
>
> The USM is a growing community of Americans that believe that the supreme laws of our Constitution must be diligently protected and upheld. Fostering the lawful rebirth of State militia is a crucial step in preserving the Republic.
>
> America promises freedom for all and we pride ourselves on being inclusive; Every Color, Every Culture, One Country.[53]

OTHER GROUPS

This study does not allow for a full explication of the various groups identified as being either patriot or militia in their orientation. The foregoing brief survey is intended to provide only a summary of some of the more active and/or expressive groups of this type.

Within the 50 states of the United States, however, there are several other groups that are consistently organized within these jurisdictions and are either particular to one state or can be found in several. Among these are the following groups:

America Can Be Free
Alaska Citizens Militia*
America First Party
Get Out of Our House (GOOOH)
Committee of Safety
Constitution Party
Don't Tread on Me
Heal Our Land
Liberty Restoration Project

Maine Constitutional Militia*
Maine Highlands Defense Force
Maine Patriot Militia*
Nebraska State Militia*
Restore the Republic
Sons of Liberty
The Heartland USA
The Patriot Network

*There is a militia group named for the state in which it is found in virtually every state.

As noted previously, the accepted authority on the tracking of patriot, militia, and hate groups in the United States is the Southern Poverty Law Center. The SPLC, founded in 1971, expresses its mission as one that is "dedicated to fighting hate and bigotry and to seeking justice for the most vulnerable members of our society."[54] The SPLC lists as its priorities fighting either for and on behalf of or against the following causes: (1) at-risk children, (2) hate and extremism, (3) immigrant justice, (4) LGBT rights, and (5) teaching tolerance.[55]

Annually, the SPLC issues reports on these topics, including lists that track the number of hate, patriot, and militia groups. As noted earlier, many who find themselves on the patriot list in particular contend that they are only expressing opposition to government programs, policies, or actions, as is their constitutionally guaranteed right. That they are labeled as hate or extremist groups begs the point that the SPLC does establish its lists in a somewhat arbitrary fashion. For instance, in a recent article published by the SPLC titled "Public Schools in the Crosshairs: Far-Right Propaganda and the Common Core State Standards," the SPLC contends that those who express opposition to Common Core standards see the educational plan as

a plan to indoctrinate young children into "the homosexual lifestyle," a conspiracy to turn children into "green serfs" who will serve a totalitarian "New World Order."

To the propaganda machine on the right, the Common Core— an effort driven by the states—is actually "Obamacore," a nefarious federal plot to wrest control of education from local school systems and parents. Instead of the "death panels" of "Obamacare," the fear is now "government indoctrination camps."

The disinformation campaign is being driven by the likes of Fox News, the John Birch Society, Tea Party factions, and the Christian Right. National think tanks and advocacy groups associated with the Koch brothers, whose father was a founding Birch member, have taken up the cause. . . .[56]

One may or may not take umbrage at the label of "far right" in the report, but the use of the word "crosshairs" invokes images of armed right-wing groups willing to fight to defeat Common Core. Such rhetoric is at best disingenuous and at worst inflammatory. If the SPLC is indeed criticizing the far right for its position, why inflame the situation by evoking such a violent image in its own report? Of course, critics of the SPLC are no more kind in their characterization of the organization. In a rebuttal to the SPLC report, author Eric Owens wrote, "Leftist, Terrorism-Inspiring Southern Poverty Law Center Labels Common Core Critics 'Far-Right Extremists.'"[57] Owens points out that those who oppose Common Core standards are labeled as "far-right extremists" simply because of their opposition to a program favored by the SPLC.

Of course, this tit-for-tat rhetoric is indicative of the level of discourse practiced by those characterized by the left as patriots and the response of these groups to the accusations that they are extremists. Unless and until there is more self-restraint on the part of those on both the left and the right to temper the rhetorical devices they use to criticize their opponents, we will likely see the continuation of such diatribes in the public press.

FROM THERE TO HERE: WHITHER THE PATRIOT?

In the early history of the American Republic, a patriot was a civic-minded individual who took pride in the uniqueness of the American experience and the "miracle" that was found in the Founding Documents of the period—the Declaration of Independence and, particularly, the Constitution of the United States of America. These patriots self-identified and were seen by the public as well as those who defended the common principles of their country. These principles included not only the parchments upon which the ideas of government were written but also the individuals who strove to carry out the meaning of the ideas that supplied the documents' meanings. It was not that Patriots may have had qualms with this politician or with that policy but that they always supported the country—the essence of "patriotism."

Yet today, although the first brand of patriot may still, in fact, exist, the more common understanding of a patriot is one who sees deficiencies in the current iteration of the government of the United States. For patriots of this ilk, the form of the government that they love and respect is present, but the substance is missing. It has been replaced by self-serving politicians who remain in positions of power for decades instead of for limited terms (as they believe most of the Founders intended). It has been replaced by policies and practices that are antithetical to the uniqueness of the American position in the world—factors that have changed the fundamental character of the United States. And, finally, the United States of America is no longer a government "of the people." Rather, it is a government that serves its own ends regardless of the implications for the people.

Of course, what today's patriots often forget is the resilience with which a government constructed more than 200 years ago in circumstances that are quite different than today has survived and endured. If government has changed, it has *had* to in order to survive. The government of the United States today reflects the adaptations that have been necessary over the course of decades to continue the mandate to serve the people. It is quite possible that there is not a single American today who believes that they live under a perfect government. There *are* imperfections, inconsistencies, and false starts. Yet this is the essence of democracy. As Winston Churchill once famously stated, "Democracy is the worst form of government, except for all those other forms that have been tried from time to time."[58] In the United States today, there is *still* freedom of speech, freedom of religion, freedom of the press, freedom to assemble, the right to keep and bear arms, and so forth. How these freedoms are interpreted and practiced continually changes according to circumstances and the time in which they are found. Are they viewed the same way by everyone? Certainly not. But they also cannot be held to an idealized version of conceptions that may have existed two centuries ago in a country that was very much different than the one in which we find ourselves today.

Unfortunately, there are those in the patriot and militia communities who do not believe that they can live under the current conditions in which they find themselves. One solution would be to foment violence to forcefully bring about the desired changes in government. There have been groups that have followed and may continue still to follow this path. But there are those who believe that the U.S. government is too broken and corrupt to be redeemed. Violence might institute new government, but innocent lives might be lost. Therefore, there are those who are determined to live apart from the conditions in which they find themselves.

Consider for a moment, the Citadel—a community of liberty. According to its website, the Citadel "is a developing community of Patriots in the mountains of Idaho who believe in Jefferson's Rightful Liberty and have chosen to live amongst one another, who have sworn their Lives, their Fortunes and their Sacred Honor to defend one another and Liberty."[59] The Citadel is currently evolving as a planned community in which residents will be bound together by their beliefs in (1) patriotism, (2) pride in American exceptionalism, (3) the proud history of liberty as defined by the Founding Fathers, and (4) physical preparedness to survive and prevail in the face of natural catastrophes or man-made catastrophes such as power grid failure or economic collapse.[60]

As noted by the community, the Citadel will be "liberty driven," a concept based upon Thomas Jefferson's notion of rightful liberty. Those who populate the Citadel will be patriots of the highest order: "Marxists, Socialists, Liberals and Establishment Republicans will likely find that life in [the] community is incompatible with their existing ideology and preferred lifestyles."[61] The community will house between 3,500 and 7,000 "patriotic" American families who agree with "being prepared for the emergencies of life and being proficient with the American icon of liberty—the Rifle. . . ."[62]

Thus, the Citadel is for those who believe that "liberty" has been missing from their lives and the lives of their family members. This community is a clarion call to those who may find themselves exhausted in waging their battles against the federal government. It may be for those who wish to find the ideal that is embodied in their own personal notion of Utopia. It may also be for those who wish to regroup and regain their strength in the face of what they believe is the inevitable showdown that must occur between those who believe that the current system of government in the United States cannot or will not reform and those who maintain that no reform is necessary. Whatever the reason, one thing is certain: the Citadel is meant to provide a refuge for those who wish to remove themselves from the current political climate so that they may maintain their allegiance to liberty.

NOTES

1. Potok, Mark. 2013. "The Year in Hate and Extremism." *SPLC Intelligence Report.* Issue 149. (Spring). http://www.splcenter.org/

home/2013/spring/the-year-in-hate-and-extremism. (Accessed February 5, 2014).

2. De Rugy, Veronique. 2009. "Spending Under President George W. Bush." Mercatus Center at George Mason University. (March). http://mercatus.org/publication/spending-under-president-george-w-bush. (Accessed March 5, 2014).

3. Westcott, Kathryn. 2003. "Bush Revels in Cowboy Speak." *BBC News* (June 6). http://news.bbc.co.uk/1/hi/world/americas/2968176.stm. (Accessed January 18, 2014).

4. Halberstam, David. 2007. "The History Boys." *Vanity Fair.* (August). http://www.vanityfair.com/politics/features/2007/08/halberstam 200708. (Accessed May 20, 2014).

5. See "Birthers' Claim Gibbs Lied When He Said Obama's Birth Certificate Is Posted on the Internet." Politifact. *The St. Petersburg Times* (July 28, 2009). (Accessed May 15, 2014); Found at http://www.politifact .com/truth-o-meter/statements/2009/jul/28/worldnetdaily/birthers-claim-gibbs-lied-when-he-said-obamas-birt/. Tomasky, Michael. 2011. "Birthers and the Persistence of Racial Paranoia." *The Guardian* (April 27). (Accessed May 15, 2014). Found at http://www.theguardian.com/commentisfree/michaeltomasky/2011/apr/27/barack-obama-obama-administration. Travis, Shannon. 2010. "CNN Poll: Quarter Doubt Obama was Born in U.S." politicalticker. . . *CNN.* (April 4). (Retrieved May 18, 2014). Found at http://politicalticker.blogs.cnn.com/2010/08/04/cnn-poll-quarter-doubt-president-was-born-in-u-s/.

6. "Bill Ayers, Communist Terrorist, U.S. Government Bomber and Obama's Book Author." 2012. *Commieblaster.com.* http://www .commieblaster.com/bill_ayers/. (Accessed May 5, 2014).

7. Ibid.

8. Potok, Found at http://www.splcenter.org/home/2013/spring/the-year-in-hate-and-extremism.

9. Ibid.

10. Associated Press. 2013. "Leading Democrat: Gun Control Faces Uphill Climb." *Associated Press.* (January 27). http://cnsnews.com/news/article/leading-democrat-gun-control-faces-uphill-climb. (Accessed March 29, 2013).

11. Sullivan, Eileen. 2013. "Maze of Gun Control Laws in U.S. Hurt Gun Control Efforts." *Associated Press.* (January 25). (Accessed September 12, 2013). Found at http://bigstory.ap.org/article/maze-gun -laws-us-hurts-gun-control-efforts.

12. Keating, Dan, and Darla Cameron. 2013. "IRS Targets Conservative Groups." *Washington Post.* (May 5). http://www.

washingtonpost.com/wp-srv/special/politics/irs-targets-conservative-groups/. (Accessed April 23, 2014).

13. Ibid.

14. "IRS Keyword Targets: Tea Party, Conservative, Patriot, Constitution." 2013. *Mercator.net*. (June 18). See more at http://www.mercatornet.com/sheila_liaugminas/view/12348§hash.fGr2uJLQ.dpuf. (Accessed May 3, 2014).

15. Avlon, John. 2013. "How Did 'Patriot' Become a Dirty Word?" *CNN*. (May 28). http://www.cnn.com/2013/05/27/opinion/avlon-patriot/. (Accessed August 6, 2013).

16. Ibid.

17. Ibid.

18. Boldin, Michael. 2013. "Nullification: Alive and Well on the Left and Right." *The Patriot Post*. http://tenthamendmentcenter.com/2011/03/18/nullification-alive-and-well-on-the-left-and-right/. (Accessed November 20, 2013).

19. Kopa, Tai. 2013. "States Seek to Nullify Obama Efforts." *Politico* (July 27). http://www.politico.com/story/2013/07/states-nullification-obama-94826.html. (Accessed August 6, 2013).

20. Ibid.

21. Ibid.

22. Ibid.

23. Ibid.

24. Whaley, Monte. 2013. "51st State Question Answered 'No' in 6 of 11 Counties Contemplating Secession." *Denver Post*. (November 5). http://www.denverpost.com/breakingnews/ci_24461077/11-counties-weigh-weigh-secession-from-colorado-formation-51st#ixzz32I5Vojvc. (Accessed November 5, 2013).

25. Ibid.

26. "What We Do." 2014. *Southern Poverty Law Center*. http://www.splcenter.org/what-we-do/hate-and-extremism. (Accessed May 1, 2014).

27. Morin, Bill. 2014. "Retired Army Colonel Plans Militia-Backed 'Operation American Spring' to Force Obama Out of Office." Southern Poverty Law Center (May 2). www.splcenter.org/blog/2014/05/02/retired-army-colonel-plans-militia-backed-operation-american-spring-to-force-obama-out-of-office/. (Accessed May 21, 2014).

28. *Southern Poverty Law Center Intelligence Report*. Spring 2012, Issue Number 145.

29. Ibid.

30. Ibid.

31. http://wearechange.org/about/mission-statement/. (Accessed May 20, 2014).

32. M., Kelley. 2010. "WeAreChange Founder Luke Rudkowski Makes SPLC's Patriot Most Wanted List!" (April 16). http://wearechange. org/wearechange-founder-luke-rudkowski-makes-splcs-patriot-most-wanted-list/. (Accessed May 21, 2014).

33. Ibid.

34. Ibid.

35. http://oath-keepers.blogspot.com/. (Accessed May 21, 2014).

36. Ibid.

37. Ibid.

38. Ibid.

39. http://tenthamendmentcenter.com/#. (Accessed May 21, 2014).

40. http://www.republicoftheunitedstates.org/. (Accessed May 12, 2014).

41. Ibid.

42. Ibid.

43. Ibid.

44. http://nullifynow.net/overview?destination=node/8. (Accessed May 19, 2014).

45. Ibid.

46. Ibid.

47. "About the We The People Organization." http://www.wethe-peoplefoundation.org/00-AboutUs.htm. (Accessed May 20, 2014).

48. Ibid.

49. Ibid.

50. Ibid.

51. http://thepatriotparty.org/. (Accessed May 23, 2014).

52. Ibid.

53. https://unitedstatesmilitia.com/forum/showthread.php?t=6437. (Accessed May 20, 2014).

54. http://www.splcenter.org/who-we-are/. (Accessed May 18, 2014).

55. http://www.splcenter.org/what-we-do/. (Accessed May 18, 2014).

56. "Public School in the Crosshairs: Far Right 2014: Far-Right Propaganda and the Common Core State Standards." 2014. Southern Poverty Law Center (May). http://www.splcenter.org/sites/default/files/downloads/publication/public_schools_in_the_crosshairs.pdf. (Accessed May 18, 2014).

57. Owens, Eric. 2014. "Far-Right Extremists. Leftist Terrorism-Inspiring Southern Poverty Law Center Labels Common Core Critics

'Far-Right Extremists.'" *The Daily Caller* (May 10). http://dailycaller.com/2014/05/10/leftist-terrorism-inspiring-southern-poverty-law-center-labels-common-core-critics-far-right-extremists/. (Accessed May 19, 2014).

58. Speech before the British House of Commons, November 11, 1947.

59. (Accessed May 19, 2014). http://iiicitadel.com/index.html.

60. Ibid.

61. Ibid.

62. Ibid.

Index

About the Author

Barry J. Balleck received a B.A. in political science and an M.A. in international studies from Brigham Young University. He received his Ph.D. in political science from the University of Colorado at Boulder with emphases in international relations, American politics, and political theory. Upon completion of his degree, Dr. Balleck joined the faculty of Georgia Southern University, where he held a joint appointment in both the Department of Political Science and the Center for International Studies. Dr. Balleck currently serves as the chair and department head of the Department of Political Science at Georgia Southern University. For the past sixteen years, he has also directed Georgia Southern University's Model United Nations (MUN) program, one of the oldest and most continuous programs of its kind in the country. Dr. Balleck has directed the Georgia Southern MUN delegation to several national awards and has conducted dozens of MUN conferences for middle and high school students from Georgia, South Carolina, Tennessee, and Florida.

Dr. Balleck has research and teaching interests in the fields of international and domestic terrorism, U.S. foreign policy, the rhetoric of politics, the United Nations, and international human rights. He has dozens of conference presentations to his credit and has published in journals such as *Presidential Studies Quarterly, Politics & Policy*, and *Peace Psychology Review*.

Dr. Balleck has been married for the past 30 years to his best friend, the former Deana Daniels. They have four children and one grandchild. When not engaged in academic pursuits, Dr. Balleck enjoys gardening, bike riding, traveling, and spending time with his family.